Justice and Space Matter in a Strong, Unified Latino Community

Yolanda Medina and Margarita Machado-Casas
General Editors

Vol. 3

The Critical Studies of Latinos/as in the Americas series
is part of the Peter Lang Trade Academic and Textbook list.
Every volume is peer reviewed and meets
the highest quality standards for content and production.

PETER LANG
New York • Bern • Frankfurt • Berlin
Brussels • Vienna • Oxford • Warsaw

Kathy Bussert-Webb, María Eugenia Díaz,
and Krystal A. Yanez

Justice and Space Matter in a Strong, Unified Latino Community

PETER LANG
New York • Bern • Frankfurt • Berlin
Brussels • Vienna • Oxford • Warsaw

Library of Congress Cataloging-in-Publication Data

Names: Bussert-Webb, Kathy, author. | Díaz, María Eugenia, author.
Yanez, Krystal A., author.
Title: Justice and space matter in a strong, unified Latino community /
Kathy Bussert-Webb, María Eugenia Díaz, Krystal A. Yanez.
Description: New York: Peter Lang, 2017.
Series: Critical studies of Latino/as in the Americas; vol. 3
ISSN 2372-6822 (print) | ISSN 2372-6830 (online)
Includes bibliographical references and index.
Identifiers: LCCN 2016033980 | ISBN 978-1-4331-3206-3 (hardcover: alk. paper)
ISBN 978-1-4331-3205-6 (paperback: alk. paper) | ISBN 978-1-4539-1783-1 (ebook pdf)
ISBN 978-1-4331-3715-0 (epub) | ISBN 978-1-4331-3716-7 (mobi)
Subjects: LCSH: Hispanic Americans—Texas—Lower Rio Grande Valley—
Social conditions—Case studies. | Latin Americans—Texas—Lower Rio Grande Valley—
Social conditions—Case studies. | Immigrants—Texas—Lower Rio Grande Valley—
Social conditions—Case studies. | Poor—Texas—Lower Rio Grande Valley—Case studies.
Poor—Education—Texas—Lower Rio Grande Valley—Case studies.
Poor—Services for—Texas—Lower Rio Grande Valley—Case studies.
Community development—Texas—Lower Rio Grande Valley—Case studies.
Community organization—Texas—Lower Rio Grande Valley—Case studies.
Unincorporated areas—Texas—Lower Rio Grande Valley—Case studies.
Classification: LCC F395.S75 B87 2016 | DDC 305.868/0730764485—dc23
LC record available at https://lccn.loc.gov/2016033980
DOI: 10.3726/978-1-4539-1783-1

Bibliographic information published by **Die Deutsche Nationalbibliothek**.
Die Deutsche Nationalbibliothek lists this publication in the "Deutsche
Nationalbibliografie"; detailed bibliographic data are available
on the Internet at http://dnb.d-nb.de/.

The paper in this book meets the guidelines for permanence and durability
of the Committee on Production Guidelines for Book Longevity
of the Council of Library Resources.

© 2017 Peter Lang Publishing, Inc., New York
29 Broadway, 18th floor, New York, NY 10006
www.peterlang.com

Printed in the United States of America

KBW: To Bart, Katrina (synonym sage), and family
MED: To Luis, Cecilia, Sebastián, and family
KAY: To Rodger, Marmie, Nick, and family

From all of us: to our co-researchers (participants),
desde nuestros corazones

In loving memory of Magnífico, who first told us about the
D.C. trip and who died in March 2016

CONTENTS

ACKNOWLEDGEMENTS

Gracias [thank you] to our co-researchers (participants), families, and friends who provided insight and support, and to Peter Lang staff, especially Yolanda Medina.
Thank you to Contributors: Claudia Troncoso and Irma Guadarrama.
Front cover design by Irma Guadarrama.
Thank you to the U.S. Geological Survey (USGS) for this map: Colonias along the U.S.-Mexico border: Texas layer.
Internal university grants supported our research.

LIST OF FIGURES

AUTHORS' PREFACE

A test
To question
1. Have you heard or read about the *bad side* of town?
2. Have you heard or read about undocumented immigrants?
If yes to question 1 or 2, open me
Yet first, we open words in the world—
Slum
Seedy
Shantytown
Squalid
Skid
Colonia
Chancy illegal
Crossing breaking neglecting
Yet colonia residents, united, *trabajan duro* [work hard]
Othering marginalizing
Stereotypical unjust
Myth
Or as Sonrisa, 11, exclaimed—
"This is my family and this is my street where I live and right here is my
brother and my mom and grandpa and grandma and we have a flag on top
of our house to represent the United States."
Come! Meet Sonrisa and her colonia, an unannexed
Southwestern settlement.

INTRODUCTION

Meet Claudia

Claudia, book contributor and former tutorial volunteer, moved to *Corazón* [heart], Texas, from Mexico at age eight. All names are pseudonyms. Claudia received a four-year academic scholarship from our university. A certified bilingual fourth grade instructor in a local public school, Claudia completed a nationally accredited master's program in counseling recently.

Claudia recollected when she and her friends cleaned mud from their clothes in the school bathroom before entering their classrooms on rainy days. On such days, either Claudia's godmother carried her to the bus stop or Claudia sloshed through the unpaved streets, sometimes with plastic bags around her shoes. Claudia appeared as the quiet girl, so school peers would not bother her; yet they would taunt Claudia's friends. When youth would start arguing, others they would sneer, "You're from [*Corazón*]," or they would say the shoes of Claudia's friends looked filthy.

Yet mud did not stop Claudia, nor did structural or societal inequities related to employment. Although she could not work as a public school teacher because she lacked applicable documentation at the time, she honed her teaching skills as a Tutorial Center volunteer, where her friend, Hermosa, also volunteers. Claudia had received tutoring at this after-school agency, so she wanted to give back to her community. We define community as kinship circles—complex, hybrid, power-laden, and place-based (Moje, 2000b).

Since 2005, Claudia and other co-researchers (participants we perceive as experts) have been collaborating with us in theatre, gardening, technology, and participatory advocacy research. The latter involves critical literacy and social justice perspectives. Participatory advocacy studies unconceal power and strata and transform relationships (Cherland & Harper, 2007). We highlight Claudia's story, not as meritocracy, or a bootstrap approach for economically disadvantaged people to achieve success. Instead, we recognize that Claudia and her South Texas community possess power. *Corazón* possesses attributes missing from pathologizing depictions. Rita, Tutorial Center coordinator, described *Corazón* families as strong, friendly, caring, spiritual, and hardworking.

We describe our relationships with many *Corazón* residents, including Claudia. We sought Claudia as a contributor to gain an emic, or insider, perspective. Although power imbalances permeate research, we attempted to right some by having Claudia write with us. Indeed, Claudia possesses etic viewpoints. Our collaborative writing blurs emic and etic perspectives. We have not lived in *Corazón*, but we are not complete outsiders, nor objective observers. Instead, we have blurred identities as teacher-researchers and activists because "one's own people are those with whom one has made a common cause" (Hames-García, 2011, p. xv).

Purpose

Research questions—coursing through this book—are, "What are *Corazón* strengths? How do we work with and in community, while coming clean with power and privilege imbalances? How do residents engage in hybrid or blended practices to confront obstacles?" *Corazón* strengths include hope, ingenuity, and unity. Obstacles include local, state, and national policies and multi-factor discrimination, treatment based on group categories, and prejudice, preconceptions about a group. Latinos/as without U.S. documentation may face hate crimes, which maintain racial hegemony (Johnson & Ingram, 2013).

Thus, we invite you to explore these questions with us and to meet people like Claudia who live in a strong, unified Rio Grande Valley neighborhood consisting of many Mexican immigrants living below the U.S. poverty line. We do not want to give the impression that a unified community signifies homogeneity. Many differences exist between residents' religious beliefs, jobs, homes, and incomes, and immigration status, e.g., first- versus second-generation immigrants, documented and undocumented. *Corazón* enjoys basic services and is organized politically; however, it remains unannexed. Many unincorporated high-poverty U.S. communities dotting the Mexico border lack running water, electricity, sewage lines, and city police protection. The previous sentence constitutes the Texas Secretary of State (n.d.) definition of colonias, a Spanish word for neighborhood. While Latin America colonias are not necessarily destitute, poverty pervades U.S. colonias, unconscionable in the ninth wealthiest country. Similar places exist in other nations, but their qualities may miss the public domain.

To some, colonias may conjure images of early U.S. colonies of European settlers, but colonialism remains and relates to subjugation and capitalism. Even the name represents colonialism: "It is not by chance that in the more rural towns of Texas Chicano neighborhoods are called *colonias* rather than *barrios*" (Anzaldúa, 1990, p. 143, original emphasis). Mexicans began to defend their communities after the 1848 Guadalupe Hidalgo Treaty against non-Mexican settlers' encroachments. Mexican-origin people found they could maintain indigenous and Spanish languages and customs in colonias and *barrios* [neighborhoods] (D. Gutiérrez, 1999).

We provide an analysis of a long-standing Rio Grande Valley colonia from our partial perspectives. While problematizing jarring systemic inequities, we also highlight *Corazón*'s strengths to parry pathologizing portrayals (Bussert-Webb, 2015). Thus, we move beyond labels. We unpack what *poor* means because *Corazón* residents possess language and literacy wealth.

We define literacy as socially embedded, ideological practices (Gee, 2012). Literacy is not neutral, decontextualized skills one (dis)possesses. For instance, creating a low-rider car represents a literacy. Additionally, print literacy skills do not ensure success, as much depends on the socio-political context. We discuss how residents' lush literacies conflicted with impoverished pedagogies vis-à-vis education and language policies (Fernández, 2001). Perry's and Homan's (2014) participant in a Mexican prison engaged in luscious, resistant literacies by placing poems and messages in soccer balls, which he sewed together for his job. Their participant and ours, behaving like lush rhizomes, found ways around barriers to parry.

Thus, if we can show the poorest U.S. neighborhood (U.S. Census Bureau, 2010) abounds in strengths, maybe we can remove the negative words and images others have produced about *Corazón* and similar communities. Diverse economically strapped Latino communities have qualities invisible to some outsiders. Therefore, we attempt to create a deeper level of understanding, from our partial perspectives, of one Latino community for a more equitable, compassionate world and to uncover and challenge power, including our own.

Furthermore, we wish to counter misperceptions about diverse Latinos/ as, who link to the U.S. future (Gándara, 2010). By 2060, one in three people in the USA will be Hispanic (U.S. Census Bureau, 2012b), and many countries have fast-growing immigrant populations. Some people may fear this boom, but culturally diverse people—immigrants and indigenous, voluntary and involuntary (Ogbu, 1992)—form the vertebrae of many nations. Immigrants possess enormous courage, faith, and diligence; as such, they can improve their adopted land.

Some believe undocumented people in the USA are hard-core criminals. Yet immigration decreases crime; anti-immigration panic relates to media- and politician-fueled xenophobia (Zatz & Smith, 2012). Xenophobia demonstrates how discourse relates to power and perception. Language and discourse frame what we believe and how we treat others and we construct and reproduce truths from our contexts (Foucault, 1972). Actually, anti-immigration sentiment and ensuing legislation relate to undocumented immigrants' underreporting of crime; the latter are vulnerable to abuse and exploitation because they fear deportation if they report criminal activity (Zatz & Smith).

Others have misperceptions about bilingualism, particularly involving Spanish. Yet, about 50% of foreign-born people in the USA speak English well or only speak English (U.S. Census Bureau, 2012b). Being bilingual or multilingual in the USA does not mean a person ignores English.

Last, few studies have focused on researchers' long-term activist roles. Our book fills this void, as we have been working with *Corazón* families and tutorial staff for years, many of which have involved gardening. Reciprocity and uncovering power issues remain essential in humanizing, social justice research (Paris & Winn, 2014). We gave back before we conducted any research with *Corazón* residents because of our commitment to equitable practices. And we stayed put. Kathy, first author, realized that gardening with teacher candidates, *Corazón* children, and parents extended her community roots. Indeed, bodily engagement forms spatial connections (Comber, 2016).

Theoretical Frameworks

Our overarching theoretical frameworks were social justice from structuralism, and Third Space or hybridity from poststructuralism, postmodernism, and postcolonialism. Alas, Post Toasties! (See Chapter 1 regarding our epistemologies, or knowledge theories, and ontologies, or human interaction theories.)

Structuralists posit human conditions relate to overarching structures, e.g., race and class. Conversely, poststructuralists favor an open approach—no categories, no one answer. We consider Foucault (1972), who refused to label or categorize himself, a poststructuralist because he did not believe power related to structures. A critic of Marx, Foucault argued power could be good and bad, intertwined with knowledge, and everywhere.

Poststructuralism sprang from political and social theories, whereas postmodernism emerged from a range of fields, including architecture, the arts, cultural studies, history, and semiotics (Hassan, 1987). Later, we discuss Deleuze and Guattari (1987), postmodernists who theorized rhizomes and who favored interconnected, nonlinear rhizomic surfaces, versus depth and linearity. Postcolonialism represents theories about historical and geographical problems related to colonialism.

Social Justice

We refrain from discrediting scholars before us, as we balance on their shoulders. South American scholars influenced Freire, as did Sartre (Macedo, 2000). In one edited book, authors argued that Gramsci, Habermas, Hegel, Marx, and Latin American liberation theologists motivated Freire (Kress & Lake, 2013). Within a structural framework, conscientization occurs when oppressed people dialogue and take action against economic, political, and social structural inequities (Freire, 2000). Some cannot reconcile Freire's Christian allusions and symbolism, such as the Easter Experience, but Freire's experiences, readings, and interpretations in colonialist South America influenced him (Lange, 1998). As Freire did, we build theories by engaging with—and valuing—others. Farmer, a physician and liberation theologist, said, "If you don't understand structural violence … you're grasping around in the dark in public health, public education [and] poverty reduction" (McElwee, 2013, para. 21).

Although social justice does call for resource redistribution and ending multi-factor oppression and exclusion (material concepts), the former embraces love and mirth, or affective concepts (Cherland & Harper, 2007). Moreover, mutual care, creative expression, and freedom and fairly representing and valuing diverse people encompass a justice perspective, as justice focuses on ethics (Fraser, 1997). For a just world, we must intervene pedagogically and ethically (Macedo, 2000).

Some dismiss class analysis, but pretending social class's nonexistence remains disingenuous. Granted, a singular analysis, such as class, ignores gender and race. Yet Freire's later works embraced complex, multifactor analysis. Freire (1997) could not understand "how, in Brazil, we can maintain feminist, black, Indian, working class groups separately struggling for a less perverse society" (p. 86). Freire recounted a family in northeast Brazil, Brazil's poorest and oldest colonial region, scavenging a landfill and finding amputated human breasts for their Sunday meal. Complex oppression issues present themselves in this breast story—colonialism, gender, and poverty, to name a few (Macedo, 2000).

Thankfully, we tell no amputated breast story from *Corazón*. However, we wish to shed light on injustices *Corazón* residents have endured and resisted. Structural inequities facing *Corazón* children have included prejudice and banking education (Freire, 2000). The latter relate to the No Child Left Behind Act (NCLB). NCLB's 2015 revision, Every Student Succeeds Act (ESSA), may diminish this banking education. Sister Joan, some participating children, and teacher candidates said educators had lower expectations after discovering the youth came from *Corazón*. An administrator told María, second author, "We receive a lot of students from [*Corazón*], but we treat them like everybody else" (Bussert-Webb, 2015, p. 56). This assertion can mean the reverse with contrastive conjunction, *but*. Sentences such as, "He has high hopes, but he's a loser" or "She's black, but pretty" reveal a conjunction's power to alter meaning. If the school administrator treated all students fairly, then why would she single out *Corazón* youth? Equality includes providing people with equal access to quality education or redistribution, and valuing diverse people or recognition (Fraser, 1997).

Other inequalities facing many *Corazón* residents relate to health and nutrition. People without U.S. documentation can receive emergency medical care, yet they may fear seeking health and social services if they or family members are undocumented. Some blame health problems on individuals, but poverty impacts health services and outcomes. Health issues relate to children's academic achievement as well because we need energy to learn. Hunger's effect on learning appears in Freire's boyhood story: "I tried to read or pay attention in the classroom, but I didn't understand anything because of my hunger. I wasn't dumb" (Gadotti, 1994, p. 5). Certainly, out-of-school factors hinder children's learning (Berliner, 2009).

Heightened border security also affects colonia residents who could seek less expensive healthcare and medicine in Mexico previously. Some U.S.-born people have been unable to obtain U.S. passports because of *partera* [midwife], versus hospital birth delivery. Midwife deliveries, acceptable in many indigenous cultures, make birth certificate issuance difficult. These systemic inequities weigh on *Corazón* families. Yet *Corazón* people may resist hegemonic (controlling) and normative (conforming) practices through hybridity and fighting myths about the colonia. Residents have garnered agency from Mexican-heritage leaders, organizations, and their own socially situated, diasporic practices.

Diaspora, a Greek term meaning scattering, refers to immigrant groups (voluntary and involuntary) who leave their homeland. Diaspora and border bleed into one another (Clifford, 1994). We discuss diasporic processes and practices. A diasporic practice from Mexico includes relationship building. Unlike some Americans who may be individualistic and civically disengaged (Putnam, 1995), many *Corazón* residents practice interdependence and civic engagement. Organizations, working with colonias, have tapped into these diasporic practices to affect progress. Thus, it took the hands and hearts of many people to initiate positive change. Much work remains regarding education.

Third Space

Freire realized space could relate to tyranny. He embraced Southern theory, which is postcolonial and Latin American (Morrow, 2013). Although Freire valued people's lived experiences and he opposed hegemony, his underlying theoretical assumption was structuralism because he discussed societal-level inequalities or structures, such as schooling. So, why do we combine structuralism, postmodernism, and postcolonialism? Granted, Third Space philosophical roots are poststructuralist, or no subject-object distinctions, and postcolonial, or a critique of colonialism. However, Foucault, a poststructuralist, and Lefebvre, a Marxist/structuralist, influenced Soja (1996), who combined structure and agency to create spatial justice. Soja (2009) focused on the intersection of class, gender, political activism, race, and solidarity in urban spaces. Even the theories in this book dialogue in a Third Space. Our perspectives complemented each other and informed our participatory advocacy research, teaching, and ongoing relationships.

This philosophical Third Space represents a mixed media we create to merge structuralism, poststructuralism, postmodernism, and postcolonialism. We fuse distinct philosophies to support each other in understanding a complex phenomenon, such as a U.S. colonia. Social justice and poststructuralist research have different ontological purposes, e.g., to emancipate versus deconstruct, and distinct epistemic purposes, e.g., to rally against one factor versus considering multiple, unstable factors (Cherland & Harper, 2007). Yet, Third Space relates to hybridity, not binaries. Do we bracket theories, as some do with language, when we dichotomize them? Cannot theories exist together in the same discursive space, not as similar theories, but as ones that enrich each other? Poststructuralism, postmodernism, and postcolonialism are not islands. *Post*, except for a U.S. cereal brand or snail mail, means after. Philosophically, *post* reacts to an(other) theory before it. *Post* stands on shoulders. Nothing can be *post* without the concept it opposes (Clifford, 1994). *Post* does not mean we forget the past or create something new. Instead, *post* means to look beyond binaries, beyond singular categories, such as only class or only gender.

It appears Bakhtin, a literary critic, informed Bhabha's Third Space theory. Bakhtin published the first of four essays in 1934; these four became eventually part of *The Dialogic Imagination*, in which Bakhtin mentioned *space* over 70 times and variations of *hybrid* over 90 times (Holquist, 1996). Bakhtin gave homage to Einstein's concept of time and space interconnections in a fourth dimension. However, Bhabha (2004) cited only Bakhtin's (1986) *Speech Genres* book. K. Mitchell (2005) noted, "… Arising from Bakhtin's analysis of hybridity was … Homi Bhabba … [who transposed] Bakhtin directly to the colonial cause" (p. 190). We mention Bakhtin, a literary critic, to show how diverse disciplinary thinkers inform our thinking. Thus, we can nudge the world forward by considering alternate perspectives.

Besides hybridity, another Third Space organizing principle focuses on fissures and heterogeneity (Gutiérrez, Morales, & Martínez, 2009). These cracks and diversity emerge in the diaspora, resulting in contradictions and change. We, as Shihab Nye (Poetry Foundation, 2010), revel in these contradictions, these spaces—fleeing and linking simultaneously. This Third Space encompasses a friction-filled crevice where cultures collide. "The non-synchronous temporality of global and national cultures opens up a cultural space—a third space—where the negotiation of incommensurable differences creates a tension peculiar to borderline existences" (Bhabha, 2004, p. 312). These contexts, contradictory and ambiguous, do not belong to any one thing or person, yet they teem with potential.

Anzaldúa, a Rio Grande Valley (RGV) postcolonial theorist, also realized simultaneous identities and burdens, such as race, class, gender, and immigration. To her, Third Space signified *nepantla*, an Aztec word meaning between worlds, e.g., the USA and Mexico. Constant *nepantla* prickles like an embedded cactus needle we cannot dislodge. Yet *nepantla* may not constitute a place where marginalized people are agents. "Most of us dwell in *nepantla* so much of the time it's become a sort of 'home'" (Anzaldúa, 2002, p. 1). The U.S. Southwest is a Third Space where marginalized people have created identities in reaction and opposition to their marginalization (D. Gutiérrez, 1999).

Since our book focuses on education, Third Space can also represent physical spaces and practices that integrate and change home and school experiences. Second space may occur in formal institutions, such as schools, while first space, often marginalized, might transpire in community settings. Third Space can break binaries to transform evolving knowledges and identities when the subaltern are agents (K. Gutiérrez, 2008). *Corazón* children have been agents in our reciprocal tutoring and gardening program since its 2006 inception. Children teach teacher candidates (TCs) how to be community-affirming educators. TCs have countered local schools' NCLB curricula through dialogue, place-based lesson plans, and valuing youths' lived experiences. Together, they create an evolving, hybrid space where school and home mesh; see Chapter 8.

We found instances of Third Space in *Corazón* contexts, including health and religion. Third Space can occur online, in schools, and neighborhoods. Third Space butts up between languages, between the real and imagined (Soja, 1996). Hybrid practices of translanguaging, or strategic, creative, dynamic language processes bilinguals and polyglots employ (García, 2009), and language brokering, or children translating into a second language for parents, signified expanses between culture, language, and literacy. This language hybridity (see Chapter 7) blurs boundaries so no one unit remains the same after the intermingling. Thus, we take a broad approach to Third Space theory to include different phenomena encountered.

To think about hybridity related to food, imagine a hamburger with *el chile piquín*, a pinky-nail native RGV hot pepper, in the mix. Removing the peppers after marinating or grilling will not rid the mouth's burn from the pepper. Indeed, hamburgers enjoy popularity, maybe too much, in the USA, but adding *el chile piquín* would be a local flare. The heat in one's mouth signifies change from the hamburger's initial state, now not quite American, not quite Mexican. This hybridity, or blending of two cultures, transforms a phenomenon. Thus, stereotyping culturally diverse people who employ hybrid practices becomes difficult. For example, what does a reader do with Hong Kingston's (1976) Chinese character who prefers chocolate chip cookies versus rice? Similarly, when asked what his family was famous for, a *Corazón* child said,

"My mom makes real good hamburgers for us and for my aunts." Those unwilling to acknowledge local knowledges may refuse the combination (Fernández, 2001). Yet, sticking to binaries becomes difficult.

Analytic Lenses

We recognize discussing structural inequities and conscientization can create binaries, so we include four analytic lenses: to bridge/a bridge, slantwise, rhizomes, and power to keep us from dichotomies. These tools serve as important elements within Third Space and social justice frameworks because *Corazón* and our relationships to it prove complex. Foucault (1972) argued we should maintain theoretical openness, which enriches our depth of understanding as subjective beings.

To bridge/A Bridge

To bridge, suspending in Third Space theory, can mean bridging language and ethnic contradictions, not to fix them, but to realize they will be liminal, in flux. A person bridges by crossing borders and changing perspectives (Anzaldúa, 2002). To bridge connotes an action a person takes to go from one place to the other. Anzuldúa perceived bridges to be places where people could dialogue about their differences and commonalities regarding class, gender, race, and sexual orientation, but we extend her bridge analysis to other factors, e.g., people helping others to achieve success. This bridge metaphor fits because our campus is a pebble's throw from Mexico. Anzuldúa also perceived bridges as *nepantla*, an Aztec word, signifying an uneasy place lacking clear boundaries; bridges span liminal thresholds. Additionally, bridges relate to social justice because we dialogue with each other along a path toward conscientization and healing.

A bridge can signify multi-factor oppression including colonialism, ethnicity, gender, language, race, and social class, also. Subjugation accumulates; we cannot separate the factors (Moraga & Anzaldúa, 1983). In this sense, we visualize a bridge as a heavy, iron-like burden for the subaltern, who carry layers of oppression on their backs. Unfortunately, others walk on bridges without acknowledging and respecting them.

In this book, many bridges existed. The mostly Mexican-heritage teacher candidates (TCs) become bridges to children during Kathy's course, as the TCs stay physically under the children's tender feet for three weeks. Another year passes. New TC bridges guide the children's passageways in academia and in appreciating their hybrid cultures. Some TCs return to work with the children. Thus, these TC bridges stay in the children's minds and hearts, and vice-versa, as the children transform the college students on the bridge. Visually, we see bridges occupying extended cognitive and metaphorical divides in nature, where Anzaldúa (2002) loved to ponder. Yet bridges can exist emotionally, as they unite our emotions and relationships. We could not have conducted this study without these bridges. *Corazón* residents with whom we established *confianza* [trust] created bridges, or connections to more co-researchers with whom we could collaborate and learn. We like Anzaldúa (2007) for another reason: she embraced tolerance for ambiguity.

Slantwise

Third Space and social justice connect to slantwise, breaking resistance and passivity binaries (Campbell & Heyman, 2007). Based on Mexican and West Texas colonia research, Campbell and Heyman coined slantwise to signify transgressions people may perform—inadvertently—to achieve conventional goals, such as providing adequate housing for their families or earning a living wage. Usually, people conceptualize agency as someone's compliance or resistance to social norms, polar opposites on an axis. However, unconventional slantwise activity does not necessarily involve any intentional political opposition. Instead, slantwise relates to improvisation, mobility, and obliquity, which challenge authority. Obliquity constitutes any angle except a right angle. Slantwise helps us to understand colonia residents' creative activities, mainstream in Mexico, but unorthodox or even faux pas in the USA.

Colonia residents may exchange labor credit to remodel neighbors' homes (Coronado, 2003). These slantwise practices help colonia residents to keep building and utility costs down. In Chapter 7, we explain how *Corazón* children may go to neighbors' homes to complete Internet-based school assignments or to print documents. Another slantwise instance (see Chapter 9), occurs when Mexican children attend U.S. public schools, while living with extended U.S. family on weekdays and parents in Mexico on weekends. Alternatively, they may cross the border, taking city busses to arrive at their schools. We witness this practice on weekday mornings by our city's international bridge; even college students engage in these slantwise activities to obtain the best education possible.

Rhizome

We thank Fernández (2001) for introducing us to hybridity and rhizomes. A rhizome signifies an organic growth branching in any direction if cut, which represents the assigning rupture principle. Other rhizomic principles relate to heterogeneity, connection, multiplicity, having many entryways, and openness to continual modification; a rhizome would never be a tree root, but would be a ginger root or crab grass because it does not like deep structure. Because a rhizome intermingles, it does not occupy any one space. A rhizome, embracing possibility, could be a *samizdat*, an underground newspaper during Poland's communist era, or a pirate radio station that plays music from one's homeland. *Corazón* children were rhizomes also because they found alternative paths to systemic barriers related to digital tools and games; see Chapter 7. Like underground newspapers and the Underground Railroad, rhizomes focus on diversity, relationships, many components and entryways, collaboration, and receptiveness to revision and growth (Deleuze & Guattari, 1987).

As with slantwise, rhizomic conceptualizations keep us from binaries (present in structuralist conceptualizations). Rhizomes, acting unexpectedly, remain free. They constitute maps, not tracings, and they can change. Outsiders may not notice rhizomes. After all, rhizomes thrive underground. Ironically, officials' neglect of *Corazón* and other U.S. colonias made these spaces stronger. Instead of relying on governments to help them, colonia residents have created political kinships, primarily from rhizomic social relationships in and out of *Corazón*. You will notice we avoid the word *network* because networks can imply rigidity; when we use kinship circle and rhizome metaphors we wish to create images of hybridity and fluidity (Deleuze & Guattari, 1987).

Yet aspects of kinships and self-help may relate to neoliberalism, e.g., governments quit paying for services so private organizations take up the slack, resulting in little political activism (Dolhinow, 2010). Programs for low-income people involving non-government organizations (NGOs), yet no government help or political activism would be neoliberal. We reject this pull-yourself-up-by-the-bootstrap, individual-level approach to poverty. Instead, we maintain that when neighbors face hardships, like rhizomes, they create hybridized, slantwise solutions (Campbell & Heyman, 2007). These moves delink from colonial rules (Mignolo, 2006).

We discovered elderly *Corazón* residents behaved rhizomically, also. They grew from the teachings of United Farm Workers' (UFW) leader, César Chávez, who believed people could accomplish much if they work *in* community.

This ginger-rootedness relates to collective impact (Kania & Kramer, 2011). Undoubtedly, Chávez influenced Luchador [Fighter]. Luchador earned this name not from revolutionary activity, but because he fought for *Corazón* services. The beloved Luchador's smile, laughter, and indefatigable spirit lives in these pages. Laughter demolishes fear. Luchador, who organized a UFW Colorado strike, worked with Chávez in California. In 1971, Luchador bought a *Corazón* home, 1,600 miles from California! Elderly co-researchers appeared proud of Luchador's César Chávez connection. Luchador agitated in *Corazón* and even in Washington, D.C.; see Chapter 3.

Power

Freire, Foucault, and Bakhtin discussed power differently. Freire (2000) said nondominant people must participate in their emancipatory process with critical awareness of their agentive roles. Thus, power, from a social justice perspective, means social privileges and hierarchies, wedded to unequal resource distribution. Yet, people have power to resist and transform their world.

Conversely, Foucault (1980) posited power is "never localised here or there, never … a commodity or a piece of wealth" (p. 98). A five year old can have power over his toddler brother and vice-versa. Power hides like a ghost and it can be like Casper or a *cucuy* [monster]. For instance, teachers in high-stakes testing environments, where their jobs and pupils' future have major consequences, fear supervisors and the media watch them constantly, so they monitor themselves by teaching to the test. This represents panopticism; *pan* means all and *opticon* means seeing. Maybe the principal watches—not. Maybe the newspaper editor (dis)likes publishing schools' inane district test scores.

Power relates to discourse, also. Discourse involves subjective, socially constructed communication systems, which include and exclude people (Foucault, 1972). We imagine people have power over us. We hear, read, speak, and enact submission, which connects to psychology and coloniality (Quijano, 2000). External oppression parallels our internalization and acting out of that oppression (Anzaldúa, 1990). However, we can counter deficit discourses.

Similarly, power relates to language. Bakhtin believed that authoritative discourse exists in dialogical relationship with the less-privileged internally persuasive word (Holquist, 1996). Centripetal (centralizing, passing inward) and centrifugal (decentralizing, fleeing the center) forces collide, as people resist hegemony, sometimes subconsciously. For us, heteroglossia represents a

Third Space, where competing ideologies and discourses counter monoglossia. We find monoglossia, steadfast utterances, in U.S. and Texas language policies and curricular standards. Although Bakhtin referred to novels, we extend his notions of power to language and education politics.

We connect these social justice and Third Space frameworks and analytical tools—to bridge/a bridge, power, rhizome, and slantwise—in a philosophical Third Space to navigate a complex topic. We mention more perspectives as they apply to a particular chapter, e.g., language loss and New Literacy Studies in Chapters 6 and 7.

In our visual book representation, Figure I.1 signifies a triadic representation between our university, *Corazón* homes, and the children's schools because universities can do more to create school-community partnerships. For example, Comber (2016) described a 30-year collaboration between university researchers, children, and classroom teachers in high-poverty neighborhoods. Third Space also occurred in the colonia's Tutorial Center, where Kathy's students tutored and where youth engaged in transformative digital practices.

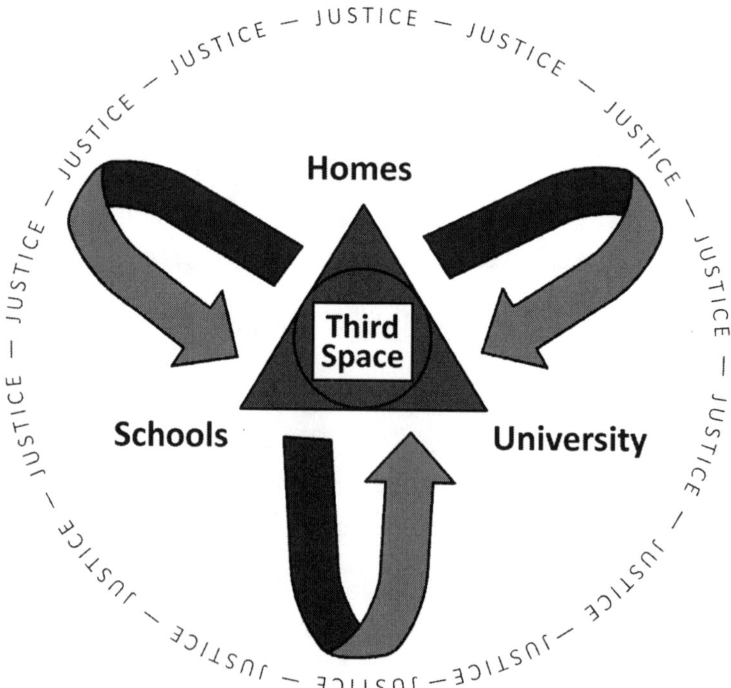

Figure I.1. Third Space and Social Justice Representation: Centrifugal and Centripetal Forces.

We also found hybrid Third Space between Church doctrine and indigenous religious practices, governmental health and *promotoras* [health promoters], and county politicians and colonia organizations. This Third Space can help centrifugal forces, such as translanguaging, to refute centripetal ones, such as negative rhetoric and totalizing education policies. Looping arrows demonstrate unending tensions and resistance to structural inequalities. We created dashes versus solid lines to resist centripetal forces, to crash through boundaries, including identities and ideologies. Additionally, the outer spaces represent dialogue's potential to break through multi-factor barriers.

Methods

In subsequent chapters, we do not mention methods much. Although we have been conducting *Corazón* case studies individually and collaboratively, we have used similar methodologies for our studies since 2006. Total co-researchers include about 200 children, 98 teacher candidates (TCs), 70 parents, 52 female walking path users, 30 other adults in and outside of *Corazón*, and seven tutorial staff [N = 457]. We collected data mainly through:

- Child and TC focus group discussions for the May programs,
- Child, parent, staff, and volunteer semi-structured and unstructured interviews,
- Child and TC daily journals and 24-hour literacy logs (documenting all reading, writing, and digital uses throughout the day) for the May programs,
- Child and TC pre- and post-reflective essays for the May programs,
- Child, staff, parent, TC, and female walking path user open- and close-ended surveys,
- Participant observation,
- Public domain Internet documents,
- TCs' reading reflections and lesson plan artifacts for the May programs, and
- Visuals (child art, visual metaphors from TC small groups, and photographs).

We audio-recorded and transcribed all focus groups. We did the same with interviews, except when interviewees told us they did not want us to record them. For focus group discussions, we asked each person to state their name when they began speaking. We typed as focus group members and interviewees spoke; we conferred with respondents later if we misunderstood something or if we wanted to explore a topic. At an interview's end, we summarized what a co-researcher said. We asked TCs to add, change, or delete any focus group transcript they perceived as incoherent, incorrect, or incomplete. Only a few revised the transcripts.

We present an example of how we established trustworthiness. In May 2015, Magnífico told Kathy he participated in an audacious Washington D.C. trip with *Corazón* activist Luchador to fight for potable water. Elderly Anglo-Saxon outsiders told Kathy they knew nothing about the voyage. Kathy searched for at least 40 hours on the Internet about this trip and discovered Patriot's 2012 obituary, which mentioned Patriot helped *Corazón* to obtain potable water. Kathy assumed Patriot was Luchador. Thus, Kathy found and messaged Patriot's surviving daughter-in-law through Facebook. Through this Facebook contact, Kathy was able to interview Patriota, Patriot's widow. Coincidentally, Patriota and Patriot were Luchador's friends; these three organized the D.C. trip! Meanwhile, Kathy interviewed community organizer Janie, who pointed us to Luchador's actual widow, Luchadora, whom María interviewed. Brother James introduced Kathy to Poeta and Esposo [Husband], two elderly friends of Luchador. All elders confirmed the trip and Luchador's important role. Yet, these existed as oral histories. Finally, Poeta and Patriota showed Kathy the lode—a historical newspaper document about the trip and Luchador, trip photos, and bus passenger rosters.

This type of confirming and disconfirming of information guided us throughout data analysis, also. We looked for patterns based on our theoretical frameworks, analytic tools, and research questions. For this book, we identified and categorized themes by making comparisons and looking for similarities and dissimilarities across all data. We kept asking ourselves, "What binds our findings?" Kathy started gathering TC data in 2006 when she taught her first *Corazón* course, but waited until 2008 to build trust before inviting resident participation.

Our long-term commitment to *Corazón* related to our evolving findings, also. When we began collecting community data, we believed outsiders had improved *Corazón*. However, when we became better acquainted with elderly colonia residents, we realized the latter played key activist roles. Thus, our relationships helped us to change a key finding—from external forces to grassroots political activism. The more people we met, the more trustworthy our findings became because we constantly compared diverse people's perspectives and different data points. As authors and contributors, we communicated constantly as we analyzed and reanalyzed the longitudinal data. Some may desire quantitative analysis, but we wish to go deeper, not broader. We are writing about a particular setting, people, and time, and our relationship with this community; see Chapter 1.

Each study related to this book has undergone rigorous institutional review board (IRB) approval and renewal processes and *Corazón* staff approvals. All co-researchers, including teacher candidates, guardians, children, staff, and adult community members, signed assent and consent forms before data gathering. We engaged in constant member checking and peer debriefing. Contributor Claudia, teacher Joy, and Brother James commented on a draft before it went to press; we made every suggested change.

Limitations

Our studies have many limitations. Because of tight timeframes of the 2006–2010, 2013, 2015, and 2016 community service learning (CSL) programs and because we wanted the children to feel at ease, we interviewed two siblings or friends together sometimes. To fit in, youth may have agreed with each other. Some did not want tape-recorded interviews, but we typed as the children spoke and we read aloud what we had typed. Next, the first child interviews during the CSL programs consisted of too many questions and topics, so we focused on particular themes, such as digital literacies, when we re-interviewed them.

Places where we conducted interviews presented limitations; some interviewees may have withheld information, fearing others would hear. Most interviews with tutorial staff, volunteers, and children took place with others present over the years. Phone calls and parents or children needing assistance interrupted interviews. Sometimes we arranged for adult interviews in other places, e.g., coffee shops or restaurants. We re-interviewed some people, also. Yet, interruptions during interviews made us more aware of co-researchers' concerns and contexts.

Additionally, Krystal used informal interpreters for some interviews because of language barriers. Krystal noticed translation loss. She would understand some interviewees' words as she typed, but the interpreter would use dissimilar words, e.g., "I feel good now" versus "I feel more confident now." Krystal describes language barriers in Chapters 9 and 10. We ponder how interpreters influenced relationships and results.

Next, the children may have stated things to please tutors or interviewers. Teacher candidates (TCs) may have done so, pining for higher grades. Social desirability permeates research. Last, we have not conducted research to determine if TCs still believe in, and practice, liberatory pedagogies, which represents another limitation. Yet long after course completion, TCs tell Kathy how much the CSL improved their social justice perceptions.

Outline

In Section I, we invite you to meet some *Corazón* people and our connections to them. Chapter 1 includes entering the field and the relationship between our experiences, beliefs, and advocacy research. We tell the stories of Kathy, María, Krystal, Claudia, and Irma. Claudia lived in *Corazón* for over 20 years and volunteered at the Tutorial Center. Next, Chapter 2 provides an in-depth analysis of Texas colonias. Chapter 3 focuses on *Corazón*'s obstacles, histories, and strengths. Chapter 4 explores organizations' efforts connecting *Corazón* residents to outsiders and promoting political activism. Thus, our findings differ from Dolhinow's (2010), who stated non-government organizations perpetuate neoliberalism by avoiding the activism of those served.

Section II focuses on the sociocultural contexts of religion, language, and literacy; we concentrate on *Corazón* children and families. Chapter 5 describes *Corazón* religious events and practices, conflicts, colonialism, and social justice. Chapter 6 relates to residents' Spanish-related purposes and practices and English-only policies, which influence church and Tutorial Center language policies. In Chapter 7, we highlight a culturally affirming, multimodal teacher, one parent's venture into the digital world, and children's digital access and practices.

Section III centers on education. Chapter 8 examines how a reciprocal project helped teacher candidates and children; both demonstrated agency. Chapter 9 explains education at every level and presents success stories because justice without hope is not justice (Freire, 2000). Chapter 10 explores lessons learned and ideas for programs and schools serving Latino/a students and families. This section brings forth a query in the U.S. educational agenda: How do we educate Latino/a children, despite systemic inequities and school failure? We yearn for you to feel *Corazón* youth's vitality and hope.

Summary

We included a portrait of Claudia to demonstrate how such a talented person faced so much difficulty because of her neighborhood, a structural inequality related to socio-economic status and residence. We explained the book's purposes: to gain a deeper level of understanding of a Latino community of promise (from our partial perspectives), to uncover power differences, and to transform the world. We do this by countering myths. Hopefully, our stories will help you to live residents' experiences, to dream with them tonight and tomorrow. Although we make no generalization attempt, we hope you can make connections to other neighborhoods of promise.

Next, we introduced social justice and Third Space frameworks and incorporated the analytic lenses of bridge, power, rhizomes, and slantwise. These theories and tools co-act to explain complex phenomena deeply and they help us to resist dualisms or binaries. We included a visual representation of how our frameworks work vis-à-vis *Corazón* homes, schools, and universities. We discussed our qualitative methods involving residents, staff, and teacher candidates. We then introduced each section and chapter of this book. Our collaboration with activists, children, community workers, families, teachers, and teacher candidates has generated knowledge and questions, as the issues prove complex. We emphasize this book represents only people we met and phenomena we experienced; we do not purport to re-present the entire community. Furthermore, we could not tell all stories we heard.

Questions to Ponder

1. How can you identify with Claudia? What makes you wonder about Claudia and her context?
2. What are dynamic factors constituting a Third Space and how are these specific to a context in your community?
3. We introduced theoretical frameworks and supporting analytic tools. Pick one framework and one tool and apply both to your context.
4. What would be a Third Space in your community? Why would it be a Third Space?

SECTION I
BUILDING BACKGROUND

· 1 ·

ENTERING—THE FIELD AND OUR POSITIONALITY

Meet Maribel and Alma

Corazón. April 27, 2006. The floor to Maribel's home sits at ground level, with no step above the elements. Only the door blocks the outside—no marble threshold, no raised platform. However, Alma represents the threshold to other realities, the bridge between Kathy, professor, and Maribel, resident. As the founding Tutorial Center coordinator, Alma assists Kathy in recruiting children tutees for our community service learning (CSL) course. For CSL, Kathy's students would tutor and garden with youth and write course-based reflections. Kathy notices handwriting on Maribel's wall by a mounted phone—numbers, names, dates. "We engaged in those literacy practices on our walls at home," Kathy recalls, then listens to Alma discuss the CSL program with Maribel. The Hungarian in Kathy chimes in regarding the food we will provide.

Introduction

This scene demonstrates Alma's role as a bridge into our *Corazón* research experiences. It also shows Kathy's Hungarian background, childhood literacy practices, and literacy knowledge. As a literacy education professor who grew up working class, Kathy perceives literacy as contextualized, power-laden, ideological practices (Gee, 2012). She values people's lived experiences and local knowledge. People do things, such as writing telephone information on the walls instead of using paper, because their sociocultural and literacy contexts. Although we may no longer write on walls, our family experiences shape our beliefs and practices. Furthermore, our theoretical positioning and disciplinary socialization informed how we gathered and interpreted data (Caelli, Ray, & Mill, 2003).

In this chapter, we introduce our institutional context. Next, we explain our experiences, disciplinary formation, ideological positions, and privileges, e.g., language, race, and socioeconomic status. We share stories of entering— and continuing—in the field as intersubjective teachers-learners.

Our positioning connects to all research facets. Maintaining reciprocal relationships with colonia leaders and residents takes time, as does conducting qualitative decolonial and advocacy research. Kathy initiates this chapter, since she began *Corazón* research in 2006. María and Krystal follow, as they entered *Corazón* later. We include Claudia and Irma, contributors. Last, we discuss our epistemologies (knowledge theories), and ontologies, (human interaction theories), which related to our research questions, relationships, data sources, procedures, and analysis.

Institutional Context

We discuss the University of Texas Rio Grande Valley (UTRGV) because we mention UTRGV teacher candidates throughout our book. We are from the UTRGV College of Education. Claudia recently completed a master's degree. Krystal, third author, is pursuing a doctoral degree. María, second author, serves as an assistant professor and Kathy is professor. Irma retired recently. Our university, nearing 30,000 students, is a designated Hispanic-serving institution. Latinos/as represent about 90% of UTRGV students. UTRGV received National Council of Accreditation of Teacher Education (NCATE)/Council for the Accreditation of Educator Preparation (CAEP) and subject-area recognitions, including English and Spanish teacher certification programs. Likewise, UTRGV is a Carnegie community-engaged campus, based on reciprocal partnerships and resource and knowledge exchanges.

Kathy's Story

Kathy's field entry connects to her beliefs and experiences. Kathy's Hungarian mother, an immigrant in Germany and then the USA, possessed a sixth grade education until Kathy pursued a master's degree. At that time, Kathy's mother received her General Educational Development (GED) diploma. Kathy's elementary teachers embraced deficit methods and shunned a second-generation child's literacies. Kathy crept along lower primary tracks, still receiving low marks for reading and writing. Yet art became Kathy's reprieve. These experiences motivated Kathy to pursue a Ph.D. in literacy and to research literacy's oppressive and liberatory roles. Her dissertation question stem was, "How does language oppress and liberate … ?" Kathy's subject area socialization focused on multimodalities, socio-psycholinguistics, and qualitative research.

Kathy began her relationship with *Corazón's* Tutorial Center so teacher candidates (TCs) could learn with children through community service learning (CSL). This type of social justice pedagogy and scholarship (Maynes, Hatt, & Wideman, 2013) enticed Kathy. Kathy's father, who possessed a GED, labored in an automobile factory. Kathy detassled corn for over seven seasons, and taught Honduran children in the U.S. Peace Corps. Yet despite her struggles, Kathy acknowledges her benefits as a: white person, speaker of the U.S. language of power, and middle class professor. These privileges tore into Kathy in June 2015, when Kathy overheard a participating *Corazón* mother say she was paying a $30 school library fine in three installments. See Chapter 9. Discussing researchers' social and language privileges helps us to recognize power issues and researcher subjectivity.

Thus, Kathy's life experiences motivated her to use CSL pedagogy. In fall 2004 Kathy required TCs in a content area literacy course to complete and reflect on five CSL hours for less than 10% of their grade. Although TCs had choices for agencies, including *Corazón's* Tutorial Center, most of the course involved TCs' lesson plan implementation in public schools. Kathy realized she was forcing CSL into an inappropriate course. However, in spring 2005 she began teaching a literacy/English as a second language (ESL) methods course. Again, Kathy included this Center as a CSL site, yet she required no school service. Joy (see Chapter 7), was enrolled in that spring course. Tim, *Corazón* priest at the time, objected to a multiple intelligences survey Joy was administering to a child. This made Alma, tutorial coordinator, question the survey, also. They thought Joy was testing the child's intelligence, so Kathy visited the Center, for the first time, to explain Joy was surveying the child to implement strengths-based lessons. Kathy parked her car on the wrong street in the evening, worrying about vandals. As with most TCs, Kathy had not entered *Corazón* before, yet believed others' negative portrayals. Kathy became angry with herself.

That spring 2005, Kathy read reflections from TCs who completed their CSL at the Tutorial Center. Their growth in realizing prejudice, systemic inequities colonia children encountered, and community strengths impressed Kathy. Thus, Kathy and Alma started planning for Kathy to teach her course there. Alma wanted to beautify the tutorial grounds, so this team project could also unify TCs and children.

During the first round of institutional review board (IRB)-approved research in May 2006, Kathy focused on CSL impact on TCs. Kathy wanted to establish *confianza* [trust] before inviting community respondents. Alma and Kathy decided to move the gardening project across the street to a parking lot for May 2007. The community needed a centralized walking path so we painted one on the lot. Most streets lacked sidewalks and dogs roamed. Additionally, *Corazón* possessed some of the region's highest diabetes and heart-related problems, related to safe outdoor places to exercise (Cohen et al., 2007).

Corazón children enjoyed gardening and spending time with TCs. As Kathy began presenting and writing articles about the CSL, people asked, "Yet how does this help the community?" Indeed, outsiders' benefits to communities are essential for decolonializing, advocacy research and redistributing power (Cherland & Harper, 2007). Engaging in these social practices make us more fully human (Freire, 2000). Thus, by May 2008 Kathy received IRB permission to invite children, parents, and adult walking path users to determine indirect CSL impact. Kathy started inviting staff from her university to present in Spanish to tutorial children, parents, and other residents about financial aid and admissions in 2009. Thus, Kathy included audience members in IRB proposals. In 2006, 2007, and 2008, Kathy gathered data by herself, but by 2009 paid graduate students began helping. María, second author, had this role in 2010. Kathy did not offer the project in 2011, 2012, and 2014 because of university service commitments. Another graduate assistant helped in 2013. Krystal, third author, assisted in 2015 and Kathy was the sole researcher in 2016. Kathy gathered data from TCs and staff, while research assistants collected data from children and parents when Kathy was unable.

María's Story

María hails from Uruguay, South America, where she obtained a bachelor's in Biological Sciences. She migrated to the USA in the early 1990's to study neurological diseases, such as Alzheimer's, in New Mexico and Texas universities. In 2001, she and her family moved to the Rio Grande Valley, where she became a certified bilingual education teacher. She earned a bilingual education master's, then a curriculum and instruction doctorate with a bilingual education specialization. She taught first and second grade bilingual education at a local elementary school for eight years.

María made contact with *Corazón* in 2008, as a doctoral student and research assistant at the local university. She joined professors who planned to conduct participatory action research with colonia youth and elders. María's main task involved participant recruitment. Team members barely knew the neighborhood. After contacting *Corazón* staff via telephone, the research team realized the Tutorial Center represented a strategic place to recruit youth.

Despite living in the surrounding city for years, María had not visited *Corazón* before January 2008. As she drove around the colonia before visiting the Tutorial Center, her childhood *vecindario* [neighborhood] in Uruguay engulfed her. Roads unfinished. Houses dilapidated. Barking dogs, unleashed. Smells from inadequate drainage. Chickens crowing and pecking. These sights, sounds, and smells transported María to her working class childhood environment. Yet seeing the *vecinos* [neighbors], particularly elders, talking in the street triggered this *déjà vu* the most. The *vecinos* reminded María of her grandparents and their neighbors, chatting in front of homes. María had not observed this in the cities where she had lived since she moved to the USA. This colonia tour gave her confidence to reach out and connect to residents. Additionally, she realized outsiders could have insider characteristics.

Searching for the Tutorial Center, María stopped by the church office. The receptionist referred her to Alma, tutorial coordinator, and Claudia, volunteer, who were preparing for children to return from winter break. As María introduced herself, Alma and Claudia expressed happiness to collaborate with the university and said the project could help colonia youth. María realized her university affiliation provided privileges in entering the field. Alma, of Mexican heritage, did not live in *Corazón*; however, she served as Center coordinator and knew many families. Alma told María, "Come back tomorrow and I will introduce to people who can help you." María realized Alma linked the team and residents, extending connections and multiplicity, like rhizomes (Deleuze & Guattari, 1987).

The following day Alma drove María around *Corazón*, introducing María to potential participating families. Alma accompanied María the first time, but then the selection of other families followed a kinship process. As María met parents and explained the project to them, they suggested other families. This experience demonstrated families knew and trusted each other and María.

Although a native-Spanish speaking Latina, María speaks Uruguayan Spanish, including Italian-inspired words, e.g., *chau* [bye]. María's dialect may have separated her from others. As researchers investigate a new community, the former may appear unnatural to community members. Furthermore, to understand how insiders make sense of their world, researchers need to engage with participants. Thus, María realized an effective way to share experiences involved volunteering at the Center. Twice weekly during two academic semesters she helped children with homework, organized a small library, and supervised children when playing outside. She also met church staff (priests, nuns, and catechism teachers) and other volunteers (mothers, private high school students, and winter Texans, or elderly retirees mostly from the Midwest).

Slowly and respectfully, María became more aware of community needs and residents' everyday lives. Participating families invited María to family events and community festivities, traditionally celebrated in Mexico, such as *la tamalada* [tamale party], *quinceañera* [sweet 15 mass and party], *El Día de los Muertos* [Day of the Dead], and *Los Reyes Magos* [Three Wise Men]; see Chapter 5.

María began collecting dissertation data in 2009. Many children and mothers knew María from her previous research and Tutorial Center service. Thus, María straddled outsider-insider roles. Her *Corazón* experiences made her aware of community dynamics; she wanted to understand how residents perceived and used their native language, Spanish. Because she earned master's and doctoral degrees in bilingual education, María's disciplinary socialization influenced her research. Main settings for data collection during her doctoral dissertation consisted of participating families' homes and the Center. However, María visited the health clinic (no longer open because of funding and scheduling issues), grocery stores, the Catholic Church, and schools *Corazón* children attended. María's involvement has continued, as either a researcher or visitor. Although many colonia aspects have changed since she first visited, e.g., sidewalks, houses, and leaders, María still feels a strong *Corazón* connection.

Krystal's Story

Krystal is light-skinned and her later childhood consisted of a mostly upper-middle class lifestyle; she recognizes the privileges and benefits associated with both. However, as a young girl she saw her mother take any job available. Krystal's mother had received a beautician's license immediately after high school, but let the license expire because of family circumstances. When her mother needed a job later, she entered the professional world with only a high school diploma. Krystal's mother worked as a clerk at a county health clinic. During this time, Krystal realized what hard work meant, regardless of a person's position or pay. Krystal's mother taught her to approach each encounter with effort, humility, and empathy.

Born in Houston, Texas, Krystal moved with her family to a small town about 20 miles north of *Corazón* in second grade. She grew up in a Mexican-heritage home, but did not learn Spanish. Krystal's immediate and extended family members speak Spanish fluently, although most prefer to speak English. Krystal ponders why Spanish disappeared in her house.

Krystal received bachelor's and master's degrees in communications and she has taught this subject. She is pursuing a doctoral degree in curriculum and instruction with a specialization in higher education. Improving adult education and bilingual youth's college access compel her. These passions inspired her to add two child interview questions about college to Kathy's institutional review board (IRB) proposal and to gravitate toward higher education when she analyzed the data. Furthermore, Krystal's disciplinary socialization in communications and higher education influenced her research questions, data gathering, and analysis. She could identify with youths' educational barriers and thus created a space where the children felt comfortable sharing stories.

In spring 2015, Kathy approached Krystal, inviting her to be a research assistant at the Tutorial Center. Every time Kathy mentioned the project, she referred to *Corazón* as a colonia. Krystal had some conceptual knowledge of colonias as she had taken Kathy's doctoral course in fall 2014, so she searched through her course binder to refresh her memory. On top of an otherwise blank page, she had scribbled, "Colonia: forgotten." After Krystal's Google image search, she believed she would be driving into an area resembling a developing country. She expected to see a community without drainage, running water, and lighted and paved streets.

Krystal erred. As she drove down the street on May 11, 2015, in a 10-year-old black Chevy truck towards the Tutorial Center, it looked like her neighborhood. Krystal noticed familiar landmarks, including *panaderías* [bakeries] and taco stands advertising *barbacoa* [tacos made from beef head] and *menudo* [soup with beef stomach].

Krystal arrived 15 minutes early to become acquainted with tutorial staff and parent volunteers. Upon entering, she saw women moving feverishly to get things ready for the children, who would be arriving soon. As she introduced herself and the women responded, it became clear the women spoke Spanish only. Discomfort's wave engulfed her. Krystal started doubting her ability to work effectively in this environment. Normally, this would not pose a problem for a Mexican-heritage 30-year-old. However, her Spanish was limited to few words. She hated that nobody ever spoke Spanish with her while she was growing up. Yet later, she read the comforting words of Anzaldúa (2007), who grew up near Krystal's home: "A monolingual Chicana whose first language is English or Spanish is just as much a Chicana as one who speaks several varieties of Spanish" (pp. 80–81). Krystal realized she should accept the language she speaks because heritage language speakers are diverse.

Krystal began to unpack her bags on a bean-shaped table, specifically designed for children, as Krystal's knees hit above the table. While Krystal organized various assent and consent forms, Kathy arrived and began introducing Krystal to the parent volunteers. Thankfully, Kathy spoke Spanish, putting Krystal at ease. As the children, exuberant and confident, began arriving, Krystal felt the energy in the building change. Two girls, in particular, placed themselves in front of Krystal and wiggled their way into Krystal's heart, convincing her that her time would be better spent listening to them read a decontextualized school passage on taxi drivers. (Few taxi drivers visit the colonia.) It became obvious during Krystal's first week at the Center the children felt comfortable studying in *Corazón* with people who appeared similar to them.

Some children would look for Krystal, which encouraged her. Almost daily, three girls visited her interview room—hanging out, asking questions about college. Krystal said she had been in school for 11 years non-stop. Dulce, 11, sat with Krystal eating cinnamon candies Krystal used as rewards for turning in permission slips. "Do you like college?" Dulce asked, spinning around on an office chair. "I love it. That's why I've been there so long," Krystal answered. Questions and spinning continued. Krystal said, "Throughout your life, people can take things away from you—your money, house, car, even freedom, but no one can take knowledge from you." Dulce froze. "Do you think I'm going to go to college?" Dulce leaned toward Krystal with a serious look. Krystal smiled, "Of course. Heck, I'll either be your teacher or a student with you." They laughed.

Contributors' Stories

Claudia

Claudia tells a different story because she lived in *Corazón* for 20 years and she teaches in a local public elementary school. Although she does not conduct formal research studies, Claudia considers herself a teacher-researcher. Claudia's childhood experiences inform her teaching and counseling beliefs. She arrived in this colonia from Matamoros, Mexico, in September 1994, at age eight. Claudia lived with her godparents, who are also her aunt and uncle, in *Corazón*. Claudia accompanied her godmother to the colonia's Catholic Church every Sunday and Claudia became acquainted with the clergy. Claudia's family moved from Matamoros to *Corazón* two years after Claudia arrived.

Claudia had an interest in learning English, which is why she came to America. She role-played with her brothers in Matamoros, Mexico, pretending to speak English. Her mom asked if she wanted to move to Texas and learn English. Claudia said yes, but adjusting to U.S. schools proved difficult. Claudia had nervous breakdowns the first few days and vomited often at school. Her godmother had to retrieve her constantly. Claudia felt lost, lonely. She missed her brothers. The pupils shocked her. Many disrespected the teachers, which she never witnessed in Mexico. Yet she adored her first American teacher, Ms. Love, a bilingual Anglo.

Claudia soared in math. Third grade U.S. peers were learning times tables, but she knew how to add, subtract, multiply, and divide fractions. Because Claudia was ahead in math, Ms. Love would let Claudia listen to books-on-tape during math instruction. To push Claudia, Ms. Love would have Claudia write English grammar rules and examples, which Claudia would take for homework. Ms. Love tailored instruction to fit Claudia's academic needs and affirmed Claudia's spoken Spanish. Group work in Ms. Love's class also helped Claudia to acquire vocabulary. Claudia's godparents spoke no English, but her older cousins did; they taught her English. By the end of third grade, Claudia knew how to read and write in English, which represents a fast academic language transition. In fourth grade, she passed the Texas Assessment of Academic Skills (TAAS) in English. She also earned the highest writing grade in her class. Her teachers were surprised, yet thrilled.

Yet Claudia remembers an incident in fourth grade related to Spanish use. The school, just a 15-minute drive from Mexico, had just started a "no speaking Spanish" rule, making it hard for Claudia to communicate. Claudia became shy. One day she and peers were working in groups; someone kept saying Spanish words. Her teacher, Ms. Smith, kept stopping the class, reminding them they could not speak Spanish in class; Ms. Smith would look at Claudia because Claudia had less time in American schools. Suddenly Ms. Smith's arteries burst in anger and she made Claudia stand in a corner—for a long time.

Claudia's heart broke. She had not received school punishment before. She did not utter a Spanish word that day in class! Regardless, Claudia could not fathom why her mother tongue reeked to Ms. Smith. Isolation and punishment because of one's mother tongue constitutes linguistic terrorism (Anzaldúa, 2007). Ms. Smith was a Latina with an Anglo surname. Nevertheless, Latinos/as can discriminate against one other because of the coloniality of power and internalized racism (D. Gutiérrez, 1999).

Around sixth grade, Claudia attended *Corazón's* Tutorial Center intermittently to borrow the computer or to seek homework help from Alma, former coordinator. Claudia organized and co-supervised some tutorial activities as part of Claudia's own course requirements. She began volunteering regularly in February 2008, by helping children with homework, collecting report cards, assisting with record keeping, and supervising soccer on the Church parking lot.

Claudia taught first grade in San Antonio at a dual-language school, but she returned to the Valley to finish her master's degree and to teach fourth grade. Based on her positive experiences with peer collaboration as an emergent bilingual child and her pedagogical knowledge, Claudia engages her mostly Mexican-heritage students in group-work and modifies instruction constantly. Because of her experiences and bilingual certification socialization, Claudia encourages students to maintain Spanish. Claudia met Kathy in 2008 when Claudia volunteered at the Center. Claudia liked the idea of Kathy's May project because many children, but few volunteers, attended the tutorials. Claudia participated in Kathy's studies and completed surveys. Additionally, she participated in María's doctoral dissertation about language use in *Corazón*. Claudia met Krystal in August 2015 when Krystal interviewed her, Hermosa, and Itza at Hermosa's home. See Chapter 9.

Irma

Born in Cuidad Juárez, Irma lived in many Texas towns. She grew up in a Spanish-speaking, Mexican-heritage home. On her initial visit to *Corazón* in fall 2014, she recalled her first assignment as a bilingual elementary teacher in a town west of San Antonio, where families faced numerous challenges, including flooding and unlit streets. After four years teaching, Irma pursued advanced degrees, but continued working in communities similar to *Corazón*.

Irma worked at our university in 2014 and 2015. Kathy's and María's research fascinated Irma. When Irma visited *Corazón's* Tutorial Center, she focused on building *la confianza* [trust], with Rita, tutorial coordinator. Irma observed the tutorial children struggling with their English homework; Irma related their difficulties with language policies.

After seeing Rita interact with the children, Irma realized Rita's tutorial and *Corazón* resident roles enabled Rita to create a cultural Third Space landscape. Rita participated in the Church's traditional practices, guiding the children in memorizing long scripts in Spanish for the *Aparición de la virgen de Guadalupe* celebration. Rita, a biliterate, bilingual resident and caring leader, affirmed Spanish and created academic bridges for the children. Upon Rita's invitation, Irma attended the December 2014 apparition celebration. By walking with the procession, taking photos, and seeing the children's reenactment, Irma learned about *Corazón*.

Our Positioning

Our experiences, perceptions, privileges, and power relate to every aspect of our advocacy research (Cherland & Harper, 2007). Our stories connect to our epistemic and ontological beliefs, which blurred often. For instance, if we believe in learning from others, then this stance is epistemic, related to knowing, and ontological, related to being in the world.

Toward Epistemic Reflection (Vasilachis de Gialdino, 2009)

- How do we know? We know by faith, relationships, dialogue, storytelling, disciplinary formation, experience, multimodalities, print, and technology.
- What assumptions underlie our processes of knowing? We know through qualitative data sources (e.g., participant observations and interviews) and from many people to establish trustworthiness. However, we cannot measure everything because many forms of partial knowledge exist. Furthermore, we know through risk-taking.

- What do we believe about generalizability? We know about particular people (not the entire colonia), and a particular place and time. We cannot generalize our findings to all of *Corazón*, other colonias, or Latinos/as.
- What is knowledge? It carries power. It is experience- and perception-based information and understanding—affirmed, shunned, (re)constructed, reproduced, and partial. Knowledge situates itself culturally, economically, historically, politically, and socially.

Toward Ontological Reflection

- We interact with co-researchers reciprocally.
- We know with—not about. Knowing with co-researchers represents ontological rupture (Vasilachis de Gialdino, 2009).
- What we know with co-researchers may not be the same tomorrow, as people change.
- We believe co-researchers and we are equal, but we acknowledge power relationships. Thus, we treat people with respect and dignity.
- We share more similarities than dissimilarities, but we value diverse persons and ideas.
- Our paradigm influences how we conduct research and co-write this book.
- We are intersubjective. Co-researchers are not objects. We are not objective.

Further Ontological Assumptions from These Stories

- We value blended, situated, and evolving identities and practices.
- We build and maintain relationships.
- We grow with others.
- We use language for communication and enrichment.
- We aspire to help others. They aspire to help us.

Summary

We discussed our institution because it relates to this book. We became involved with *Corazón* with different goals, as students and professors at this community-engaged university. We explained how our experiences influenced our research, starting with Kathy, who began teaching and researching at the Tutorial Center in 2006. María followed, describing her roles as a volunteer, doctoral student, research assistant, and researcher. Krystal and Irma learned about *Corazón* recently, while Claudia arrived in the colonia during third grade. We unpacked our privileges and epistemological and ontological beliefs. Knowing our backgrounds and positions may help you to realize how we reached conclusions. Giving back, researching and writing with participants as co-researchers, and coming clean with our privilege are decolonial.

Related to ontology, we recognized this book came from the community when Brother James, after reading a draft, met with Kathy and offered a least 23 detailed suggestions. He said, "We don't want to say that … Our book … We want the reader to …" We agreed with him and made the changes. As we continue to explore possibilities of developing reciprocal, long-lasting partnerships with residents and staff, new questions arise, each one challenging our understanding of how to work with *Corazón* children and their families and to engage in socially just, decolonizing community-based research.

Questions to Ponder

1. This chapter addresses our research processes. How would you conduct community-based research? What ontological beliefs (human interactions) undergird your ideas?
2. What benefits arise in emic (insider) and etic (outsider) perspectives in this chapter?
3. Explain some of your epistemological (knowledge) beliefs related to conducting research. How are they similar to and different from the ones we discussed in this chapter?
4. Why should researchers interrogate their privilege?

· 2 ·

TEXAS COLONIAS

Introduction

Because we have not visited another colonia besides *Corazón*, we do not start with a scenario. Chapter 2 consists of a literature review and interviews with some adult *Corazón* residents. By applying the imprimatura or toned ground for Chapter 3, Chapter 2 begins with the Rio Grande Valley. It focuses on colonia demographics, histories, and economies along the Mexico-Texas border. Next, we explain why colonias are important for policy and research, and how colonia case studies may help us to understand culture, education, language, literacy, neighborhood, social class, slantwise, diasporic (motherland) practices, and neoliberalism. Slantwise, discussed in this chapter, signifies unorthodox practices for socially-acceptable ends (Campbell & Heyman, 2007). Next, people who live away from their homeland may engage in diasporic practices, e.g., using Mexican oregano tea for respiratory infections. Neoliberalism, an old concept, resurged in the 1980s with Margaret Thatcher and Ronald Reagan (Duménil & Lévy, 2013).

Neoliberals focus on laissez-faire economics and less government spending on environmental and social programs. Profits drive neoliberal ethics (Freire & Macedo, 2000). Vincente Fox, a neoliberal, led Mexico for six years

(S. A. Day, 2004). Neoliberalism relates to Mexican professionals' exodus to the USA and billions in remittances sent to loved ones in Mexico, more than combined manufacturing and tourism revenues (Greenberg, Browning-Aiken, Alexander, & Weaver, 2012). Calling someone a neoliberal is an affront, as neoliberals may avoid this term to describe themselves.

Rio Grande Valley

El Valle [the Valley] occupies the southernmost Texas tip. About 1.3 million live in the Rio Grande Valley (RGV), the fastest growing U.S. region. Approximately 92% of RGV residents are Hispanics, a U.S. government term for Spanish-origin people. About 29% of RGV inhabitants possess less than a ninth grade education, compared to the USA's 6%. Fifteen percent of RGV residents earn associate's (or higher) degrees, compared to the USA's 29% (U.S. Census Bureau, 2010). This low RGV achievement relates to income; the RGV has the highest U.S. poverty level (U.S. Census Bureau, 2010). The McAllen-Edinburg-Mission area, constituting Hidalgo County and 775,000 people, ranks in the top 18 for U.S. metropolitan area unemployment (U.S. Department of Labor, 2015b).

The RGV belonged to Mexico until the 1848 Treaty of Guadalupe Hidalgo, signed after the Mexican War. RGV Mexican-origin people became orphans of Mexico, yet racially discriminated against in the USA. Mexican and U.S. governments have marginalized this hinterland historically (D. Gutiérrez, 1999). Residents without English-speaking skills may receive paycheck penalties and those with inadequate English select lowest-paying jobs frequently (Richardson & Pisani, 2012). Because scant RGV industry existed before 1970, many RGV residents sought seasonal farm work in other states. In the early 1980s and in 2014, the Valley experienced an influx of Central Americans. Most of these migrants have been poor, but many upper-middle and upper-class Mexicans have fled Mexico. Migration reasons for children and adults may range from home-country extortion, poverty, violence, and/or family reunification. Last, many immigrate to subsist. Like Francisco Jiménez's family in *The Circuit* (1997), migrants move to different states to survive.

Four counties (Cameron, Hidalgo, Starr, and Willacy) constitute the RGV. The Rio Grande River, separating the USA and Mexico, remains undrinkable in some areas (Satija & Ura, 2015). This river's pollution may connect to increases in border dumping and *maquiladoras* [U.S. factories], which sprang up after the 1992 North American Free Trade Act (NAFTA). Furthermore, border dumping relates to the abrupt 1994 Mexican Peso devaluation and increased costs of disposing hazardous waste (Matthiesen, 1997).

Regardless of its pollution, the Rio Grande constitutes the main RGV water source. *Resacas*, channels, meander ubiquitously. *Resacas* formed when the Rio Grande changed course over time. This sea-level area exemplifies a geographic misnomer. Certain sections, such as the South Padre Island dunes, have higher elevations. However, some posit developers created the name, Valley, in the early 1900s to lure investors and tourists.

Lack?

The Cranston-González National Affordable Housing Act of 1990 defined colonias as: (1) identifiable communities in (2) Arizona, California, New Mexico, and Texas, (3) within 150 miles of the U.S.-Mexico border, with (4) inadequate water and sewer systems and sanitary, safe housing. Inadequate housing infrastructure, such as building codes and inspections, characterizes colonias (U.S. Department of Housing and Urban Development, 2014). Yet these definitions focus on lack.

What more are colonias? What strengths do they exhibit? How do colonia residents support each other? As explained in our Book Introduction, many colonia residents exemplify neighborliness. Residents care for each other, as their lives depend on resource sharing amid poverty. Mexican diasporic practices may relate to sharing, also. Inhabitants may value colonias and other high-poverty Southwestern places for non-material reasons, also (D. Gutiérrez, 1999).

Additionally, colonias provide housing, not only for transnational residents crossing the U.S.-Mexico border, but also for seasonal or migrant workers. Ramshaw (2011) shared a story of a Matamoros, Mexico, mechanic, who bought land with his wife in a Rio Grande Valley (RGV) colonia for $9,500, but who could not afford to build a home. Instead, the couple and their three teen sons lived in a dirt-floor rental shack on their land. The mechanic yearned to give the land to his oldest son, a U.S. citizen: "We're here so he can get an education, rise up. God willing, he will build on this land" (para. 12). Some colonia residents, such as the Matamoros mechanic, started as migrant workers, whose pay hangs below the poverty line. Magnífico, an elderly activist said, *"Eran puros labores"* [Only labors lived here] when he bought his *Corazón* lot in the mid-1960s.

Because colonias are high-poverty neighborhoods, municipalities do not annex them. We draw images of abandonment and cruelty as we consider the exclusion. Picture a hen taking chicks under her wing, yet leaving a scrawny one alone to starve, thirst to death, and freeze. This signifies life in a colonia—cut from the wing of most government care. This neglect represents a structural inequality, involving city, county, state, and national governments. Coloniality could be another way to characterize how and why colonias exist and continue. They represent a caste-like system in a capitalistic society, which encourages profit over caring for the most vulnerable populations (Quijano, 2000).

Most Texas colonia residents share Mexican roots. Texas boasts the most colonias and largest U.S. colonia population. Thus, we focus on Texas colonias, specifically colonias in the RGV, which has the largest colonia population; see Figure 2.1. Approximately 2,294 colonias dot the 1,250-mile Texas border; 500,000 people live in Texas colonias (Federal Reserve Bank of Dallas, 2015). About 1,524 Texas colonias existed in 1999, so the 2015 estimate constitutes a 51% increase. Texas colonias wear these bright names: Angel Haven, *Casa del Rey* [King's Home], Four Sure All Right, Stardust, and *Tierra Bonita* [Beautiful Land] (Texas Department of Transportation, 2004).

One RGV colonia, with a name reminiscent of the sitcom, *Green Acres* with Eva Gabor, represents travesty. In 2008, Hurricane Dolly left the Green Valley Farms in Cameron County in floodwaters for over three months (Brezosky, 2012). Residents could not enter or leave with vehicles. Although many RGV colonias sit on flood plains, some West Texas colonias occupy arid places.

History of Colonias

In the 1950s, colonias began to represent a way of life for low-income families when avaricious developers created subdivisions in unincorporated rural areas by subdividing poor farm land. An elderly *Corazón* resident said building a colonia home is more cost-effective than growing crops on colonia soil. Because the lots existed outside of city limits, authorities did not enforce subdivision codes. Furthermore, colonias propagated because many developers contributed to county officials' political campaigns and some county commissioners owned or invested in the developments (Ward, 1999).

How can people with little money buy land? Developers sell unwitting buyers land as a contract for deed. This constitutes predatory financing. The

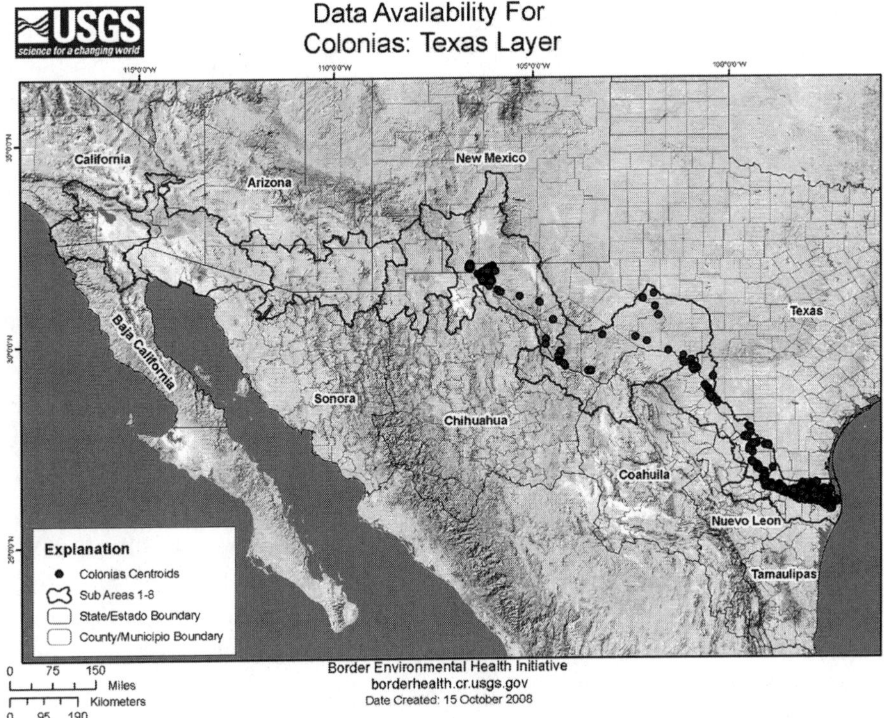

Figure 2.1. Colonias along the U.S.-Mexico border: Texas layer. Used with permission from the U.S. Geological Survey (USGS).

buyer cannot obtain the title until s/he pays off the house or land. Sellers, bypassing banks, engage in seller-take-back deals with unsuspecting buyers. If a person owes only $500 after paying off $8,000 of the principal, the seller can confiscate the land.

Colonias did not capture much public attention until the late eighties, when people debated the environmental impact of North American Free Trade Act (NAFTA) on southwestern border towns. Environmentalists anticipated, correctly, an increase in dumping hazardous waste into the Rio Grande River related to NAFTA. Environmentalists, the media, and politicians mentioned colonias when discussing border and NAFTA problems (Matthiesen, 1997).

Additionally, inadequate infrastructure has been problematic since the existence of U.S. colonias. Because of the serious consequences for public health, a concern regarding colonias has been living conditions. Some activist religious leaders, especially in the Catholic Church, have improved colonia conditions; see Chapters 3 and 4. Some clergy affiliated with Valley Interfaith, a national social justice organization. In his case study of some Valley colonias and schools, Shirley (2002) documented Valley Interfaith's role in local school reform since 1981, working with local and state politicians to get laws passed.

Some Laws Concerning Colonias

People have attempted to confront socio-economic and environmental challenges of U.S. colonias, where a dream becomes a nightmare because of promised, but undelivered services. Certainly, Texas colonias have received help since their abysmal conditions began to draw state and national attention. This chapter does not attempt to cover most laws concerning colonias. Instead, we highlight some important laws.

Texas Senate Bill 585 initiated colonia water and sewage infrastructure in 1987. Many Texas Senate and House bills followed. Brother James, retired Catholic clergy, said Senate Bill 2 (SB 2) of 1989 helped *Corazón* much. SB 2 established the Economically Distressed Areas Program (EDAP) to provide water and wastewater services in new and existing colonias. In 1995, Texas House Bill 1001 gave county governments the power to impose platting and service requirements on property sellers. This meant basic amenities in colonias became legally mandatory. From 1987 to 1999, many colonia water bills created facilities, funding, planning, quality, and supplies for indoor plumbing, sewer, and water hookups; federal block grants helped. In 1999, Texas authorized a colonias initiative, including a director and six ombudspersons to coordinate colonia improvements (Texas Secretary of State, n.d.).

Laws authorized county district attorneys and the Texas Attorney General to prosecute violators of the Model Subdivision Rules *and* counties that failed to enforce these rules. House Bill 1001 imposes civil and criminal penalties for noncompliance. Since 2002, the Texas Attorney General has sued more than 70 developers for marketing substandard land (Brezosky, 2012). However, the dearth of state legal employees impedes suing counties for inadequate enforcement (Ward, 1999). Moreover, developers may hide assets and file bankruptcy to avoid providing services (Matthiesen, 1997).

Some U.S. colonias lack services most Americans consider essential, e.g., potable water, sewage, electricity, and paved roads. Improvements happened slowly. In 2006, about 145,000 people resided in colonias with at least basic infrastructure, including sewage and paved roads (versus 194,000 inhabitants in 2010), a 33% improvement. About 63,000 people lived in colonias with no drinkable water or drainage in 2006 (versus 45,000 in 2010), a 35% improvement (*The Economist*, 2011). Despite advances, 45,000 people living without necessities in such a rich country ires us. Laws may not change developers' coloniality mindsets (Mignolo, 2006). Hiding colonias from view relates to racism and fear of foreigners: "While the rest of the nation is just waking up to its love-hate relationship with immigrants, the Southwest has been aware of this relationship for years, and the colonias developed in part as a solution to this problem of xenophobia" (Dolhinow, 2010, p. 4).

How Colonias Help the U.S. Economy and Other Neoliberal Ideas

Some people believe colonia residents burden, instead of help, state and national economies. However, colonia residents, like others who live in the USA, pay sales taxes on goods purchased. Texas colonia residents may not pay city taxes because colonias are unannexed, but they do pay county taxes. Texas has no state income tax. Additionally, anyone who works in the United States with a U.S.-provided social security number must pay federal income taxes. Colonia residents are also creative, problem-solving entrepreneurs; see Chapter 3. Undoubtedly, the USA has benefitted from the consumption, labor, and taxes of Mexicans in the diaspora (Greenberg et al., 2012).

Unfortunately, many colonia residents earn low wages, allowing businesses to sell products inexpensively for higher profits (Coronado, 2003). This bothers us from a social justice viewpoint because it exploits workers with little choice. Yet low wage/high profit constructs align with ignoble, neoliberal U.S. business practices and coloniality regarding capitalism and domination (Duménil & Lévy, 2013).

Next, some institutions appear unappreciative of the language brokering children provide to adult family when youth translate official documents, a service governmental institutions should provide (Orellana, 2009). Having children redress the dearth of governmental translators relates to neoliberalism. Virginia has only 2.3% of the U.S. immigrant population, while Texas has 10.4% (U.S. Census Bureau, 2012a). However, Virginia employs more interpreters and translators per thousand jobs (0.54) than does Texas (0.35) (U.S. Department of Labor, 2015c); the site made no distinctions between sign and foreign languages.

Next, colonia residents without U.S. documentation may avoid social welfare programs because they fear deportation. The scant housing organizations applicable to colonia residents may have waiting lists of over 3,000 families (Arizmendi, Arizmendi, & Donelson, 2010); thus, few colonia residents receive benefit from government housing programs. Oftentimes, colonia residents turn to friends, families, churches, and non-government organizations, but governments should help.

Colonias as Policy and Research Sites

Policies

Studying colonias, and one colonia in depth, can guide us regarding policy. For instance, we can see how Texas, the second largest U.S. state in size and population, manages rural affairs and enforces laws. Furthermore, we can realize implications of the No Child Left Behind Act on colonia families. Despite the law's appealing title, many colonia children lag behind academically; see Chapter 9. Other policy implications relate to diverse disciplines, ranging from economics and immigration to healthcare.

Slantwise, Diasporic Practices

Colonias provide novel research perspectives related to hybridity. Residents' nonlinear border zigzagging relates to slantwise; many colonia residents travel to other states as migrant farm workers, also (Campbell & Heyman, 2007). Yet anti-immigrant hysteria and ensuing laws have affected the U.S.-Mexico border permeability after the 9/11 tragedy (Zatz & Smith, 2012). Additionally, 9/11 halted negotiations between Vincente Fox and George W. Bush regarding guest workers and Mexican migrant amnesty (Dolhinow, 2010).

Although legal and physical walls have slowed transnationalism, colonia residents still engage in slantwise diasporic practices. Some *Corazón* neighbors shared electrical costs by stringing orange electrical cords between homes, slantwise for economic survival and relationships—not defiance. Thus, colonias have Mexican-inspired attributes sparse in many U.S. neighborhoods—*convivencia* [coexistence]. An attendee of the bi-annual *Corazón* Catholic Church *kermes* [carnival], held on the Church parking lot, may notice over 200 youth and adults shaking hands, embracing, and talking, eating, and dancing in small groups. Rare stands the loner. Living *in* community, not just in a community, characterizes colonia residents.

Language, Literacy, and Education

As language and literacy researchers, colonias excite us. Colonia demographic characteristics, such as U.S.-Mexico border mobility, provide unique knowledge. The border, this special place Anzaldúa (2002) called *nepantla*, has been shifting its socio-cultural landscape, offering language and curricular transformation for nondominant people in a hybrid Third Space. Colonias represent some of the most bilingual U.S. communities, as many colonia residents self-identify as bilingual English and Spanish speakers. Moreover, we can understand the literacy practices of people who have experienced Mexican and U.S. educational systems and Spanish-language marginalization in local schools (Smith & Valenzuela, 2012). Bilingualism relates to ethnic homogeneity in colonias, as over 90% of colonia residents are of Mexican origin. We wonder how the border wall may affect Spanish maintenance. However, Smith and Valenzuela found only 12% of research about colonias relates to literacy and/or education.

Case Studies

We build on the qualitative colonia-related cases of: Arizmendi et al. (2010), Coronado (2003), Dolhinow (2010), Richardson and Pisani (2012), Shirley (2002), Smith and Murillo (2012), and Ward (1999). Colonias lend themselves to case studies because of their geographical boundaries. A case study constitutes a single example, bounded physically and temporally, which fits *Corazón's* physical demarcations and our emphasis on a particular data gathering time, e.g., 2006–2016. While we do not generalize all colonias, case studies constitute necessary social science methods (Flyvbjerg, 2006). A case affords an in-depth analysis of a particular group, place, and time. Cases, situated within broader themes, such as discrimination, can make concepts salient, but we invite readers to make their own connections.

Sociocultural, Education, and Neighborhood Intersections

We can learn much about culture, education, neighborhood, and social class from colonias. Some official and educator marginalization of *Corazón* astonishes us, considering most local officials possess Mexican roots and 87% of local teachers are Latinos/as. Culture constitutes many facets. Furthermore, exclusion relates to power and social justice. Anzaldúa (1990) stated Mexican-heritage people's marginalization of each other demonstrates colonialism still exists—internally and externally: "They have us doing to our own ranks what they have done and continue to do to us—Othering people" (p. 143).

Summary

Although ubiquitous in Texas, many misunderstand colonias. We focused on economics, histories, and laws of Texas colonias. We discussed why colonias might help us to understand policies, slantwise and diasporic practices, culture, education, language, literacy, social class, and neighborhood. Colonias constitute a Third Space, a boundary blurring. "You won't find the Borderlands marked as a spot or shape on a map. Consider it a Third Space, one that is neither Texas nor Mexico, but contains the blood, voices and language of both" (M. Ortiz, 2014, p. 23). Borderlands exist when spaces between individuals and cultures shrink with intimacy (Anzaldúa, 2007). Third Space colonias can challenge colonizers, also. We hope this chapter has created an interest and a rhizome, or organic shoot, to the next chapter.

Questions to Ponder

1. Before reading this chapter, what did you know and perceive about colonias? Which concepts surprised you from this chapter? Why?
2. How are colonias different from urban slums? How are they similar?
3. What slantwise activities have you noticed in other economically disadvantaged neighborhoods or among nondominant people?
4. We discussed laws related to colonias. Research and discuss instances in which laws changed and did not change people's behaviors.

· 3 ·

CORAZÓN

Meet Poeta and Esposo

Esposo [husband] and Kathy squirm from the back of Brother James's car, Esposo with his walking cane, Kathy with a digital recorder. Standing upright now, the sight before Poeta's [Poet's] and Esposo's home makes Kathy's head reel. At least 75 cracks in the cement driveway greet us, with brave white and fuchsia *teresitas* [Vincas of Madagascar] in every crevice. Each *teresita* bears testimony, not to a single blossom, but to innumerable curved friends. Each bouquet stands 10 inches tall—at least. The fenced-off driveway waits not for cars, but for the careful to admire and skirt. *Las teresitas* mock the harsh cement, the impossible. What began as a talk with *los señores* [the men] transforms into an understanding about how *las señoras* [the women], have fought.

Kathy encounters Poeta, who uses a walker, at the threshold. Brother James, a trusted friend on both sides, lived in *Corazón* for many years, but Poeta squints with suspicion at Kathy. As per the phone call, Poeta already knows about the research project. Poeta considers the consent form. Kathy says, "I'll change all names, even the colonia's." Poeta asks, "*¿Entonces, cómo va a saber la gente la verdad si cambias todos los nombres?*" [So how will people know it's the truth if you change all of the names?] Kathy says she and her colleagues will write with enough detail that people will know it is true. Satisfied, Poeta and Esposo sign the forms.

Introduction

For Chapter 3 we inquired: What are *Corazón's* struggles and strengths? We answer this query by telling stories, from partial perspectives, of our relationships to Mexican-heritage people, such as Esposo, Poeta, Magnífico [magnificent], Luchadora [fighter], and Patriota [patriot], hard-working activists who improved the colonia. Chapter themes relate to *Corazón's* characteristics, systemic inequalities, and activism. In presenting our themes, we describe *Corazón's* location and demographics, and issues related to *Corazón's* unannexed status, such as water, sewage, streets, homes, electricity, police, and transportation; the outskirts lack some services still. We include *Corazón's* progress and some residents' perceptions. Finally, we underline *Corazón's* positive aspects, including: activists getting results, unity, stability, community pride, entrepreneurialism, ingenuity, and freedom.

Most data involved interviews; see the Book Introduction for methodology. Co-researchers consisted of elderly community activists, adult volunteers, staff, parents, teacher candidates, and Tutorial Center youth. We do not generalize this diverse community; we could not interview every resident. However, we can report U.S. Census (2010) results, which places *Corazón* below the Texas average for: median household incomes, house values, and higher education attainment. From the same Census data, *Corazón* remains significantly above the Texas average for Hispanics and foreign-born populations.

Characteristics

Demographics

About 1,850 households on 1,624 lots comprise *Corazón*. This colonia occupies approximately 60 blocks, with 0.6 square miles (1.6 km²) or 401 acres. Approximately 40% of households share or rent lots with other families. About 99% self-identified as Hispanic; 97% reported speaking Spanish at home (U.S. Census Bureau, 2010).

About 39% of foreign-born people (mostly from Mexico) reside in *Corazón* (U.S. Census Bureau, 2010), which may be inaccurate, as residents may fear revealing undocumented U.S. status. About 50% of Latino/a adults in the USA were foreign-born (Pew Research Center, 2014). Census workers attempt accurate demographics, but residents may report slantwise information to protect themselves and neighbors. Furthermore, Census enumerators may not know on which doors to knock, since some residents create improvised residences and occupy many homes per lot (Campbell & Heyman, 2007). Immigration laws and enforcement terrify close-knit residents, who fear separation from families and friends; thus, residents may change residences within the colonia. The children told teacher candidates during our May sessions that immigration officers raided neighbors' homes.

Additionally, *Corazón* constitutes the most impoverished U.S. neighborhood for its size, with a per capita income of about $7,700 and a median household income of $25,000; 54% of residents live below the poverty line (U.S. Census Bureau, 2010). *Corazón's* per capita income is similar to El Salvador's gross domestic product (GDP) per capita, an accepted measure of a country's wealth; El Salvador represents one of the poorest countries. *Corazón's* economic hardships represent structural inequalities related to annexation and education; see Chapter 9.

However, some residents (1.3%) do possess advanced degrees and earn an average income for their families, including their parents, grandparents, and siblings. Residents' occupations vary, from entrepreneurs (mentioned later in this chapter), to white-collar jobs. Some residents are teachers, school administrators, and nurses. *Corazón's* most common male occupation relates to construction and extraction (27%), followed by maintenance and building and grounds cleaning (15%) (U.S. Census Bureau, 2010). We could find no Census data on female jobs, but based on our long-standing knowledge of *Corazón*, most adult female *Corazón* residents work in the service industry, e.g., education, housekeeping, health professions, and food services.

Location

As Figure 2.1 in Chapter 2 showed, most Texas colonias exist along the U.S. border. Arriving to *Corazón* entails traveling close to the border by the Gulf of Mexico. *Corazón*, a Census-designated place (CDP), is within one hour of South Padre Island and five international airports, three in the USA and two in Mexico. A *resaca*, meandering channel, loops around *Corazón's* north and east boundaries, a drainage canal borders the south, and a main road to the west divides *Corazón* from the surrounding city.

Unannexed

Although a city has surrounded *Corazón* for years, city officials have refused to incorporate the colonia, perhaps because they believe it would be a fiscal drain to repair the residences; many *Corazón* homes do not follow building codes. Many cities shrink at providing costly services to colonia residents. Pastor Sabio, *Corazón* Baptist Minister, stated, "They figured out already that whatever taxes they raise on us won't be enough payoff." We wonder how much of a burden 7,000 people could be on a city that receives substantial state and federal grants. However, the surrounding city is one of the most economically strapped in the USA (U.S. Census Bureau, 2010).

Thus, discrimination against the colonia and geographic area layers like tree rings, or an aged trunk's cross-section, as no major interstate runs west of the Valley, disastrous if a major hurricane hollers from the north. This marginalization demonstrates European colonialism's legacy, such as social stratification (Quijano, 2000). Related to this tree-ring metaphor and coloniality, Knoll (2012) found Latino assimilation levels predicted Latino anti-immigrant nativism.

A city commissioner said the city does not wish to incorporate *Corazón* for an altruistic reason; the colonia would not receive as much federal funding if the city incorporated it. Federal monies set aside to help colonias face underutilization, however. Nowadays some *Corazón* residents do *not* want the city to incorporate it because they feel service costs and taxes will increase without the city reinvesting into the colonia. *Corazón* activist Janie asked, "What's in the city that can be offered to us, other than standards?" She chuckled. *Corazón* residents mentioned trash pick-up and a centrally located soccer field as the only assistance the city could provide. Many children play soccer on asphalt because the grassy soccer field occupies *Corazón's* southwestern periphery.

Marginalization

Corazón faces another type of marginalization—negative portrayals. When Kathy analyzed a local new station's words and images about *Corazón* over a 12-month period (2013–2014), the most common topics involved criminals, drug users, illegal immigrants, and neglectful parents. Indeed, news stations report crime in nondominant, poor communities as texts of terror (Rappaport, 2000). Pastor Sabio mentioned drug dealing occurs in the local country club, too. Due to *Corazón*'s marginalization, one might compare *Corazón* to Harlem. Matthiesen (1997) described colonias as rural slums. Colonias and ghettos share middle class outsiders' avoidance behaviors (Bussert-Webb, 2015). Many Latino/a teacher candidates (TCs) in Kathy's course feared *Corazón* initially. Mabel, a May 2015 TC said:

> The majority of the comments … might just be gossip. Everything they own is due to their hard work. I noticed how the students' parents all know each other … chitchatting or laughing together. They are a united community, not like many upper class communities where not many people know who their neighbors are. [*Corazón*] people are humble and nice, but they are also protective of their family.

Brother James refuted outsiders' portrayals, but added, "It takes a long time for the community to change their image." Janie agreed.

Many people call neglected urban areas surrounded by wealthier areas donut holes. This exclusion and discrimination fits *Corazón* because it sits physically in a city, but *Corazón* remains unwelcome. *Corazón* residents cannot vote for city commissioners or the mayor. Imagine walking in a U.S. town, then suddenly descending into a void not *technically* America. You are physically in the city, right? We must fight to change this treatment based on neighborhood status because residence can represent destiny for diverse children in poverty (Orfield, 2014). We can see this destiny with *Corazón* college graduation rates, versus the surrounding city and Texas; see Chapter 9. *Corazón*'s marginalization explains, in part, basic service problems, such as water, sewage, and police protection.

Police

Teacher candidates (TCs) saw no city police in *Corazón*. When TCs and children crossed the street with children for our gardening project, some motorists ignored speed limits or stop signs, making driving and walking dangerous. Although city police do not patrol, in 2002 Texas paid for a regional sheriff's substation in the colonia. Police visibility can decrease crime in U.S. cities, especially if officers walk around and develop positive relationships (Novak, 2013). People in Spanish-speaking Chicago neighborhoods reported more fear of crime and less police contact than English-speaking residents (Skogan, 2006).

Local police represent the Valley ethnically, which relates to representative social justice, e.g., nondominant people holding positions of power

(Fraser, 1997). The city surrounding *Corazón* is 93% Latino/a (U.S. Census Bureau, 2010). Based on Kathy's open record request, 89% of officers speak Spanish and are Latinos/as; the chief is Latino. However, Spanish-speaking Latinos/as are sparse in most U.S. police forces (Skogan, 2006). Instead of racism, no city patrols relate to *Corazón's* unannexed status. Undocumented people may not report crimes due to deportation fears (Zatz & Smith, 2012).

Transportation

Children reported not visiting city libraries (over three miles away) because their families lacked transportation. Keeping a registered, inspected, insured car in good condition may be difficult for colonia residents. Coronado's (2003) participant, a colonia mother, could not attend a far-away school meeting because the family car lacked gas. Spaces can be unjust, but diverse people in poverty can fight to have spatial justice (Soja, 2009), such as bus routes, because inadequate transportation leads to isolation.

Water and Sewage

Many assume all U.S. residences have potable water. However, easy access to clean water can signify privilege and power (Comber, 2016). Before 1993, *Corazón* residents used septic tanks and outhouses and lacked tap water. They had to draw water from the polluted *resaca* for drinking, cooking, and bathing. Luchadora narrated the difficulty of living without potable water, "*Con el agua batallamos mucho. Acarreábamos los tanques de agua desde allá de la resaca para bañarse, lavar la ropa y las vasijas*" [We struggled with water. We had to carry tanks full of water from the channel to have a shower and wash the clothes and dishes].

In 1994 local government employees attempted to install water and sewer services to 1,000 homes from a grant, but only 150 homes received initial connections to water and wastewater systems (Ward, 1999). Some residents could not afford to connect water and sewage lines, which cost less than $850. Many fear making homes to code will increase housing costs, which might leave them without affordable housing. A former *Corazón* resident said most elderly residents could not afford to comply with state law regarding sewage because they must pay at once, not in installment plans, to remodel their bathrooms to code and to connect sewage lines to streets. Some opted for latrines or outhouses. More water and sewage connections occurred later.

Corazón, like many Valley colonias, sits on a flood plain; water engulfs homes after torrents. Kathy's students walked children home from the Tutorial Center in 2006. Some dwellings, flooded after heavy rains, jolted these teacher candidates. Drainage canals surround much of *Corazón*, so heavy rains cause frequent colonia flooding. The irrigation district does not allow *Corazón's resaca* to circulate into other waterways and the Texas Water Quality Board refuses to get involved; providing the citation would breach confidentiality. A Level 5 hurricane may obliterate most of *Corazón*.

Corazón's resaca collects toxic waste, which Peña (1999) described as environmental racism or racial discrimination in environmental policies. Matthiesen (1997), appalled by national and state callousness and ineptness, called Texas colonias environmental border cesspools. Pesticide exposure threatens residents' health because a developer built *Corazón* on farm fields. Other colonias sit atop pesticide-laden land. *Corazón* and similar locales need environmental justice and the Texas Water Quality Board could help.

Figure 3.1. Littered water channel bordering *Corazón*. Photo by Kathy Bussert-Webb.

In Figure 3.1, you see a beautiful *resaca*. These native Valley waterways abound. However, litter overflows the banks and water. Ed, a teacher candidate in Kathy's May class and a *Corazón* resident, said outsiders dump refuge in the *resaca* because they face no official repercussions. What would happen if people deposited trash in a lake beside an upper-class neighborhood? How long would the trash remain?

Streets, Sidewalks, and Paths

Kathy, holding the historic December 1961 *Corazón* plat, eyed wide streets and street names. Yet Brother James said the developer used tiny garden flags to demarcate street names. No official forced him to create real streets. Leti, a co-researcher in her seventies, said residents created makeshift streets: "*Cuando llovía salíamos con mucha dificultad, pues era puro lodo, nuestros muebles se atascaban bien feo*" [We faced many difficulties when it rained. It was pure mud. Our cars became stuck in the muddy roads]. *Mueble* signifies a border term for car. Muddy roads meant mail carriers and emergency vehicles could not enter. People parked cars on *Corazón's* periphery during heavy rain. Others climbed in and out of car windows. Luchadora said, "*Yo veía pasar a la gente con sus bolsas de mandado y los garrafones de agua*" [I saw them walking with their bags full of groceries and big tanks of water].

Activists got street drainage culverts and improvements in 1996 and 1998 and the streets paved in 1998. However, county workers used recycled asphalt in some places and paved some streets incompletely; they have not made street repairs since 1998. Tim, former clergy, replaced his vehicle axels often from driving on inadequately paved streets.

Corazón streets have some litter. As mentioned, teacher candidate Ed said people dump trash here because no one will arrest them. Peña (1999) refuted characterizations of Chicanos as ignorant natural resource abusers. Most *Corazón* residents care deeply about their neighborhood and try to keep it clean. When Ed would see people discard shabby furniture from their trucks, Ed threw rocks at them until they left. This was his community, Ed said, and he would defend it. Until around 2009, *Corazón* had no formal, systematic rubbish retrieval. County workers eventually created some raised wooden boxes so dogs could not knock over the garbage cans. Although trash pick-up happens now, many families cannot afford the fees.

County workers created some *Corazón* sidewalks in 2010. A walking path exists at the colonia's southwestern boundary. Parents, children, teacher candidates, university clubs, and Kathy created a centrally located path in 2007 on the Church parking lot. From our university's $500 grant, we bought flora and signs for the path name, lap and mile/kilometer conversions, and warm-up/cool-down exercises. Kathy convinced county officials to stripe and delineate a path. The path benefitted adult women's emotional and physical well-being and camaraderie (Bussert-Webb, 2012). Alma, former tutorial coordinator, wrote:

> When the project was completed, community members continued planting and weeding the area. The children from the Tutorial Program presently enjoy daily-planned, hour-long exercise classes. An aerobics class does their warm-up exercises in the area. The walking path has become a popular place for families to gather, where native plants grow and where butterflies abound!

Homes

Most *Corazón* homes sit atop concrete blocks as one-story wood dwellings; see Figure 3.2. Some lots take up little space. Thus, 40 homes can occupy a block. State law mandates one residence per lot, but officials enforce this for new structures only.

Discarded trailers serve as some homes; see Figure 3.3. A teacher candidate from Kathy's May program wrote: "My tutee, he lives in a trailer. No running water. No power. Same shirt every day" (Bussert-Webb, 2015, p. 55). Using discarded mobile homes, 18-wheeler trailers, and school busses confounds officials, unaccustomed to residents' improvisational houses and migratory habits (Campbell & Heyman, 2007). Because most residents ignore expensive building codes, homes can face rain, wind, and flood damage.

Acquiring or remodeling a colonia home contrasts with the regulated marketplace, which most Americans expect. Colonia residents beautify their homes when they can spare funds, apparent with beams and bricks outside of *Corazón* homes. A family may live in a trailer as they build their wooden house on the same lot. When they finish enough to live in the house, they convert the trailer into a garage or sell, rent, or loan it. Unorthodox building and remodeling techniques demonstrate slantwise practices by colonia residents, adept at making things work with limited resources (Campbell & Heyman, 2007). For instance, in Figure 3.5 the air conditioner [AC] sits on the roof. Tailor-made colonia homes prove economical and functional (Coronado, 2003).

Corazón residents with limited resources pride themselves in owning homes, challenging because they cannot obtain mortgages. Many have limited

Figure 3.2. Wooden home on cement blocks. Photo by Kathy Bussert-Webb.

credit access, disdain for debt, and no checking accounts (Coronado, 2003). They rhizome around barriers by purchasing inexpensive land. *Corazón* activist Poeta explained:

Figure 3.3. Trailer Dwelling with Dog on Chain. Photo by Kathy Bussert-Webb.

Pues lo que pasa es que los hispanos de condición pobre, muy pobre, estas colonias es donde nos venimos porque está barato el terreno, y no hay tantas exigencias, entonces sólo nos preocupamos de estas colonias [This happens to Hispanics who are destitute. We came to the colonias because the land was cheap, and few requirements exist; we are the only ones who worry about colonias].

Magnífico disliked the muddy streets, so he bought a colonia lot on *Corazón's* perimeter for $750 in 1967, which cost more because it bordered commercial property and measured 100 by 200 feet, bigger than most colonia lots. Magnífico said a *Corazón* lot might have cost as low as $150 in 1967, but most cost about $200 at that time. Janie's home was worth $13,000 in 1995 and $20,000 in 2015. Another resident reported few lots empty because of recent Mexican and Central American influxes, related to those countries' present instability. Demand exists for *Corazón* lots.

Additionally, *Corazón's* median value of owner-occupied housing units is $48,000 (U.S. Census Bureau, 2010). This higher-value relates to some large, middle-class homes in *Corazón. Corazón* home conditions vary because older folks who advance financially tend to stay; this staying put relates to neighborhood and family ties. Thus, run-down $500 trailers and uncompleted houses stand beside fancy structures. However, residents do not grumble when newcomers park trailers beside finished homes. Instead, they may say, "That was how we started 10 years ago and look at us now" (Coronado, 2003, p. 195).

Many colonia residents, innocent and trusting, believe banks are unnecessary. Janie said they buy land through a deed of trust (or contract for deed) instead of a bank-involved warranty deed. Sellers took advantage of weak local governments and divided tiny lots to poor migrants and Mexican-heritage people, desperate for inexpensive housing (Ward, 1999). If an inhabitant cannot pay one month's mortgage, the developer forces the buyer to leave; the payment cycle starts with new occupants. Thus, a developer turns over a lot many times without inhabitants accruing equity. Janie's mother lost her home after paying the seller for many years; Janie's mother had to pay for the lot twice because she missed one payment. This angered Kathy, but Janie said her mother knew the rules, but failed to abide. Colonia residents believe building their homes and buying lots as contracts for deed are better than paying rent (Coronado, 2003).

Electricity

Although homes received electricity soon after *Corazón's* inception, Poeta said installation related to companies smelling profit. Three companies provide electricity to homes in different sectors. Street lights appeared in 2009, over 45 years after *Corazón's* founding. From a government grant of about $55,000, a power company installed 84 street lights, challenging because residents had to agree to extra county taxes for energy costs. Janie said Brother James convinced county officials to add *Corazón* street lights to tax assessments and maintenance.

And Yet ...

Activists Get Results

Brother James' advocacy, as well as the advocacy of Luchador, Luchadora, Poeta, Esposo, Magnífico, and others, helped *Corazón* to move from the margins. Community organizer Janie said, "All of these things that happened ... were from leaders who cared." Husband and wife teams working for the common good impressed Janie because they modeled activism to youth.

Luchador died in 2006, so Luchadora (his widow), Poeta, Patriota, and Magnífico told Luchador's story, which we verified with a historic newspaper article. All witnessed what happened in the early eighties when *Corazón* residents collaborated. See the Book Introduction and Chapter 5 about Luchador. Poeta stated, "*Él, como nosotros, había enganchado terrenos aquí*" [He, like us, got tricked with property here]. Poeta said Luchador taught them to walk toward him if police tried to arrest Luchador during a protest because police cannot arrest a multitude at once. Luchadora recounted how Luchador gathered residents: "*Iba a las casas y también tenía una bocina y les hablaba a la gente para que se junte. Toda la gente se juntaba aquí, en mi solar*" [He visited the houses and used a loud speaker to announce the meetings. Everybody was gathering in my backyard]. Driving through the streets with a loud speaker was slantwise. Most people would conjure up images of football coaches and authorities with loud speakers, barking orders, not a man in poverty. Moreover, the reunions took place in Luchadora's and Luchador's home, which demonstrated slantwise, grass-roots efforts.

Residents made key decisions during those backyard reunions, including a Washington D.C. trip for potable water and food. Magnífico first told Kathy of it; six interviewees confirmed it. Magnífico, Luchador, Patriot, and Patriota rode the two busses. Magnífico, Luchadora, Poeta, and Esposo were living in *Corazón* during 2015 data gathering. Patriota, who resided in a nearby U.S. town, immigrated to the USA at age 13 from Guadalajara, Mexico, and was a migrant child. Although Patriota had never lived in *Corazón*, she and Patriot, a Mexican-heritage Vietnam Veteran, befriended *Corazón* residents. Patriot had attended a Chicano university in Mercedes, Texas; Patriot and university staff participated in Chicano political and social movements.

On May 7, 1981, Rio Grande Valley (RGV) Latinos/as boarded a Greyhound bus and a yellow school bus for over a 1,700 mile or 2,700-kilometer journey. Patriota and Magnífico said the school bus displayed a homemade banner, hanging by threads and proclaiming, "*Viva la raza!*" [Long live the Mexican race]. This pro-Chicano banner may have represented *La Raza Unida* [The United Race] political party, formed in 1970 in Crystal City, Texas. The party assisted with the Civil Rights movement. Mexican-heritage people won Crystal City elections in 1963 and their party morphed into *La Raza Unida* (Acosta, 2011). Anzaldúa (2007) explained the Chicano party's formation, César Chávez's fight for farmworkers (which Luchador also led), and the realization of Chicano Spanish. Alternatively, *la Raza Unida* banner may have symbolized the nearly inseparable Lady of Guadalupe and Mexican race.

Yet *Corazón* life was challenging physically. In 2015, Kathy held the 1961 plat, which allowed an unscrupulous developer to create *Corazón* with no basic services. Kathy saw only Anglo-Saxon names, nine exactly, on the plat. Brother James explained, "All the rulers were Anglo." He said things started to change when Mexican-heritage people became elected. Besides little political power, Mexican-heritage people faced other types of discrimination in Texas. District officials in Driscoll, Texas, just north of the RGV, forced Mexican-origin children to stay in first grade for up to three years (Martínez, 2013). Perhaps Driscoll leaders wanted emergent bilinguals to drop out to prevent these youth from garnering power. Mexican-heritage people had little political power in Texas after the 1848 Treaty of Guadalupe Hidalgo and they felt (and feel) stereotyped and discriminated against (Ortiz & Telles, 2012).

Patriota said both sets of RGV bus passengers experienced much discrimination from many white people on the D.C. trip. Of the 28 passengers, 10 (36%) were from *Corazón*. Magnífico said he was proud he went. Recollecting the journey, he smiled and pretended to lean back to rest in the Greyhound bus with air conditioner (AC). Magnífico took three subsequent bus trips to Austin to fight for more *Corazón* services. Patriota narrated a different D.C. bus experience: The school bus "was full [of people] … it did not have AC … We had 10 gallons of water in case it overheated. We carried a mechanic with us, a guy from [*Corazón*]." The bus overheated often, possibly because of the 94 degrees Fahrenheit, 34 Celsius, outside temperature. The Greyhound driver and accompanying car drivers would wait until the mechanic fixed the school bus. In Figure 3.4, D.C.-bound passengers stand outside of the broken-down bus. A faded cloth sign, exclaiming ¡Viva la raza! dangles under the bus windows.

These RGV risk-takers relied on African Americans, who guided their journey. Some whites along the way refused Latino/a passenger bathroom use. In places with no African American friends to tip them off about friendly and unfriendly gas station staff, the RGV passengers would tell gasoline station clerks they would purchase gas elsewhere if the passengers could not use the toilets. This mistreatment transpired in 1981, despite the Civil Rights Act of 1964, barring discrimination in public places based on color, national origin, race, or religion. Patriota said:

The black people, they would all tell us, "Oh, don't go in there, they don't want you; they're only for whites. You'll get in trouble; you'll get arrested." You know, along the way we had our same people really, that would tell us where to stop, where not to stop.

Figure 3.4. Yellow school bus—Washington, D.C. bound. Photo by Patriota (pseudonym).

We interpret Patriota's statement "our same people" to mean African American friends who shared racism's burden. Patriota took more trips to represent RGV residents' rights; she and others would stay with African Americans. Thus, these trips demonstrated rhizomic heterogeneity and connection between Latinos/as and African Americans. D. Gutiérrez (1999) discussed historical documents in which Mexican-heritage people of the U.S. Southwest claimed whiteness and Spanish heritage to avoid racial discrimination by whites, but we found no indication of this racial distancing in our longitudinal *Corazón* research. In fact, the shared black and Mexican racial struggles propelled the RGV group. Yet, the discrimination for both groups continues. Negative reaction to dark-skinned undocumented U.S. immigrants relates to race (King & Punti, 2012). Undocumented Irish face less discrimination than undocumented, darker-skinned immigrants in the USA (Duffy, 2014). Immigration debates have framed Mexicans and other Latinos/as harshly.

In D.C. in 1981, the RGV group had an appointment to see their U.S. representative, Kika de la Garza, but his secretary said he had left. The RGV group then barged into his office anyway, finding the legislator at his desk. Patriota said, "We went in by force and we were all Hispanics in raggedy clothes, babies crying." To commiserate matters, unbeknownst to the group, a member hid in her suitcase bug-infested cornmeal and flour bags, old food the government earmarked for the RGV. The female, flinging the food on Kika de La Garza's shiny desk, shouted, "*Mira! Esto es el mugrero que nos están dando de comer*" [Look! This is the stuff they give us to eat]. Beetles from the spoiled food scrambled.

Patriota:	(Sucking in air) We were, like, "*Beatriz, qué hiciste?*" [What did you do?]
Kathy:	Then what did he [the representative] do?
Patriota:	(Shaking head sideways) "This won't happen again. I will take care of it." … He said that he would and put some bills in and stuff, but I don't feel like they did much.

The Honorable de la Garza left office in 1997. In his defense, only six other Latino legislators were in Washington during this time, which may have related to racism against Latinos/as. It must have been difficult for the Honorable de la Garza to convince others to help colonia residents. On June 20, 1987, Texas Governor Clements signed the Texas Water Code, Chapters 15–17, authorizing the Texas Water Development Board to provide colonia loans and grants for potable water and wastewater services. However, it took more legislative acts and RGV activism for the rest of Corazón to get sewage and water systems. According to historical newspaper articles, the [Corazón] Betterment Committee helped to get this 1987 bill and subsequent bills passed. Additionally, Valley Interfaith, Patriot, Patriota, and others helped in kinship circles (Moje, 2000b). Why does this trip captivate us?

- The trip was anti-colonialist. The Chicano and Civil Rights movements empowered RGV passengers. They had the "*Viva la raza!*" banner displayed on the bus exterior.
- The RGV people showed no fear. They persevered for human rights and dignity.
- The group believed the trip would affect change. Otherwise, they would have stayed home.
- The trip was a sacrifice. It was at least a two-day drive D.C. The school bus had no AC, the outside temperature soared, and the bus kept breaking down. Furthermore, taking this trip signified time away from family and/or work.

- Passengers faced much discrimination, but African Americans reached out to them along the way, in solidarity of racial struggles.

Besides the Texas government, the Quaker Church also helped the RGV activists to buy water and sewage pipes for *Corazón's* water, Patriota said. "The Quakers are the ones who gave us money to buy the pipes. Maybe it was for something else, but we used it for the pipes." Patriota's statement (and her one about vouchers) demonstrate ways communities, not far-away outsiders, however well intentioned, know what is best for a community, and clean water remains essential.

We can perceive, throughout the activist process to obtain potable water, a range of slantwise behaviors. Patriota and *Corazón* women prepared tacos and sold them for the trip. They also received money from the Friends Church (Quakers), activists in the anti-slavery movement and the Underground Railroad. Patriota recalled using the Quakers' vouchers to help fund the trip: "The people would cash the vouchers in a little store they had. The guy would trade the vouchers to get the money so we could go to D.C. ... They all agreed on it." Using vouchers for other purposes was unorthodox, but effective.

The RGV group engaged in additional slantwise practices. Patriota said someone donated the school bus, but the RGV group lacked money for a professional sign, so they hung a homemade banner, which is slantwise. The group typed correspondences, including a press release announcing the first Texas Senate Water Bill in 1987, on that rummage-sale typewriter. A local newspaper printed the press release. Patriota, studying to be a teacher at the time, said, "We didn't have stamps; we didn't have computers." These slantwise, grass-roots activities demonstrated socially accepted goals: community improvement.

Rhizomic principles abounded in the D.C. trip, also. In every trip aspect, the RGV group used ingenuity and relationships to circumvent barriers. The group brought their own food, drinks, mechanic, and radiator water, involving multiple entryways and assigning rupture. They relied on African Americans for safe passage, related to connection, heterogeneity, and multiplicity. This is because people can rework a rhizomic map (Deleuze & Guattari, 1987). We argue the group functioned as a map, connecting locations, people, and events. Thus, this map, this group, adapted to circumvent racism. *Corazón* activists and Patriota's group intersected to become one RGV group. In turn, the RGV group reached out to other activists, which demonstrated heterogeneity and multiplicity. Likewise, the RGV group demonstrated that squeaky-wheel activism achieves results for colonias (Arizmendi, Arizmendi, & Donelson, 2010). We found colonia activists collaborated with insiders and outsiders to affect change. This RGV group demonstrated sparks of collective impact, but lacked shared measurements (Kania & Kramer, 2011).

The RGV group's collective efforts and local politicians' resistance represented centrifugal and centripetal tit-for-tat, also (Holquist, 1996). The group attempted to break colonialism, while we perceive many officials sought to maintain it. We now discuss how local politicians attempted to bar Patriot (a key player in the D.C. trip) from helping *Corazón*:

Poeta:	"[Patriot] *estuvo aquí con nosotros en la lucha*" [Patriot fought with us].
Esposo:	"*Él nos ayudó mucho, hasta lo corrieron de aquí*" [He helped us, so much that they ran him off].
Kathy:	"*¿Quién lo corrió?*" [Who ran him off?]
P:	"*Pues los enemigos que estaban en contra de ayudarnos*" [Well, the enemies who were against helping us].
Kathy:	[Confused] "*¿Pero cómo pueden?*" [But how can they?]
Poeta:	"*Que él no podía meterse aquí porque él no vivía en [Corazón]. Pero nos quería ayudar*" [They told him he wasn't allowed to get involved here because he didn't live here, but he wanted to help us] … "*Como diciendo, 'Tú vete de aquí, tú no tienes nada que hacer aquí, tú no vives aquí'*" [They said something like, "You get out of here. You don't have anything to do here. You don't live here"].
Kathy:	"*¿Pero todavía ayudó?*" [But he still helped?]
Poeta:	"*Si, nos apoyó mucho. Nos orientó mucho*" [Yes, he helped us. He oriented us].
Esposo:	"*Él anduvo escarbando aquí para meter el agua. Él era otro guerrillero, que en paz descanse*" [He was here digging for the pipes. He was the other guerrilla. May he rest in peace].

This exchange demonstrated Patriot oriented the colonia activists politically. We ponder whether Patriot's bodily involvement in *Corazón*, e.g., digging for the pipes, deepened his place-based connections. Patriot labored for *Corazón*. He felt her warm earth and soiled his fingers for her. Additionally, these elderly colonia activists appreciated and loved him, e.g., "May he rest in peace." Some local officials believed they owned colonia residents, that they could make Patriot disappear. The Spanish conquistadors and U.S. colonialists divided and conquered in indigenous genocide. This relates to an Iberian Middle-Ages concept, called patrimony or paternalism, in which authorities feel they own and control people with less power (Eakin, 2007). After all, everyone has power. RGV officials, like Kika de la Garza in Washington, D.C., might face marginalization at state and national levels, but in their backyard, they appear to ignore or strong-arm Mexican-heritage people in poverty. Anzaldúa (1990) disliked nondominant people discriminating against each other; she believed this internalization of oppression stemmed from colonialism, in which native people believe their values and systems are unworthy. Many Spaniards thought indigenous people, who were often slaves to the Spanish, had no souls (Eakin).

In fact, an unwitting Mexican-heritage politician spurred *Corazón* residents and clergy in the mid-1990s. When they asked the local politician for help getting streets paved, he asked, "Why should I? You don't vote. You don't have a voice." They asked, "How many votes do you need to get action?" The official said 300, unaware of how channeled anger propels activism. In a massive voting campaign, these Catholic activists went door-to-door, encouraging all people with U.S. documentation to vote; this resulted in an 800% voter participation increase, according to a former *Corazón* resident. During Tim's tenure as priest, residents conducted their own slantwise census and helped to start the Civic Organization; see Chapter 4. Indeed, *Corazón* boasts one of the highest voting South Texas precincts. Tim stated that residents were excited and proud to vote for the first time.

Furthermore, *Corazón* residents have attended neighborhood, city, and county meetings for many years, fighting for necessities. When we saw online meeting records, we spotted familiar colonia activist and clergy names. *Corazón* has made much progress because of this collective action. Religious leaders encouraged resident activism and helped the latter to obtain services. Although pious neoliberalism relates to religion because of self-help rhetoric, our religious focus relates to unpacking complex factors and demonstrating religion's role in political activism. Pope Francis, who critiqued laissez faire economics and a structurally perverse world economic system, appears to dislike neoliberalism (Burke, 2015). Neoliberalism connects to laissez-faire economics, reduced government spending on social services, and an increased private sector role.

Our findings differ from Dolhinow (2010), who found New Mexico non-government organizations (NGOs) reinforced neoliberal ideas and did not connect colonia women to outsiders. Dolhinow stated, "Without NGOs it would be more difficult for the state … to cut back its social service provision" (p. 9). Conversely, political activism remains essential for the Civic Organization. Janie, a Mexican-heritage woman from *Corazón*, encourages residents to engage in their community and to develop solutions. She teaches them to work with other organizations, insiders, and outsiders. Janie invites elected officials to *Corazón's* monthly town hall meetings. Last, *Corazón* NGOs and Catholic Church leaders and laity demonstrated social justice passion. Similarly, Arizmendi, Arizmendi, and Donelson (2010) discovered equal partnerships among Southwestern colonia organizers and residents.

Children's and Parents' Perceptions of *Corazón*

Highlighting strengths from a social justice framework may avoid deficit conceptualizations. Additionally, from a Third Space, postcolonial framework, exploring co-researchers' evolving identities helps us to contest categories. Children and parents described their neighborhood quite differently than the media and local politicians (Bussert-Webb, 2015). From unpublished May 2013 data, 30 child interviewees said:

> Everyone helps each other. That they don't do bad things. Peaceful, nobody gets in trouble. My mom has friends here and they hang out with her when she picks me up at school. I get to play with my friends who live next door. We all play soccer. My mom takes me to the park. I got a lot of friends here. The way it looks, it looks like, when I pass by, all the houses look clean. My neighborhood is not so loud. It has many trees. Gathering with people and playing outside. How the people are—I know a lot of people and they are all very nice, older ladies, kids. Ducks and dogs.

The child's comment about ducks and dogs demonstrates *Corazón's* liveliness. Unpublished data reveal mothers' views of a collaborative neighborhood with educational opportunities:

> *"La convivencia con la comunidad"* [life together], *"Que existen oportunidades"* [Opportunities exist], *"La ayuda que dan a nuestros hijos para que pasen del año"* [The help they give to our children so they can be promoted], "They can walk in the park," and *"Que existen lugares como* [Tutorial Center] *y les ayudan a nuestros hijos"* [Places that help our children].

Participating parents valued their community, perceived the Tutorial Center as integral, and supported their children's education. Participating mothers expressed dreams similar to other Latino/a parents (Nora & Crisp, 2009).

Unity

Despite *Corazón's* hardships, researchers have discussed positive colonia aspects. Colonias constitute popular places for recent immigrants because these dynamic sites meet cultural and physical needs. Financial struggles, diasporic practices (such as Day of the Dead), and Mexican and Spanish-language heritages unite them. Because of similarities, many residents trust each other and live peacefully. Other strengths include exchanging skills, knowledge, and goods. Residents may exchange kitchen cabinets for electrical wiring (Coronado, 2003). Neighbors allowed children to use their digital equipment; see Chapter 7. Participating teacher candidates stated, "This is a family-based community" where parents care about their children's education and "work harder than we could ever imagine" (Bussert-Webb, 2015, p. 49).

Stability

Corazón is also stable. Despite the conditions of some houses, 77% of Texas colonia residents own their own home, above the 64% national average (Federal Reserve Bank of Dallas, 2015). Home ownership may help the stability of neighborhoods; 72% of *Corazón* adults are married and live together; less than 2% are 65-year-old or older living alone (U.S. Census Bureau, 2010). Instead of nursing homes, the elderly live with families.

Many white Americans tend to move out of high-poverty neighborhoods once they become well-off (Sharkey, 2013). However, this practice may be an aberration for African-Americans (Rothstein, 2014). The same could be said of middle aged and older Latinos/as in U.S. colonias. For instance, book contributor Claudia lived with her parents and four brothers in a trailer. When her family could afford it, they moved to a bigger *Corazón* home. Claudia feels connected to *Corazón* because Claudia's parents, brothers, cousins, uncle, and aunt live there. In fact, *Corazón* remains significantly above the Texas average for length of stay in one residence (U.S. Census, 2010).

Coronado (2003) noticed college graduates lived in trailers in the same lot as their parents because the former wanted to build their own homes. Teacher Joy, featured in Chapter 7, said a newlywed school administrator grew up in *Corazón* and still lives in *Corazón*. If some residents leave, they may return because they miss the unity and speaking their mother tongue with neighbors. One interviewee, now in his early thirties, moved to another state at age seven, but returned to *Corazón* when he entered high school. He said,

Cuando me fui de [Corazón] de chico, era aceptado que yo tenía que hablar el inglés pues era Colorado; yo soy un caso diferente de los otros jóvenes de aquí, pues yo fui separado de la cultura por un tiempo [When I moved from *Corazón* as a child, I was expected to speak in English because I was in Colorado; I am a different case from other youth who lived here because for a while I became separated from the culture].

For him, immersion in a different environment signified ethnic and linguistic isolation.

Green Thumbs

Although many *Corazón* families struggle financially, residents take pride in their homes and yards. In fact, some have thriving businesses selling flowers and trees. Most children co-researchers knew much more about planting and taking care of flora than university science majors; see Chapter 8. The native flowering trees, shrubs, and flowers create olfactory and visual delights. You may wander 100 feet in any direction to smell and see fragrant lime trees, *flamboyán* trees with blood orange flowers, jacarandas with delicate lavender buds, and wild olive trees bursting almost year-round with white flowers, as hummingbirds flit around in dizzy ecstasy. If you take a walk-about, as Kathy does with her students and the Tutorial Center coordinator (see Chapter 10), probably neighbors will give you starts of these beautiful trees. The native flora require less watering in the drought-stricken Valley, and the flora provide needed shade, as many homes have no air conditioning.

Entrepreneurialism and Ingenuity

This section focuses on the entrepreneurial spirit and sense of trust of many *Corazón* residents, which Kathy tapped into when she needed mile/kilometer and warm-up/cool-down signs installed for a walking path she co-initiated. Through the grant described in this chapter, Kathy paid a *Corazón* business, consisting of a married couple and their son, to create and install the signs. The business also makes round concrete tables and benches encircling them, with inlaid cobalt blue ceramic tile. This company's table and bench set have adorned Kathy's back patio for eight years.

Many businesses, such as the sign/table company, sell two completely different goods, which we interpret as slantwise, or an unconventional practice to earn a living. For example, a *taquería* [taco restaurant] also has an air/water pump station and a cell phone sale/service company offers a drive-through grocery store on the premises. These examples demonstrate how residents find ingenious ways to make money by offering different products under the same business name.

This ingenuity and entrepreneurialism are essential for a country's vitality. We welcome new immigrants, regardless of their education and income, because they have much drive and tenacity. A drive along any *Corazón* street reveals locally owned businesses. Residents seem engaged in the work ethic symbolizing the "American Dream." If this *sueño* seems within reach, residents will strive toward its achievement. These economic efforts pay off because many homeowners remodel. Not every entrepreneurial activity proves legitimate, as local news media have reported some *Corazón* drug busts. However, the energy propelling the hard-working residents vibrates, and people rhizome around impediments through personal connections.

A survey of *Corazón's* entrepreneurialism produces an album of working residents, bearing testimony to self-sustaining and creative people. Along the zipping four-lane street, *Corazón's* western boundary, over 25 businesses operate. Dominoes of businesses follow: a fish restaurant, a chicken stand, three *taquerías*, two bakeries, four car repair and tire shops, kickboxing center, eyewear store, beauty shop, adult daycare, LICENSED childcare center (original emphasis), cell phone store, laundromat, thrift store, insurance company, meat market, boat repair shop, and doctor's office; contributor Claudia and her family are patients of the latter. A drive-through grocery sells cell phones, too. Houses and apartment complexes snuggle within this one-mile space.

Although businesses deep within *Corazón* seem to maintain economic vitality, they lack fancy facades. Certain houses double as repair shops, as evident in small engines, lawn mowers, refrigerators, and bicycles in front of some homes. Car, small engine, and tire repair shops abound. Other centrally located companies include grocery stores, taco stands, beauty shops, and a business that rents tables, chairs, tents, and inflatable bounce houses. People line up on Sundays for *barbacoa* [cow's head], served with piping-hot tortillas at one stand. We hear *el camión de helados* [ice cream truck] music often in *Corazón*. *La paletería* [frozen treat] shop also offers a poster menu and drive-through to purchase selections.

In Figure 3.5, you can see this poster menu nailed to a palm tree, which we interpret as a cost-saving technique; perhaps the menu, at least 20 feet from the window, keeps air conditioning (AC) costs low. A window can remain open for less time if a customer decides in advance. Other drive-through businesses carry snacks, beer, wine, and mixed alcoholic drinks, such as *el sencillo* [simple mixture] and *la bomba* [the bomb]. An AC unit on the roof may prevent vandalism or theft. See Figure 3.5. We interpret these unorthodox *la paletería* moves as slantwise. These actions, probably done for practical reasons, may bypass regulations for businesses and structures.

Figure 3.5. *La Paletería* Drive-through. Photo by Irma Guadarrama.

Additionally, organizational means remain unstructured regarding supply/demand dynamics. Some businesses may lack full colonia support, as three fireworks stores compete. Some *taquerías* may play politics by displaying rivals' campaign posters side-by-side, obscuring the intentions of owners and politicians. The placards could be slantwise, because colonia residents may have unpredictable political loyalties (Campbell & Heyman, 2007).

Corazón residents and businesses may avoid receipts because they have built trust. In high-context cultures, receipts and checkbooks may be unnecessary because trust is more important than formal transactions, unlike low-context cultures (Hall, 1976). Although it stereotypes high- and low-context cultures, Hall's analysis may explain why few businesses provide receipts. Absence of receipts and bank checks help residents to participate in an informal economy. Although residents may not pay taxes on transactions, they lack sick leave, paid vacations, and retirement benefits. Since many residents cannot verify employment or have low-paying jobs, they have limited credit and cannot obtain home mortgages (Coronado, 2003). This border region has the strongest underground and informal U.S. economies; few governmental controls, the porous border, poverty, and belief systems favor informality. A third of Valley residents participate in underground exchanges and these informal economies increase when residents perceive illegitimate State government intervention, e.g. labor laws; however, labor abuses abound (Richardson & Pisani, 2012).

Many *Corazón* adults also offer services as landscapers and housekeepers at substandard pay, yet elderly activist Poeta (see Chapter 10), stated residents can do much more. One parent, Daniela, has a bachelor's degree from Mexico, but cannot work in her profession in the USA because she lacks official U.S. documentation and speaks no English. Daniela labors at a dry cleaning store under the table (without official payment) on some days and cleans homes on other days. Employed in mostly low-wage jobs, residents work beneath their status and training, despite advanced degrees and experiences. Their inability to work officially may relate to English proficiency and U.S. documents. Poets, singers, and storytellers have vocalized these survivalist practices along the border. These types of double, and even triple, work lives constitute slantwise activities because they arise from necessity.

Freedom

We have noticed some *Corazón* residences function as businesses, an infrequent practice in many U.S. residential areas. We have seen hens and roosters in yards and these signs outside of homes, *"Se venden gallos"* [Roosters for sale] and *"Hay huevos"* [Eggs for sale]. Normally, roosters, because of their lusty crowing, are nonexistent in city limits. Joy, who teaches across the street from *Corazón*, said, "When I get out of the car [to start the day], the roosters are welcoming me from right across the street." A child said he enjoyed living in *Corazón* because "I can have any kind of pet." The law and enforcement lacuna may help residents to be resourceful and earn money for their families. Selling and making food or cutting hair without licenses could be slantwise because residents may overlook ordinances for economic survival and flexibility.

Having no covenants or ordinances can liberate *Corazón* homeowners. Colonia residents may dislike living in public urban housing, perhaps because of inhabitant capacity restrictions per home and how long visitors may stay (Coronado, 2003). Janie mentioned the freedom residents have in building a home alongside a mobile home, which the surrounding city forbids. Pastor

Sabio said annexation might mean colonia residents giving up freedom; see Chapter 4. Yet, limits to freedom exist. Residents would shun a business conflicting with cultural norms. For example, we have not seen porn shops, probably because most residents are family-oriented and deeply religious. Although some drive-through stores sell liquor, these shops sell mostly food.

Summary

We asked this inquiry question: What are *Corazón's* struggles and strengths? We described obstacles related to marginalization, water, sewage, streets, sidewalks, homes, electricity, police, and transportation. Despite struggles, *Corazón* abounds in strengths, such as unity, stability, entrepreneurism, and community pride. In this chapter, we also discussed activists' strides in improving the colonia's living conditions. As you continue reading, we hope you fall in love with *Corazón* residents, key spaces, and places because love implies connection.

Questions to Ponder

1. What additional topics could you explore in communities such *Corazón*? Which theoretical frameworks would you use to examine these topics?
2. What lessons or implications exist for educators, policymakers, students, or researchers regarding this neighborhood?
3. What are positive and negative aspects of an underground or informal economy?
4. How does this colonia differ from other U.S. communities that live under the poverty line? How is *Corazón* similar to other low-income communities?

· 4 ·

KEY PLACES AND SPACES

Meet Janie

Kathy had sent Janie, community organizer for the Civic Organization, two query emails and two texts from January 2015 to May 2015, name-dropping a mutual friend. No result. Yet after Kathy interviewed Sister Joan in June 2015, Sister Joan escorted Kathy to the office of Janie, in the same building as *Afinidad* [Kinship]. "Dr. Webb [from the local university] wants to know some historical information," Sister Joan said, as the physical and metaphorical bridge. Janie beckoned Kathy to sit beside her.

Kathy bounded toward Janie's desk, recounting residents' trip to Washington, D.C. See Chapter 3. "Do you know about this trip?" Kathy asked. "No," Janie responded, walking across her compact office to retrieve a three-inch white binder, packed with *Corazón* contacts. After finding an elderly man's phone number, Janie texted him about the D.C. voyage and the ¡*Viva la raza!* banner on the school bus. While waiting for the man's response, Kathy continued about the trip, which Magnífico related to Kathy just days before. Kathy mentioned Luchador and Janie's eyes opened like O's. "Luchador? This name rings a bell!" Janie exclaimed. Janie began examining residents' photos, with accompanying names and phone numbers, on her laptop. Janie showed Kathy the man Janie had just texted and continued scrolling through electronic photos. Kathy saw a picture of Tim, former *Corazón* clergy, with former

Texas Governor Ann Richards. Janie said Ann Richards and *Corazón* clergy did much for this community.

Meanwhile, the cell phone interlocutor responded he was unaware of the D.C. trip. Janie texted back about Luchador. No memory. Next, Janie used her office phone and called another elderly resident, asking him about the trip. No, he said, but he did know Luchador's widow and explained where she lived. Janie thanked the man, hung up, and told Kathy that Janie had started monthly gatherings with elderly community leaders who had told her about Luchador.

After Kathy obtained the name and approximate address of Luchador's widow, who lived between a bakery and tire store, Kathy told Janie about her work with the Tutorial Center, featured in this chapter, and that Kathy was trying to change people's perceptions of *Corazón*. Janie said people remember the mud, unpaved streets, and crime and "they think we still live like that." She added, "It might have been true at the colonia's beginnings in the sixties, but it's hard to put food on the table if one does not have a job. It's not an excuse, but they had to survive." Janie coordinates visits from medical students, who express surprise at *Corazón's* organization and no galloping horses along *Corazón* streets. As Janie talked, Kathy noticed a cloth American flag and a plastic one on the walls. A heavy young woman was typing on a desktop five feet away. The woman turned to Janie, asking, "Is [Name] in Hidalgo County?" Not missing a beat, Janie said yes, and continued talking with Kathy.

Introduction

This story highlights our social justice and Third Space frameworks because Janie allowed Kathy into her transformative space, showing Kathy how Janie worked as a *Corazón* activist. We asked these inquiry questions: What are key *Corazón* places and their characteristics? How do organization leaders work with others to affect change? Although we are Third Space theorists, our social justice and ontological beliefs ground us in personal relationships. Thus, we value people-centered approaches and believe the key places in this chapter also involve key people.

Primary data sources consisted of interviews; see our Book Introduction for more methodology. Co-researchers were mostly adult volunteers and staff. Emerging themes were political activism and sparks of collective impact, or a structured process involving shared agendas and measurements and mutually reinforcing activities (Kania & Kramer, 2011). However, a shared measurement system among these six organizations appeared missing: (1) *Afinidad* [Kinship], (2) Civic Organization, (3) Tutorial Center, (4) Catholic Church, (5) Baptist Church, and (6) *Convivio* [Fellowship]. We featured the first two organizations at the chapter's onset. We chose these six key places based on a convergence of data. We asked interviewees, "What key places exist in this community?"

This chapter's beginning demonstrates analytic tools of rhizomes, slantwise, and power. Rhizomic principles of connections and multiple entry points (Deleuze & Guattari, 1987) became apparent when Sister Joan introduced Kathy to Janie, when Janie—through text messages, phone calls, and digital images—led us to Luchador's widow. Thus, an important research facet involved relationship building and trust. Next, Janie possessed hard copies of people's names and maintained positive relationships with residents. Janie could pick up a phone and call or text residents and they would help her. The way Janie explained how to find Luchador's widow shared similarities with the way Kathy writes letters to Honduran friends from towns and villages with no street names, e.g., *Profesora Erlinda Silva, al lado de la farmacia* [Professor Erlinda Silva, beside the pharmacy], and then the recipient's town and department, similar to a state or region. This unorthodox street address method is slantwise because it remains grassroots and valid for residents (Campbell & Heyman, 2007).

Additionally, Sister Joan's introduction increased Kathy's personal power and made encountering Janie possible. Power can be good. Kathy was acceptable to Janie, from the Civic Organization, because Sister Joan vouched for Kathy. Perhaps Janie doubted Kathy was really the friend of a friend when Kathy had messaged and emailed Janie previously.

Afinidad

In June 2015, Kathy encountered many vehicles in the *Afinidad* parking lot. Kathy began sending her students to *Corazón* for field experiences in 2004, but she had only been involved with staff from the Catholic Church and the Tutorial Center, both two blocks away from *Afinidad*. To Kathy, the packed *Afinidad* parking lot signified a happening, happy place. Kathy parked across the street, in front of homes. A contrast—on *Afinidad*'s side—immaculate. On the other—crooked, dented mailboxes. The open gate displayed a "Private Property" sign.

A 12' bush with vibrant red flowers greeted Kathy. The headquarters occupied the biggest building. The other buildings, diminutive, displayed saints' names beside each room. The lawn and landscaping were crisp—no blade out of order.

A chain link fence surrounded the *Afinidad* complex, consisting of a handful of grey mobile homes and a bigger modular home, trimmed in white. A local Catholic school had used these homes as portable classrooms and sold them to *Afinidad* at $10,000 each. Now the buildings serve for ceremonies, classes, health screenings, meetings, and volunteer dormitories.

In the tallest building, Kathy asked for Sister Joan, the program's founder. Two Latinas at the counter were sharing a slick magazine. When Kathy asked for Sister Joan, first in English and then in Spanish, they exchanged glances, unsure of what to do with the request. A Latina, polished, with hair in a tidy ponytail, said she would tell Sister Joan of Kathy's arrival. She brought Kathy a bottle of water—unchilled, encircled with a white paper napkin. Later Kathy worked with the polished woman in publicizing a fundraising event.

As Kathy waited, she saw a woman with ash hair and glasses sitting in front of a computer. "Probably a nun or sister," Kathy thought. Kathy peered down the corridor and saw a wall with stones, perhaps a fireplace. "Odd," Kathy thought, "in this Valley heat?!" Yet the stone wall made the building more home-like. In front of Kathy sat a wooden rocking chair with a padded seat. Behind her was a room partitioned with orange and yellow flowered curtains. Latinas passed Kathy. Kathy had only seen women at the complex.

Kathy considered a sign by the main door, "No Smoking, city ordinance." She smiled at the irony. The colonia exists in a donut hole, but it is not part of the city. *Corazón* registered voters cannot participate in city elections. Another sign—*Zumba gratis* [free Zumba exercise class] beckoned Kathy to take another gander because of the neon words in Spanish about ropes, steps, weights, and other exercise terms and equipment.

History and Purpose

Soon Sister Joan, a registered nurse, strode toward Kathy and shook Kathy's hand. She beckoned Kathy to follow her and they entered a room in an adjacent building with no air conditioner. It was at least 100 degrees Fahrenheit outside and 85 degrees in the room.

Sister Joan recounted *Afinidad's* fall 2003 beginning when it received national non-profit status. In 2004, *Afinidad* surveyed 800 *Corazón* residents to determine community needs. *Afinidad* started on Catholic Church grounds in *Corazón*. The Church gave *Afinidad* two lots a few blocks away and Sister Joan bought property from colonia residents. Sister Joan and other clergy affiliated with *Afinidad* work in *Corazón*, but live in a nearby town. *Afinidad* works with universities and local, state, and national agencies and organizations for funding and services. Some funders exist at the national level, while others are local. While grants prove essential, an annual fundraiser, featuring famous speakers and a nice lunch, also occurs. *Afinidad* has staff for Facebook, Twitter, and other social media sites. Staff place notifications of upcoming *Afinidad* events in the local newspaper, which helps to change outsiders' perceptions.

Much of *Afinidad* focuses on health promotion. However, this organization (with paid employees, volunteer nuns, and other volunteers) has other outreach programs, including education, immigration, and civics. As in nature itself, some programs overlap, as stress management falls under education and *promotoras* [health promoters] help with encouraging people to vote. *Afinidad* takes a holistic approach to community empowerment. According to Sister Joan, "Many times we have integrated services and we can refer them [clients] to several programs." Thus, this method helps the whole person and the entire family. In the following section, we focus on what we found as *Afinidad's* greatest contributions: health, education, and women's empowerment.

Community Contributions

Health

As health relates to sanitation, *Afinidad* teams up with *Convivio*, an organization featured in this chapter, to offer free trash and brush pick-up to *Corazón* residents twice a year. They offer this service because most residents cannot afford a private company's trash and brush pick-up charges. Thus, this service helps to keep the community clean and disease- and rodent-free. Sister Joan said that about eight huge trucks carry the discarded items to a local landfill twice yearly.

Food and shelter also relate to physical health, and *Afinidad* refers people to the food bank of the Catholic Church, another key place mentioned in this chapter. *Afinidad* also collaborates with the St. Vincent de Paul organization, which visits families and may help in providing food, rent, and electricity; food and shelter represent basic physiological and safety needs. Regarding health management, *Afinidad* offers free: health screenings; stress management; nutrition and cooking classes; a community garden; adult and child Zumba classes; and a community-wide Zumba-thon. An *Afinidad* female group walks around the church parking lot/walking path. Other programs relate to child and adult prevention classes in obesity and major health problems, a certified diabetes empowerment program, and flu vaccines.

Claudia said these services are essential: "We have a lot of diabetics who have no clue how to take care of themselves. The *promotoras* teach them … to exercise, how to eat healthy." Additionally, *Afinidad* creates awareness on diseases common in the colonia and the Valley, such as diabetes, obesity, and heart-related issues. These health problems relate to structural inequities. Poverty increases the propensity of people suffering from diabetes and obesity and inadequate outdoor exercise places correlate with waist circumference (Harrington & Elliot, 2009). Sister Joan said the numbers served relate to *Corazón's* and surrounding communities' health needs: "We served 28,000 individuals from 2014 to 2015. There are 1,000 diabetic patients … we are following." Sister Joan explained *promotoras* visit clients' homes every three months to perform insulin checks and to put clients into contact with people who can help them daily with their diabetes.

Afinidad uses a portable lab for cholesterol, diabetes, and so forth; blood test results appear immediately. This lab possesses a certificate of waiver, since it performs simple tests with few risks of error. *Afinidad* uses A1C tests, which provide a person's average blood glucose over a three-month period. Sister Joan lamented most clients for these tests come from outside of *Corazón*, "There are still some people in the colonia who don't even know we exist. People in the colonia often have two jobs, so they are busy."

Sister Joan said *Afinidad* employs mostly *promotoras*; 18–20 are state certified and 8–10 are community health worker (CHW) certified. The state certified folks can give continuing education classes to the *promotoras*. Claudia discussed the work of her friend, Hermosa, a *promotora* for five years:

> They trained her. She does get stipends. She makes presentations about obesity, diabetes, and heart problems … Let's say she would come to my house. I get to invite my neighbors, family members, or friends to come, so they come and they sit though the presentations. She makes her own visuals and she will get them from [*Afinidad*] … She has drawings of different body parts. She has a poster board, plus she has PowerPoint presentations made out for her. She brings a computer. [*Afinidad*] lends her a computer. She studies the PowerPoints. She googles stuff. She goes to YouTube. Whatever she is talking about, she will watch videos about it to understand it.

Hermosa took *promotora* classes, for which *Afinidad* paid, at *Convivio*. As a certified *promotora*, Hermosa trains four leaders weekly. Hermosa's role involves more than giving classes, "*Estoy entrenando. Voy a las casas y doy las clases de salud, diabetes, colesterol, hipertensión arterial, depresión, etcétera. Tenemos como 80 temas, pero tenemos que cubrir 24 en un cierto período*" [I train others. I visit houses and teach health classes about diabetes, cholesterol, hypertension, depression, etc. We have about 80 different topics, but we need to cover 24 in a certain timeframe]. Each leader must invite five people to the leader's home for every presentation Hermosa gives. Leaders must attend monthly health trainings at *Convivio*, also.

We wonder if the state certification and guidelines diminish traditional Mexican healing practices because we have never heard the *promotoras* discuss using *manzanilla* [chamomile] and other Mexican remedies. However, these transnational socio-cultural health practices, skills, and knowledge represent Mexican-heritage people's strengths and literacies in the diaspora (Jiménez, Smith, & Teague, 2009).

Education

Education programs include: summer Bible classes (taught by youth group members), the Tutorial Center's after-school program (featured in this chapter), anger management, stress management with Tai Chi, adult English as a second language (ESL) classes, and an active parent-teacher organization (PTA); we discuss the PTA in this chapter. *Afinidad* also offers birth-to-age-four child development classes, mostly in Spanish, focusing on mothers teaching math and reading concepts to their children. This program and similar ones must have a positive effect because colonia kindergarten children scored at the top of our region on the Early Development Instrument (EDI). Providing the citation would give away our site, but the EDI is valid and reliable (Janus & Offord, 2007); see Chapter 9.

Sister Joan also described ways people can advance through educational programs, starting with the adult General Educational Development (GED), which local school district personnel offer: "We have step-up programs: GED, ESL, citizenship." After people pass their GED tests, in Spanish or English, they go on to ESL classes. After that, they take the citizenship classes. "All of these are for people to be able to get better jobs," Sister Joan said. Receiving an associate's degree is easier with a high school diploma or equivalent. Thus, the GED paves the path to a higher education and income for many adult colonia residents.

Women's Empowerment

Positive interpersonal communication and female empowerment remain the focus of one *Afinidad* grant-funded family program. Sister Joan mentioned one man refurbished 20 old computers, trained 20 *Corazón* mothers how to use them, and then gave them the computers to keep. Female participants sign a three-year contract and commit to monthly classes, with topics such as self-esteem, parenting, finances, and nutrition. In the third year, participants become involved in social issues related to their families and set two short-term and one long-term goals with their families. The program coordinator visits their homes to discuss their progress. The program encourages them to enter the workforce and start small businesses, also.

Raising Leaders

Promotora leaders train others; once leaders finish their work, they receive $75. To us, this seems like much work for little pay, but it provides colonia women with stepping stones to higher paying, more prestigious jobs in and outside of *Corazón*. Some have earned state-recognized certifications, which help them to become more marketable. As per public domain sites, the women like being *promotoras* because they are making a positive regional impact, and many perceive their jobs as missions. Sister Joan discussed how she selects *promotoras*, based on personal connections: "I know them. They went to a class. They know us. They volunteer first. They have to be here for so long [as volunteers] before they are hired." Sister Joan practices an empowerment type of leadership and she has trained colonia women to be in charge of key organizations. These women, in turn, train other colonia women, and the mentoring cycle continues. Many women begin as clients, Sister Joan said.

Dolhinow (2010) critiqued non-government organizations (NGOs) in New Mexico because they recruited women by emphasizing caretaking, which depoliticized women's efforts. Additionally, the NGOs did little to help women to become politically active and to establish egalitarian, meaningful connections with non-colonia residents. Dolhinow argued NGOs perpetuated neoliberalism because colonia residents' relied on NGOs. Yet, in our longitudinal study, we found NGOs have helped *Corazón* residents to become politically active in and outside of *Corazón*. When asked about the impact *Afinidad* has had on the *promotoras*, Sister Joan replied, "A huge impact. We have *promotoras* going into the home. They start out as volunteers. As they get better, we hire them." Sister Joan mentioned two employees, whom she called "success stories." Some have been with *Afinidad* for years. "They give workshops and they start programs. We not only develop the community, but also the staff."

Hermosa said being a *promotora* has helped her confidence and activism, *"Tengo más confianza en mí misma, pues antes era más tímida. Casi no hablaba, pero ahora hablo más"* [I'm more confident in myself. I used to be more timid. I hardly spoke, but now I speak more]. When asked if she was an activist, Hermosa responded she was *"activa"* [active]: *"¿Activistas, no son las personas que andan allá arriba?"* [Activists, aren't they the people who run up and down?] She raised her arm up and waived it like a protest sign or flag. She continued to use the same word, *activista*: *"Activistas son las personas que andan ayudando a otros, que motivan"* [Activists are those who help others, who motivate]. Over time, we have noticed many college students' and participants' reticence to affiliate with social justice, perhaps because of the coloniality of power, which pervades the borderlands. In Chapter 3 Poeta and Poet explained that officials tried to run Patriot out of *Corazón*, claiming non-colonia residents, such as Patriot, could not help *Corazón*.

However, Hermosa demonstrated activism in her efforts to help residents in myriad ways. *Afinidad* featured Hermosa recently in Facebook; Hermosa was speaking into a microphone with one hand and holding a banner with the other. Furthermore, Hermosa serves as a Parent Teacher Association (PTA) officer. Although this PTA has *Afinidad* affiliation, the former has its own bank account and board. This PTA enjoys national accreditation. Sister Joan mentioned other community-based PTAs throughout Cameron County. Hermosa meets with officers and members monthly. Her group provides information to *Corazón* residents concerning primary and secondary schools, e.g., Texas House Bill 5 (HB 5), which restructured school curricula, graduation requirements, assessments, and accountability (Texas Education Agency, n.d.). Sister Joan said HB 5 relates to tracking nondominant youth, which represents a social injustice related to equal opportunity. Hermosa said:

Bueno, esta ley es una ley que … los catalogan a los estudiantes. Las materias básicas ya no van a dar crédito. Y ahorita nos mandan cartas, que híjole! Que ese niño no sirve para las matemáticas, que ellos se van a encargar de catalogar a las personas. Uno tiene que estar al pendiente. Por ejemplo si nos dicen, "Su hijo ya no va a tener álgebra", debemos preguntar, por qué no? … Estos son límites que les están poniendo a los estudiantes para que no entren a la universidad [Well, this law categorizes children. Basic subjects won't have any credit. And now they send us letters, that goodness! These letters say things like,

"Your son isn't good in math." A person has to be aware. For example, if they tell us, "Your son won't have algebra." And we should ask, "Why not?" These are limits the State puts on children so they don't go to the university].

Hermosa perceived HB 5 to be drenched with racism and classism, and her PTA group has experienced much success in informing parents about the lower-track HB 5 forms from middle and high schools. "*Sí, por eso uno está luchando para que quiten eso. Y nosotros nos estamos encargando de eso. Ya han hecho varias juntas de esas, de HB 5. Y ahora ya hay mucha gente que sabe en la comunidad*" [Yes, for this reason people are trying to repel this law. We are in charge of this in the PTA. Already we have had many meetings about HB 5. And now many residents know about it]. The efforts of Hermosa and her PTA group relate to research on high expectations. Children who take higher level courses (e.g., calculus versus general mathematics) increase their chances of attending, and graduating, college, and teachers in advanced classes expect more and offer more rigorous curricula (Haycock, 2001). HB 5 also relates to the enduring legacy of colonialism in which the Spaniards divided indigenous people to conquer them. Again, we return to Chapter 3 and officials' attempt to separate Patriot from *Corazón*. After reading this manuscript, Teacher Joy understood HB 5's racist overtones. She added, "I just know that [over] testing is hurting our kids."

Sister Joan told the story of a woman who arrived in *Corazón* from Mexico; the woman finished the *promotora* training and soon led others. This Mexican native now supervises parenting classes, a summer Bible program, and other *Corazón* programs. Sister Joan explained how *Afinidad* helped to nurture yet another woman to become politically powerful and a force for good, "One woman, she represents [town 20 minutes away]. She is the representative of her community. If someone needs something related to citizenship, housing, or whatever, they call on her." This woman, whom Sister Joan helped to train, now lives in another town and continues to work for *Afinidad* to help others. Sister Joan said her organization employs *promotoras* from outside of the colonia also, but all meet formally at least once monthly; both groups of women train and assist others regionally.

Thus, our findings about NGO's and political activism differ from Dolhinow's (2010), not only because of different locations, but also because *Afinidad* commits to female empowerment and activism. We interpret *Afinidad* as a female-friendly organization. Few males appear employed or on the organization's board and *Afinidad* appears keen on female youth and woman leadership. *Afinidad* employees and volunteers also participate in National Women's Day, inviting colonia women to presentations and group walks around the colonia; during the walk they give red carnations to colonia women they meet. This event raises awareness of gender equity. Social-justice oriented U.S. nuns clashed with the more conservative Vatican under Pope Benedict; however, the Vatican, through the social justice leadership of Pope Francis, has ended an investigation of U.S. nuns.

Afinidad's role relates to Third Space theory, especially when the Family Program coordinator visits the homes of female participants to discuss goals and when *promotoras* enter homes to train women in health-related matters. Resident female leaders build bridges between residents and federal agencies, such as Census Bureau enumerators, also. These home visitors create a link between governmental resources (the public sphere) and homes (the private sphere). Additionally, *Afinidad's* PTA functions as a slantwise, grassroots, activist organization. PTA officers, all colonia residents, attempt to affect change by informing parents about Texas House Bill 5.

Civic Organization

Afinidad finances and oversees the Civic Organization; the latter focuses on advocating for *Corazón* residents, encouraging residents to advocate for themselves, making officials responsive to *Corazón* needs, and increasing voter turnout. We featured Janie in the chapter's beginning; Janie, the Civic Organization's founding community organizer, began as a *promotora* for *Afinidad*. Janie worked as a migrant in Indiana and Michigan, as a seamstress for a large clothing factory, and as a certified medical assistant. Janie lost her clothing factory job when the company moved to China. A developer repossessed the home of Janie's Mexican-born mother because Janie's mom failed to make one payment after 19 years. Thus, Janie knows what exploitation feels like, and she wants her community to progress.

History and Purpose

The Civic Organization grew from an *Afinidad* outreach eight years ago. The Civic Organization focuses on empowering low-income communities by increasing involvement in the political process. This organization joins forces with other residents and asks officials for improved services. This entity has secured over one million dollars in infrastructure improvements, e.g., street lights and paved streets. According to contributor Claudia, the Civic Organization:

> ... is a bridge to fill in the gap of ignorance from both sides—politicians who have
> no clue about the people of [*Corazón*], how they live until someone brings them, and
> the people don't have any idea about what their rights are, how they can approach
> their politician.

Thus, the Civic Organization functions as a Third Space where colonia residents become agents through mentoring and bridging. This organization also increases state and national activism by taking *Corazón* residents to forums, political meetings, rallies, and workshops.

Kathy summarized Dolhinow's (2010) findings to Janie, regarding non-government organization (NGO) support of neoliberalism and colonia residents' reliance on NGOs. Janie, brows furrowing, exclaimed, "That's not us. Our mission is to empower low-income families." Janie also said colonia residents have become political activists who confront officials and that everyday *Corazón* residents collaborate outside of the colonia to do this. Colonia residents have learned to work for the common good, according to Janie.

Community Contributions

The Civic Organization does much in collaboration with residents and groups. Many colonias throughout the Southwest fare worse, mostly because their residents demonstrate less political activism (Dolhinow, 2010). In the coloniality of power, Mexican-descent people in poverty may fear activism because of reprisals. However, Janie wants *Corazón* residents to use their voice for the betterment of their community and she shows them *how* to do this. Arizmendi et al. (2010) connected female colonia activists to Freire and revolutionaries. Instead of women with guns, we picture women collaborating with others to affect change.

The Civic Organization helps to register voters in county, state, and national elections, and encourages entire families to vote by discussing issues in Texas and other states, e.g., Arizona politicians signing Senate Bill 1070 regarding immigrants. The Civic Organization's strategy involves one-to-one conversations with potential voters. Janie, *Afinidad's* youth group, *promotoras*, and others have coordinated voter participation. Janie beams about her precinct, which represents 75% of registered *Corazón* voters; her precinct had the second highest county turnout in 2013, just behind the wealthy South Padre Island. Although more *Corazón* residents vote in presidential elections, the percentage of overall voter turnout has increased about 20% in each election. Few RGV registered voters participate in non-presidential elections, so the Civic Organization's technique of encouraging *Corazón* residents to vote when propositions appear on the ballot has paid off. A November 2015 proposition passed for elderly and disabled voters to pay less school district property tax. High voter participation and political strategizing contrasts with *Corazón's* mid-1990 gloom, when a local politician said *Corazón* would receive no county services because only two *Corazón* residents voted; see Chapter 3.

Claudia discussed the efforts of Hermosa, *promotora*: "[She] does volunteer during elections, passing out flyers, not for a certain candidate, but to promote the vote." *Afinidad* divides the *promotoras'* streets so everyone has an equal amount of homes to visit. Hermosa said visiting homes has presented challenges: "*Una vez me topé con un señor que dijo no, que eran unos rateros, no más, y no quizo votar*" [One time I came across a man who said they (the candidates), were only rats and so he didn't want to vote]. "*Y le dije, 'entonces, con permiso' y me fui. Nos topamos con personas a veces que ni siquiera quieren abrir la puerta*" [And I said, "Ok, excuse me" and I bolted. Sometimes we run across people who don't even open the door].

Besides voting efforts, the Civic Organization participates in monthly town hall meetings with these *Corazón* entities: *Afinidad*, the Tutorial Center, the Catholic Church, the Baptist Church, the Pentecostal Church (not featured in this book), and *Convivio*. These slantwise meetings involve *Corazón* activists creating their own grassroots political system (unbeknownst to many outsiders) for socially accepted goals—improving *Corazón's* conditions and increasing residents' participation and empowerment. Town hall meetings take place at *Convivio*; each leader must bring at least two *Corazón* residents, so residents can talk directly to officials. Sister Joan said, "Every third month we bring in different people [officials]. It's non-partisan." Once the seven-member leadership team brought in animal control because of *Corazón's* stray, unneutered, and unspayed dog packs. These leaders invited a light company because some street lights did not work. They also invited sheriff employees. Sister Joan said, "There was a traffic accident at an intersection, and we brought the security in to solve the problem [with the intersection]."

Janie used the 2015 intersection problem to demonstrate how she empowers the community. Residents complained to her that they had traffic accidents at an intersection because a local entrepreneur had cars for sale that were blocking intersection visibility. Residents had spoken to the owner to no avail. Janie and others investigated the scene. Next, Janie instructed them to call the sheriff's department every morning and afternoon for a few weeks. After this, Janie invited sheriff officers and the complaining residents to attend the monthly meeting; over 40 residents appeared. Janie believed the officers were favoring the business owner, the sheriff's friend. One officer alluded to residents' inadequate drivers' licenses and insurance. A resident retorted, "You do your job! Don't you worry about this!" Janie told the officers she and residents would complain to higher authorities if the officers did not resolve the issue. Incessant phone calls to the sheriff's office, high resident meeting turnout, and dialogue resolved the situation. Through this process, residents learned to complain to a perpetrator first (e.g., the business owner), call authorities, attend town meetings, and voice concerns to officials. Janie said, "We teach them how to get their needs met, not how we are going to meet their needs."

Next, the Civic Organization has coordinated Mexican Embassy and U.S. Citizenship and Immigration Services visits. Sister Joan said, "Once a year we bring in the Mexican Embassy so people can get Mexican IDs." The Embassy comes with an automatic identification maker, and people meander in lines to receive services. The IDs represent an important step in getting official U.S. documentation because applicants for U.S. citizenship need official birth certificates and other identification. Additionally, the Civic Organization provides year-long citizenship classes, preparing adults to become U.S. Citizens. Adult students received information about why to vote and how to read ballots. A few months ago, 60 adult students sat in a tiny classroom and learned about the voting process. Tuesday classes are in English, Wednesday classes are in Spanish. If citizenship students pass the Civic Organization's mock test, the organization files the N100 form for free. For the first time in fall 2015, the U.S. naturalization ceremony took place in the colonia. Moreover, the U.S. government field-tested the online naturalization form in conjunction with the Civic Organization and U.S. staff members returned to Washington with many needed changes on the online form. This demonstrates the positive relationship Janie has with that U.S. branch.

Raising Leaders

Civic Organization committees create advocates and leaders. For instance, the Civic Organization takes colonia residents to meetings and demonstrations in Washington, D.C., and Austin, Texas. Moreover, residents accompany the Civic Organization and *Afinidad* to county commissioner meetings and to state representatives' offices to demand colonia changes. Janie said attending meetings and visiting officials yield results because officials see the colonia cares. Based on Kathy's observations of Janie's texting and phone calls to elderly residents, Janie stays in contact with the community. Janie has mentored youth, particularly the youth group, in carrying the social justice torch, also.

Afinidad's 30-member youth group differs from the Catholic Church youth group; the former consists of socially and politically active youth, ages 13–21. Both types of *Afinidad* activism focus on raising leaders. Regarding social activism, two female college youth members received Sargent Shriver awards for service and used the money to improve the colonia. One winner focused on ending childhood obesity through guest presenters and a child Zumba-thon; the other promoted voter participation. Furthermore, *Afinidad* trains youth group members and then the latter run summer Bible school for children. Youth group members decide on projects, ranging from ending family violence to painting murals. Projects might be colonia-based (painting house numbers on curbs for 9–11 purposes) or regional (promoting bicycle lanes) and may involve other Valley groups.

Related to political activism, some colonia youth group members attend Deferred Action for Childhood Arrivals (DACA) and Deferred Action for Parents of Americans and Lawful Permanent Residents (DAPA) conventions to learn about college assistance and overcoming immigration-related obstacles. The youth group has provided information on propositions and ensured people got rides to the polls. Sister Joan said the youth group even marched "against those who do not give salaries when people have worked," which relates to unjust labor practices. Sister Joan said this youth group even helps to run *Corazón's* town hall meetings, providing youth with leadership experiences. Thus, these non-government organizations counter Dolhinow's (2010) finding. Indeed, these *Corazón* NGOs do much to increase colonia residents' activism in and outside of *Corazón*.

Tutorial Center

To our knowledge, *Corazón* has two child tutorial entities—the Tutorial Center, in the colonia's center, and *Convivio*, at the southwestern outskirts. We discuss both in this chapter. Claudia attended the central one as a child and volunteered there; we call it the Tutorial Center or Center. During the academic year, about 30 elementary children attend the Center from Monday to Thursday regularly. Middle and high school students come after school on

Fridays. Some come intermittingly for project help. If we estimate the Center has no more than 100 children attendees per year, then less than 4% of *Corazón* children attend the Center. Children represent 2,800 (40%) of *Corazón* residents (U.S. Census Bureau, 2010). The low youth attendees served is not because staff and volunteers shun children. However, limits exist for space, funding, and staff. Based on evidence of the Center's effectiveness, if more children attended the Center, the colonia's high school graduation rate would be better.

Many have said the Tutorial Center represents a key *Corazón* site. A Center staff member said, "*Yo creo que el principal centro de apoyo para la educación de los niños de [Corazón] somos nosotros, el programa de tutoría. Los padres se apoyan en nosotros para ayudar a sus hijos*" [I believe the primary center of support for children's education in *Corazón* is our tutorial program. The parents support us in helping their children]. When they drew visual metaphors of the May 2015 session, all teacher candidate (TC) groups drew the Center. The groups drew industrious ants collaborating; parent volunteer ducks nurturing ducklings; and glue, needle, and thread representing how the Center connects families and helps children. Another group drew a Christian cross to represent a safe haven. They explained orally, "The Tutorial Center is a place where they don't ask, 'Are you legal?' The children don't have to worry about this [question]." U.S. Border Patrol officers avoid church-affiliated places when searching for undocumented people.

Unfortunately, few professors require TCs and in-service teachers/graduate students to complete field experience or service learning at the Center. Claudia said, "We have days where we didn't get any volunteers, so we would have those 30 students to ourselves." Kathy's TCs have tutored at the Center for eight May sessions, but few TCs help during the school year. Local Catholic high school students help, as do people completing service due to minor offenses, e.g., traffic violations. The latter assist with cleaning. The Center employs a coordinator, an assistant, and an American Association of Retired People (AARP) worker; the latter prepares snacks and cleans.

History and Purpose

The Tutorial Center started in a tiny building on Church property in the early 2000s. About 11 years ago the Center became part of *Afinidad*, Sister Joan's organization. *Afinidad*, private groups and individuals, and a local social services agency fund the Center. Alma, a Mexican-heritage woman from another border city, was the founding coordinator; Rita, also of Mexican heritage, took over as coordinator in 2014 when Alma retired.

The Center focuses on assisting colonia children, regardless of religious affiliation, with homework. However, we noticed other purposes, which include: developing positive reading and study habits, helping children with general math and reading skills, engaging youth in enrichment activities, providing children with resources, mentoring children academically, providing a safe hang-out, learning about college from staff and tutors, and teaching parents how to be proactive with educators and children's achievement. Additionally, youth seek advice of trusted tutorial staff and volunteers. Many youth have attended the Center for years.

This occurs routinely: Youth arrive, sign in, wash their hands, take out school homework worksheets, and complete homework. Monday through Thursday sessions focus on tutoring, while Friday sessions involve mentoring youth. When the children finish homework, they play soccer or other outdoor games, socialize, and eat Mexican-style snacks prepared by the parent volunteers and staff, e.g., soft tacos or fruit with spicy powder. One time during a May session class, Kathy brought peanut butter, jelly, and white bread for snacks; the children and moms ate the sandwiches, but Alma said they preferred Mexican-style food.

Tutorial children also eat special food for celebrations, such as *tamales* [corn meal stuffed with meat and steamed in corn husks] at Christmas; *pan del Día de los Muertos* [sweet bread] for All Saints' Day, and *pan de rosca* [sweet bread] for Epiphany. Diasporic celebrations weave into Center life. The university's Spanish Club has provided parties and piñatas for Christmas and for *El Día del Niño* [Day of the Child], in which children play games and hear stories in Spanish. For the *Día de la Aparición de la virgen de Guadalupe* (see Chapter 5), the children have long scripts to memorize; tutorial staff help with this annual event.

Other enrichment activities have included free ballet classes, which a local dance company provided. When the National Writing Project experienced extensive funding, a mother and daughter team engaged children in summer writing workshops, focused on community strengths and higher-order concerns, such as voice and detail. Tutorial children have attended summer zoo and art camps. Children, with help from Kathy's adolescent literature students, performed a play based on *To Kill a Mockingbird* from a National Endowment for the Arts grant. In summer 2014, tutorial children performed the musical, *Annie*, with the help of a university student on her own volition.

Regarding resources, children may attend the Center to use computers, printers, Internet, poster board, paper, glue, and markers for projects. The Center boasts a library with over 1,200 books, also. A teacher candidate wrote, "Having the resources available is important for the students living in this neighborhood. All the information she needs to learn is at the Center, and there are people available to help her."

Alma taught parents how to ensure children completed homework (even if the parents lacked English) and to read school schedules and report cards. Claudia marveled that Alma "would show them [the parents] the page number, the story" so Spanish-dominant parents could rhizome around the obstacle of English homework. Additionally, Alma encouraged parents to have their children read to them in English. Alma would say, "Although you don't understand, they can still be reading to you." Claudia said:

> She met with moms in a more personal way because … they could relate to her as a mom. [Alma] would like to have talks with them about parenting and things that you could see that are common sense, but that some moms wouldn't have thought of, like checking your child's homework.

Alma advocated for the children, families, and teachers; she taught parents how to fight for their children academically. Alma visited school teachers and staff if parents asked for her help. In so doing, Alma created a bridge between home and school. According to Claudia, "Some parents don't feel comfortable enough to talk to the teacher or principal. Some of them would feel ignorant." Yet whenever parents would complain about the teachers, Alma would help them to see teachers' perspectives because she was a certified teacher herself. Alma held parents and students accountable, also. Claudia said, "That's the freedom you don't have in the [public] school. If you would see the student wasn't bringing his homework or didn't want to work, we could easily call the parent and tell them to pick up their child."

Community Contributions

The Tutorial Center contributes the most to children's academic success. Elderly activist Poeta said since many parents know no English, they cannot help youth with homework, "*pero siempre aprendían bien pues tenían la ayuda de tutorial* [sic]" [but the children always learned well because of the help from the Center]. As demonstrated, the Center impacts more than homework help or English acquisition. It affirms Mexican identities and attempts to move beyond remediation. Because of collective efforts, most regular Center attendees graduate high school. Tutorial staff encourage former tutees to share their academic triumphs, e.g., high school and college graduation. For example, Frank participated in Kathy's May programs. Now as a high school student, Frank visited the Center in 2015 when Kathy was present. To track children's progress, tutorial staff make copies of children's report cards. The children's good grades help funders to see the Center's success.

In 2010, local university staff, a Texas foundation, Alma, and Kathy organized a bus tour from the local university to *Corazón* and Alma gave a PowerPoint presentation to foundation representatives from Texas and throughout the USA. The Tutorial Center impressed some representatives so much that the latter donated money to it. While other organizations in this chapter have raised leaders, the Center has other foci. However, with increased funding and staff, raising children activists could be a possibility.

Catholic Church

Although other *Corazón* churches exist, e.g., Pentecostal and Jehovah's Witness, the Catholic Church boasts the most members, with 400 registered parishioners, including children; about 85% of *Corazón* Catholic Church parishioners are colonia residents. Rita, Tutorial Coordinator, said parishioners fill every Spanish-speaking mass nowadays, with scant parking space.

History and Purpose

Corazón's Catholic Church started in the 1960s as a mission of another Church about five miles away. Eventually, Father O'Sullivan from the church five miles away bought two lots (some say with his own money) and constructed the parish hall. Magnífico said colonia residents then built half of the adjacent church and closed the wall. When they had enough money, they built the other side.

Corazón has had one Marist Brother (Brother James) and five priests, in this order: Father O'Sullivan, Father Cruz, Tim, Father Lucas (who left Mexico as an adult), and Father John (not from the Americas or Europe). Although all have been Spanish and English bilingual and biliterate, they demonstrated different foci. Father Cruz appeared passionate about his Catholic radio and television show, sponsored by the diocese, while Father Lucas focused on rules and his friendship with the now-retired diocesan bishop. Father O'Sullivan, Tim, Father John (current priest), and Brother James (current volunteer), were Anglo. They denoted social justice and youth leadership foci. An avid gardener, Father John is akin to *Corazón's* Johnny Appleseed and Kathy brings him starts often. Claudia said,

> Although Father [John] is not Hispanic, we can relate more to him. In his homilies Father [John] talks a lot about his personal life … Whereas Father [Lucas], his homilies were very, how can I say? Dry? He talked about things we couldn't relate to, people we couldn't relate to, books we couldn't relate to. Father [Lucas' belief was], "Follow the rules," whatever the diocese would ask, I think he would put that first … Father [Tim] would put his people first. At least he wouldn't explain everything he had to do. Father [Tim] had much support, many sponsors who would come to the church. And they left, or the majority, left when Father [Tim] left, so I think that was hard for Father [Lucas]. Financially, they would donate stuff [during Tim's tenure].

Claudia said *Corazón's* Catholic Church had a close community when Tim served from 1996 to 2008: "Everyone knew each other. The church was always up to capacity. Everything changed when he left. It was heart-breaking for us." Claudia said her church lost many people when Tim left, but now are people starting to return with Father John, which demonstrates church leaders are important regarding financial support and church attendance.

Claudia, a former catechism teacher, said the Church serves as a moral compass and aims "to guide our morals and values, which are important to bring back, because many lack those." However, Claudia repudiated rumors about *Corazón*. Father John said this specific congregation blends Catholicism and Guadalupan beliefs, or the veneration of the Lady of Guadalupe, Mexico's Aztec Princess. This exemplifies Third Space; see Chapter 5.

Community Contributions

The Catholic Church celebrates sacraments, including baptism, communion, confirmation, marriage, and non-sacramental, but important events, including *quinceañero/a* masses, and feast days. The Church has a building set aside for weekly Alcoholics Anonymous (AA) meetings. Additionally, the Church has hosted Al-anon meetings for friends and families of problem drinkers. Parishioners and staff serve by having a weekly food bank (with a focus on fresh produce), helping the destitute with rent and utility bills, and distributing clothing and shoes.

Regarding education, church staff mentor youth regarding financial aid and admissions and they introduce Kathy to these youth so Kathy can join them during meetings with university staff; thus, we bridge and rhizome. Related to literacy, Kathy saw a woman returning a *Son of God* movie on CD to the church secretary; Kathy discovered the Church had a regular lending library with English and Spanish movies and printed materials! Church members rhizomed around inadequate public library and bookstore access. The parish library was also a slantwise, grassroots effort. Like an interconnected rhizome, the Church enjoys quid pro quo relationships with colonia organizations. The Church rents a building to *Afinidad's* Tutorial Center; the same building is for catechism, prayer groups, and meetings. *Afinidad* hosts aerobics, Zumba, and dance classes in the parish hall.

Raising Leaders

Some clergy have tried to raise leader activists. Claudia remarked about Tim:

> I remember he was a lot about promoting the vote and civil rights and he would do a lot. He would educate people about voting, bringing candidates to the church. He, along with Brother [James], did a lot to get lighting in our streets and to get the streets paved.

Claudia said when Tim served as the priest, he organized a census:

> We conducted our own Census. I was in high school. We were volunteers. Each person got their own streets. We knocked on each door and asked, "Are you registered to vote?" If not, we gave out flyers [about how to register]. We also asked if they were Catholic.

The slantwise census, a bottom-up attempt at a U.S. practice, represented socially acceptable aims—to determine registered voters and to reach out to church members. Volunteers discovered at least 70% of colonia residents were Catholic.

The Church also offers youth group programs and summer camps to grow leaders. Father John invited Kathy to present media portrayals of *Corazón*, youth perceptions of *Corazón's* strengths, and how youth could help *Corazón*. The youth worked in pairs to jot down email addresses and phone numbers of officials, based on the contact list Kathy started. Tim and Sister Joan also spoke to the youth about activism and colonia needs. Kathy attended a June 2015 talk, given by a Holocaust survivor. This 90-year-old Jewish man, living in the mostly Mexican, mostly Christian RGV, spoke about his concentration camp experiences so youth honor all people and know an oppressed group's history. Kathy realized the irony of a Holocaust survivor speaking in one of the most marginalized U.S. communities.

Through these presentations and much dialogue, Father John was teaching these youth how and why they needed to be activists. He also wanted them to lead young children in the children's summer camp. Thus, Father John felt the Latino/a youth needed to learn about social justice and diversity. We must learn each other's histories because misinformed people remain subjugated (Anzaldúa, 1990). In summary, the Catholic Church remains a vital, welcoming part of *Corazón* by attempting to raise socially-just youth.

Baptist Church

So far we have discussed organizations related to the Catholic Church. This section focuses on the Baptist Church. "Did I pass it already?" Krystal, third author, wondered as she drove down the street, looking for a Baptist Church with a Spanish name. She rechecked Google Maps. Although she had ventured into *Corazón* previously, not seeing the church made her nervous. "These houses are too crowded together; it doesn't make sense that a church could comfortably fit here," she thought. She then saw refurbished school busses with the church's name and about 25 parking spaces. The church buildings seemed to create a "C" shape, encircling a hangout area, including a concession stand. The more Krystal took in the parking lot, the more confused she became. "Many people must walk here because 25 spaces do not seem like enough parking for a church this massive," Krystal thought.

When Pastor Sabio, a greying Mexican-origin man, arrived, Krystal could tell his time was valuable. His phone rang incessantly, but he appeared engaged in the interview; he even gave Krystal a tour afterwards. As Sabio had the grounds-keeper open up every room, Sabio explained each room's purpose.

History and Purpose

Sabio said five families, including his, founded the Baptist Church on April 19, 1980. A day later, they established church bylaws. In December 1980, church members began meeting; soon they constructed the church building. Sabio said in those days *Corazón* consisted of about "150 homes, no running water, no electricity, no amenities of any kind." He said the families who organized the Baptist Church 35 years ago came because they saw spiritual need. Now 200 people are committed members. Sabio said, "I have no millionaires here. A few business men, upper- and lower-class people, 'cause we minister to all."

Community Contributions

The Baptist Church engages in various types of community service, including monthly participation in town meetings. Sabio and other leaders decide on key issues to tackle. According to Claudia, Sabio spoke at *Corazón's* Catholic Church years ago, saying, "We are all brothers and sisters in Christ. We don't have to fight." Tim visited the Baptist Church to talk to members, also. Father John converses regularly with Sabio. These exchanges demonstrate rhizomic relationships because they focus on connection and multiplicity, as Catholic and Baptist theological beliefs differ like the sun and moon.

The Baptist Church hosted forums for candidates running for county commissioner so *Corazón* residents vote wisely. Sabio once ran for county office just so people would know the colonia needed its streets paved. He stays attuned to city and county politics so he can fight for *Corazón's* rights. He said, "In the colonia, I'm involved. Any little thing that will help this neighborhood, if we're gonna pick up trash, anything that I can contribute." Sabio votes and encourages people to vote to increase their voice. He cares about his colonia and wants service improvements; however, he believes incorporation by the city will drive up taxes without improving services and colonia residents will lose freedom: "No more weedy lawns because [the city] says you gotta weed your lawn. I don't know what it's going to cost to give up our liberty." He said many colonia residents vote and stand up for their rights. "So, that is dangerous territory when you have … voters that can communicate and all of a sudden you decide that you're going to incorporate and tax them." See Chapter 1 regarding freedom.

Church staff and members constantly brainstorm ways to provide community services; they offered a school and a tutorial program before. Brenda, a long-term member, said, "There's a camp in Edinburg that the church takes the kids to every summer." Her teenage son and daughter love it and raise money to pay their way. Sabio also mentioned offering a computer class: "I had someone come in and give computer classes … It helped a lot of people."

The church provides family, marriage, and parent counseling, and even took in pedophiles (and counseled them) for service work to pay off their sentences. Because the church is open from Monday to Friday with no children around, the church decided to provide counseling and vigorous work for a cast-out lot. Sabio said, "But they [the offenders] needed to do service and few places will accept a pedophile. We gave them counseling and work, and I mean work. I'm of the philosophy if you don't work, you don't eat."

Every Saturday, about 30 church members go door-to-door, offering bussing services. At least five busses take youth and adults from *Corazón* and the surrounding city to and from church services and events, which costs the church over $2,500 yearly. By offering transportation, the church aims to make it easier for children to receive biblical teachings, anti-drug messages, and motivational messages.

Raising Leaders

Sabio declared himself "a realist by nature." He believes in co-existing "in the real world," either through education or a learned trade. He wants residents to seek formal education so they can become leaders and help *Corazón*. Brenda began attending the church through her boyfriend's mother (now mother-in-law) and Brenda serves as a Sunday-school teacher, a leadership role. Sabio beams about his church's educational mentoring:

> By the time the kid is a freshman, I will have had this conversation: "What do you want to be when you graduate from high school? What do you want to study?" And if they say, "I don't know," that's an unacceptable answer. "I want you to know. What are you good at? What do you like to do? Math? You can be an engineer." We have role models.

Sabio and friends search for motivated children who need mentoring. He said he met a little girl through his church's bus outreach with little family support. Sabio recognized the child's potential and helped her to enter a dual enrollment high school program. Now she is pursuing a Master of Science in Biology. Sabio's church has empowered other youth to pursue college, also. For example, Claudia, a devout Catholic, said the Baptist Church gave 10 youth, including Claudia, $1,000 each to attend a local university; Sabio deposited the scholarship money directly into the students' bursar accounts. Claudia said the only requirements were their *Corazón* residence and enrollment in a four-year university. They needed *ganas* [desire], not high grades. Claudia said Sabio "gave me the impression he believed in us." Besides mentoring youth to pursue an education, the church also has a youth leadership club: "It's a type of Boy Scout/ Girl Scout type of club … We teach kids all the way from kinder to high school. They earn patches and it kind of prepares them for leadership." Sabio said:

> I take a person as far as I can take them … The nature of our people is to come to the leader for guidance and direction. I work at breaking this monopoly every day of my life. I like to empower people, I like to create leaders, free thinkers … Once you open a man's mind, once you train him to think for himself, two phrases my daddy beat out of me as a child: "*No puedo y no sé*" [I cannot and I do not know], he said they both really came from the root word, "*No quieres*" [You do not want].

The Baptist Church has provided colonia opportunities through counseling, mentoring, leadership training, and service, emphasizing empowerment. Based on Krystal's interviews with minister Sabio and member Brenda, this church has functioned as a Third Space—between the community, education, and employment. Although Sabio strives to put members on a successful path, he did not discuss education for personal or religious fulfillment. Instead, his statements related to education as a commodity, a banking education concept (Freire, 2000). Although career and college readiness remains the dominant U.S. discourse, adult education classes can create a Third Space; students can share poems and journals and can participate in book clubs (Perry & Homan, 2014). Aesthetic reasons for literacy education are just as important as efferent ones; we create the aesthetic versus efferent binaries (Rosenblatt, 1978).

Convivio

This last section focuses on a non-religious public organization, located on *Corazón's* outskirts. Colonia residents have mentioned that *Convivio* has faced stigma. When people were building *Convivio* over 17 years ago, a man molested a toddler girl inside of a big cement construction tube on *Convivio* grounds. Brother James said the Church now teaches the children to scream and run if they see, hear, or experience sexual misconduct. *Corazón* neighbors searched for the man, who had ran away. Joy's students said a *Corazón* man caught the perpetrator in the act and adult residents chased and caught the offender. Claudia did not know the man's neighborhood, but she said it remains easy for outsiders to jump the short fence to enter *Convivio's* park. According to some, the locale has another stigma: drug dealing. Joy's students told her, "We don't go there, ma'am. The last time we went, it smelled like weed over there by the soccer boys."

Additionally, either county officials or a Texas university (pseudonym Ranch University) appointed a woman (many used the word *divisive*) to be *Convivio's* Coordinator; she reigned for years. A local leader stated this woman "represented the worst example of *patronismo*, rewarding those who worked with her and punishing those who questioned her leadership." She called herself the mayor of *Corazón*, but began as the colonia's Valley Interfaith leader.

As Krystal pulled into *Convivio's* parking lot for the first time, the one large dull building felt like a government organization. It had few windows in the front. Inside, a teenage girl with headphones sat on a chair. A waist-high sliding window and room separated visitors from staff. Whoever designed the structure did not appear to trust *Corazón* residents. Krystal had set up interviews with *Convivio's* coordinator, Alegría [Happiness], and assistant, Fuerza [Strong]. *Convivio* has a park (at least 100 square feet, about 9.3 meters), including a walking path, an impressive playground (including a wooden jungle), covered basketball court, and soccer field—all in good condition. County employees renovated outdoor facilities lately (with a $500,000 bond); outdoor facilities belong to the county. Claudia sees people using *Convivio's* walking path for walking and running. "Many kids go there and play soccer," she said. Proximity to parks relates to physical activity and health (Cohen et al., 2007).

History and Purpose

Ranch University, about seven hours north of *Corazón*, assisted in erecting *Convivio* in 1993. Sometime later, the county purchased the building and grounds, making it part of the county park system. In 2015, Kathy saw a car at *Convivio* with a huge outreach sticker from that university on the driver's side, so we assume the person drove from Ranch University. *Convivio* endeavors to provide *Corazón* residents with resources. Alegría said *Convivio* serves as a "one-stop information center" by providing counseling, giving courses, and even helping residents to find bus routes.

Community Contributions

Adult Programs

Convivio teaches *Corazón* residents how to apply for or renew benefits for the Texas Supplemental Nutrition Assistance Program (SNAP), Medicare (federal assistance for qualifying elderly people), or Medicaid (state assistance, under federal guidelines, for any age). Fuerza said *Corazón* residents "may not understand documents or may not have Internet access," so staff can help them at no cost. Volunteers or representatives of outreach agencies teach the classes, according to residents' schedules. New programs and classes spring up. Fuerza and Alegría offer whatever will help the community.

Convivio offers free adult classes year-round, including English as a second language (ESL), knitting, sewing, and jewelry-making. The local school district offers adult ESL classes at *Convivio*; because colonia adults are predominately Spanish-speaking, this class has helped them to become more marketable. A non-profit family literacy program, *Apasionados por la Lectura* [Passionate for Reading], offered reading workshops to mothers in Spanish for years, with the goal of developing parents' literacy skills in their first language (L1). While taking domestic-skills classes (such as knitting) might not lead to something lucrative, they help adults to create things and can be a source of supplementary income. Claudia said, "[Hermosa] would go there for jewelry classes." Hermosa made Kathy an elaborate pale pink, beaded necklace and presented it to her years ago during a May session award ceremony.

Convivio offers yoga classes, also. Fuerza explained a volunteer yoga instructor from an exclusive spa gave classes. *Corazón* women fell in love with yoga and began recruiting friends and family. Fuerza said residents could not afford these classes if they had to pay for them. Thus, *Corazón* women reveled when they could gather and enjoy the luxury.

Another adult class involves computers. Fuerza described teaching computer fundamentals to *Corazón* residents. The class attracted grandmothers, young mothers, and some unemployed men. Initially, attendees could not turn on the computer or check email. Despite their fears, they completed the course. Fuerza lit up as she recounted her students' progress, "They loved it and it gave them a sense of freedom." *Convivio* has a computer classroom. Claudia said, "The one time I went there as a student the computers did not work." However, this occurred over 10 years ago. Nowadays *Convivio* has 12 computers in total, all working with free Internet and printer access for *Convivio* program participants. The computer lab hours depend on instructor or employee availability to assist with technical issues.

Ranch University's colonia program delivers *promotora* classes at *Convivio* with the aim of promoting healthy lifestyles. Sister Joan's organization, *Afinidad*, pays for the classes, but selects *promotora* candidates. Claudia, said, "[Hermosa] had gotten some certificates and they have [Ranch

University] on the certificates." Another health-related program informs young mothers that breast-feeding develops healthy child immune systems.

Family Programs

Convivio staff assist with child and adult emotional and physical wellness. Regional outreach agencies teach youth about harmful effects of drugs, alcohol, and tobacco and an outside agency provides a free licensed family counselor for parents and children with school or home problems. The counselor, serving as an intermediary between the parent, school, and child, works to get the child on track. A free health fair occurs yearly. For one or two weeks every summer, U.S. soldiers give free medical and dental check-ups to all, including those without official U.S. documentation. Local emergency and safety officers provide hurricane awareness and free emergency medical kits, also.

Youth Programs

Convivio also offers tutorials and summer classes to primary and secondary school children, but rivalry appears between *Afinidad* and *Convivio* tutorial programs, perhaps because they compete for colonia children attendees. We have seen parent volunteerstutoring and preparing snacks for children at *Afinidad's* Tutorial Center (featured in this chapter). However, Claudia, former Center volunteer, said, "They [*Convivio* staff] don't help them the way we do here [at the Center]." This might be because *Convivio* experiences inadequate tutorial staff. *Convivio* offers free summer breakfasts and lunches Monday through Friday to children up to 17 years old, and has summer activities, such as basketball, soccer, and crafts. Claudia said outdoor *Convivio* volunteers appear to be high school or university students.

Voting

Convivio functions as a polling place for city, county, state, and national elections. Although *Corazón* and non-*Corazón* residents can vote at *Convivio*, *Corazón* residents cannot vote in city elections because the colonia remains unincorporated. Confusing, right? *Convivio* works with various organizations, including *Afinidad*, to encourage voting. People can vote for amendments and candidates to affect change. Alegría told Krystal enthusiastically,

We put up signs to get the community to vote. We encourage the voting. I had a young man that just turned 18 during the last election season ... I took a picture of him out in front ... with his voter registration card. It was a milestone for him because it was his first opportunity to vote ... It's not always as successful as we would like for it to be. But we're not just going to sit back; we still go out and try.

Raising Leaders

Convivio hosts monthly meetings, as described previously. Alegría, *Convivio* director, said, "We invite the community as well to bring their voice." We found no other examples of *Convivio* leadership, however. Despite stigma associated with *Convivio* because of tragic incidents and previous leadership, *Convivio* aims to empower *Corazón* residents through various services, most of which focus on education. This section demonstrated *Convivio's* key role in *Corazón*.

Summary

We posed these inquiry questions in this chapter: What are key *Corazón* places and their characteristics? How do organization leaders work with others to affect change? The six key *Corazón* places are: (1) *Afinidad*, (2) the Civic Organization, (3) Tutorial Center, (4) Catholic Church, (5) Baptist Church, and (6) *Convivio*. Characteristics connected to organizational histories, purposes, services, and ways of creating leaders. Entities improved the community by inviting participants of all ages, establishing trust, and offering various services (e.g., education, health, and voting). Claudia said for a colonia resident to express a concern about a teacher or an issue, "It has to be someone they trust, so it has to be someone from the [Tutorial] Center, from the church."

Claudia believed these key places teach colonia residents, who may lack formal education, about their rights, which relates to social and political empowerment. Claudia stated, "Many are not formally educated so they are ignorant of their rights." Alegría mentioned it takes several organizations to help *Corazón*: "They say it takes a village to raise a child. It's the same thing with a community. People need to work together to be able to improve their environment." Schools, universities, and governments dwell in that village, also.

Questions to Ponder

1. Pick a site from this chapter. Compare and contrast this site to one in your community. What transpires there? What has transpired? What should transpire?
2. Identify key *Corazón* leaders. Discuss their commonalities and their influence on residents. What does it take to improve one's community?
3. Why do women play leadership roles in *Corazón?* What other activist roles could they have?
4. *Convivio* offers numerous classes. What additional classes could empower *Corazón* residents personally, socially, and politically?

SECTION II

SOCIOCULTURAL CONTEXTS OF RELIGION, LANGUAGE, AND LITERACY

· 5 ·

RELIGION AND A SPACE FOR JUSTICE

Meet *la virgen de Guadalupe*

December 12, 2014. 71 degrees Fahrenheit, 22 Celsius. *La Aparición de la virgen de Guadalupe* [Appearance of Our Lady of Guadalupe] event begins. Tutorial Center children sit on a float with Christmas lights dazzling. Behind the float, about 50 *Corazón* residents walk or use wheelchairs—singing hymns, meandering toward the Catholic Church. Once inside, a teen narrator behind a podium welcomes attendees, then children reenact the story of *la virgen de Guadalupe*—in Spanish. A boy and girl in costumes perform with respect the roles Juan Diego, peasant, and *la virgen*, who appeared to him on the Hill of Tepeyac, now part of Mexico City. Other children represent an incredulous, powerful bishop and his assistants. The reenactment ends when fleshy, rare roses fall from Juan Diego's *tilma* [agave-fiber cloak], encrusted with *la virgen*'s image.

Introduction

The Virgin Mary, the Blessed Mother, appeared to Juan Diego, the first Roman Catholic indigenous saint of the Americas. The Holy Mother of Jesus symbolizes the Roman Catholic faith, but the *virgen de Guadalupe*, who spoke to the humble peasant in Nahuatl, the Aztec language, represents the Mexican culture and indigenous tongue. Latinos/as who follow her are *guadalupanos/as* [Guadalupans]. Her Nahuatl name, "Quat-la-su-pe" means she who crushes the serpent's head. "She was in Indian dress, her hands joined in prayer. Her features were Indian and of startling beauty" (Hardon, 2003, para. 48). Our Lady asked Juan Diego to build a church on the spot where he saw her. The once doubting bishop granted her wish; now millions visit her shrine yearly.

The Apparition of the Virgin event demonstrates the blending of religion, culture, language, social class, and justice in diasporic *Corazón*. The flowers on Juan Diego's cloak can represent the colonia children as well, because such beautiful florets blooming against great odds leaves us breathless. This yearly reenactment reminds *guadalupanos/as* to remain faithful, also.

For Chapter 5 we asked, "How does religion connect to colonialism, culture, gender, language, socio-economic factors, and social justice?" Primary data sources were interviews and children's drawings of *Corazón*. Co-researchers were religious workers, volunteers, teacher candidates (TCs), Tutorial Center children, and adult residents. See the Book Introduction for more methodology. Themes include religious celebrations; clashes; intersections between religion, culture, class, language, and neighborhood; colonialism; social justice; and *Corazón's* Baptist Church.

The Catholic Church plays essential diasporic roles by offering Mexican-focused celebrations, services, and religious classes in Spanish. Although we discuss Catholic and Baptist denominations, we focus on Catholicism because most *Corazón* residents are devout Roman Catholics, even if they do not attend *Corazón's* Church. We base the latter statement on interviews. Most U.S. Latinos/as are Roman Catholics who attend church regularly (Pew Research Center, 2014). *Corazón's* Baptist Church, which does not venerate *la virgen*, has increased in membership and has incorporated Mexican cultural values, e.g., family, unity, education, and morals.

Although we discussed *Corazón's* Catholic and Baptist churches in Chapter 4, the present chapter relates religion to *Corazón* residents' daily lives. Christianity matters to many Latinos/as in the diaspora. Indeed, religion can serve as a cultural landing point, a key setting for the survival of new immigrants (Farr & Guerra, 1995). Most new Latino/a immigrants find the Catholic Church welcoming and lively (Pew Research Center, 2014). To a recent Catholic immigrant unaware of the new country's culture or language, the Church can represent a space, a reprieve, where newcomers feel safe and know the rituals and language. Thus, the Church provides a shelter and helps Mexican-heritage people to feel at home in the diaspora.

Religion and Culture

Diasporic Celebrations and Third Space

Our Lady of Guadalupe

As mentioned in the chapter's beginning, Tutorial Center children and the tutorial staff present a yearly reenactment of the *Aparición de la virgen de Guadalupe*, an important Mexican event for colonia residents. See Figure 5.1.

Figure 5.1. *Virgen de Guadalupe* Apparition Reenactment. Photo by Irma Guadarrama.

Non-colonia residents attend this event, also. After the float procession and reenactment, mass begins. For his homily in Spanish, Father John, *Corazón's* priest for the past few years, connected this Mexican celebration to the Virgin Mary and discussed how people from throughout the world, including Bosnia and Herzegovina, have recently spotted the Blessed Mother. Father John even sang a song in his native tongue (not English, not Spanish) about the Blessed Mother and then translated the song into Spanish. Based on Kathy's interpretation of the mass she attended, Father John invited other perspectives (not Anglo, not Latino) to widen parishioners' lenses. By singing in his native tongue and mentioning Virgin sightings, Father John's homily occupied a

Third Space, inviting language and culture crossing for *Corazón* parishioners. Yet he and the congregation moved beyond this spot, as stories can take us to other realms. Father John, an outsider to the Americas and to Europe, bridged cultures and served as a threshold to other realities.

Father John related the *la virgen de Guadalupe* to official Catholic doctrine, honored the Mexican tradition, and added many countries. Bhabha stated in an interview that slight displacements and alterations signify a transformative process (Mitchell, 1995). Father John explained the power of hybridity:

> The people of the colonia are *guadalupanos*. They might not go near a church, but they are *guadalupanos*. They've got statues in their yard and 250 in their house. The Virgin of Guadalupe goes back to the Aztec Princess. She's their Aztec princess. It's great. It's popular religion. You've got accept it and walk with it. Grasp the popular religion. I've been in different places and the *güeros*, the *gringos* [white Americans], would say that you have to get all of this stuff and get back to change, take the religion and purify it.

Father John said many Protestants, such as our Baptist co-researchers, reject mixing popular religion with Christianity; however, Father John accepted Guadalupan beliefs, while introducing Catholic doctrine. Remembering the statue of *la virgen de Guadalupe* on her grandmother's altar, Anzaldúa stated Mexicans blended indigenous religions with Spanish Catholicism in an attempt to retain their indigenous customs after the conquest: "... A lot of my people kept some of their old gods and goddesses by integrating them into the Christian ones. So now *la virgen de Guadalupe* contains within her ... the Aztec creation goddess" (Moraga & Anzaldúa, 1983, p. 230). Other Mexican goddesses may relate to *la virgen* (Ahlstrom & Hall, 2004). Historian Eakin (2007) stated *la virgen* asked Juan Diego to build her a church on a hill associated with the Aztec earth goddess.

Since *la virgen's* apparition, millions of Mexican-origin people, including many *Corazón* residents, have attached much power to her. Mexican women identify with her, feeling strengthened (Moraga & Anzaldúa, 1983). In the 1800s, *norteños* [Mexicans living in what is now the U.S. Southwest] self-identified as Catholics (D. Gutiérrez, 1999). *La virgen's* syncretism or hybridity grew the Church—kind of. According to Eakin (2007), folk Catholicism [Catholicism of the people] in Mesoamerica exemplifies "the failure of the spiritual conquest" (p. 131). Some Mexican-origin religious practices are not completely Western, e.g., *la quinceañero/a* [a fifteenth birthday celebration] and *el Día de los Muertos* [Day of the Dead], explored in this chapter.

Full-fledged spiritual conquest would have been Spanish Catholicism—not an Old World/New World combination, but a blending (Eakin, 2007). *La virgen's* cultural hybridity and the importance many Mexicans have placed on her blended identity and Mexican symbol captivate us. Mexicans remain proud of this cultural Third Space. Undoubtedly, *la virgen* exists in many hearts and even in pop culture.

The *Quinceañero/a*

Besides the Feast of Our Lady of Guadalupe, the Church celebrates and preserves other hybrid indigenous/Catholic events, such as *quinceañeras* for girls and *quinceañeros* for boys. Kathy attended her male student's *quinceañero* event in 1996 when Kathy was a RGV high school teacher. Father John said *Corazón* families take these *quinceañeros/as* seriously, paying much money for this important event. This religious and cultural celebration for 15-year-old Mexicans, marking the transition from childhood to adulthood, originated in Aztec and Mayan cultures. For Aztecs, it marked the mid-way point in which a girl transformed into a woman (Dávalos, 1996). Thus, the *quinceañera's* orgins are female. Father John, when delivering his *quinceañero* homily to a male, connected the *quinceañero* to some male Native Americans' rites of passage and vision quests. In so doing, Father John created a transformational Third Space where cultural and gendered polarities do not apply, a place where a Mexican-heritage teen could connect to other indigenous cultures.

Although the *quinceañero/a* did not begin with Christianity, Spanish missionaries incorporated this indigenous tradition into Catholicism—wisely (Conway, 1990). Some scholars, such as Conway, have placed the *quinceañero/a* in the past only and have not examined how colonialism devastated the Americas in other ways (Dávalos, 1996). Although this rite of passage has continued, the conquering Spaniards blotted out many native celebrations and customs.

Another *quinceañero/a* detail captured Kathy's attention, recorded in field notes:

> Abby, shuffling carefully in her starchy floor-length pink *quinceañera* gown, walks with Father John to the left side of the church, where a six foot by eight foot painting of the *virgen de Guadalupe* and an altar with candles and empty glass vases wait patiently. "*Madre María* … " [Mother Mary …], Abby says, repeating each phrase after the priest. Next, Abby offers flowers to the *virgen* and asks for blessings.

This prayer and Abby's renewal of baptismal vows were part of the *quinceañera* mass. Father John said the *quinceañero/a* would be *vacío* [empty] without the mass, which includes: the Act of Contrition (confession), Old Testament readings, responsorial Psalms, Gospel reading, homily, Lord's Prayer (Our Father), communion, and the child kneeling on a pillow and saying prayers with her/his mother and father and grandparents standing beside her/him. All attendees give each other the sign of peace. A dinner and dance at a reception hall close to the colonia follow. Father John reiterated the importance of this indigenous celebration in *Corazón*:

> Take the *quinceañera*, for example. It's an Aztec rite of passage. The girl comes before the altar to renew her baptismal promise. It's kind of like confirmation. It's not a sacrament. It's popular. It probably means more to the people, to the families. The way they get dressed up and all of that. They are willing to spend $10,000 on this. The dad … the *quinceañera* is important to him. He is proud and grateful to God for his daughter. The fathers cry.

To prepare for the mass and party, friends must practice group dances for months. A family spends years amassing money for shoes, clothes, decorations, drinks, flowers, food, invitations, a band or DJ, photographs, and reception hall rental. Co-researchers mentioned expending great effort finding *padrinos* [godfathers] and *madrinas* [godmothers]. As we have observed in *Corazón*, sometimes extended family celebrate two *quinceañeros/as* simultaneously; if one child turns 15 and the sibling or cousin is a bit younger, the family may wait until the younger one turns 15. A joint ceremony and party mean half of the cost. We interpret joint celebrations to represent cost-saving, slantwise moves (Campbell & Heyman, 2007). Some families use the *tanda* [group saving pool] to save for this event, a slantwise alternative to an official bank. For a *tanda*, the Ramírez family may contribute a certain amount (for example, $100) per month; if 10 families in the pool put in the same amount, by the end of 10 months the Ramírez family will receive $1,000. Thus, a *tanda* can help a family pay for a costly event.

Another slantwise move involves the celebrant's family asking adult family, friends, neighbors, and employers to contribute financially, by being *padrinos* or *madrinas* of certain *quinceañero(a)* aspects. Years ago, Kathy contributed $100 to a *quinceañera* of a friend's daughter; Kathy was *una madrina* of flowers. Having godmothers and godfathers honors contributors, helps families who struggle financially to pay for the event, and preserves this important Mexican tradition. This is slantwise, as other Latino cultures may not ask guests to contribute. Additionally, these techniques demonstrate rhizomic principles related to navigating around inadequate economic resources and connectedness (Deleuze & Guattari, 1987).

Day of the Dead

Next, many parishioners celebrate el *Día de los Muertos* [Day of the Dead], a week-long event in late October/early November and another example of hybrid Third Space. Many *Corazón* Catholic residents construct family altars with *ofrendas* [offerings] to coax the dead to visit. On their family altars, people place items the deceased enjoyed, such as pan dulce [sweet bread] and toys. Altar elements may include fire (candles), water for the deceased to drink and to bathe after the long journey, earth (flowers and food), and wind (papel picado, or delicate paper with cut-out images). Often crucifixes adorn these altars.

The Day of the Dead revives believers' spiritually, also (Eakin, 2007). Parishioners create an altar with photos of deceased loved ones in the Church. Itza, a community activist, stated, *"Ponemos el altar en la iglesia"* [We put the Day of the Dead altar in the church]. We consider this slantwise because the Day of the Dead altar is not part of Christianity, but sits in the *Corazón* Catholic Church during the Day of the Dead. Kathy asked Itza if Halloween blended with el *Día de los Muertos*. Itza said no. *"Damos a los niños bolsitas de dulces por el Día de los Muertos"* [We give the children little bags of treats for the Day of the Dead]. When asked what the Tutorial Center did for Halloween, Itza lifted her arm, motioned a shooing-away gesture to signify the streets, and said, *"Ellos van allá"* [They go there]. This represents an important finding, signifying a reinforcement of Mexican traditions at a Center affiliated with the Catholic Church. The tutorial children receive treats at the Center for the Day of the Dead, a Mexican tradition, but not for Halloween. The latter represents a U.S. tradition of giving treats to children in costumes on the night of October 31.

Unlike Halloween's commercialism, the Day of the Dead focuses on family. This may have been why Itza said tutorial staff and parents did not hold Halloween celebrations for tutorial children. María, second author, comes from Uruguay. María had never heard of Halloween before the 1990's, but many people celebrate Halloween now in Uruguay, over 5,000 miles from the USA. Brandes (2000) explained:

> *… el Halloween y el Día de Muertos, festejos que provienen de una fuente común y que aún muestran muchos rasgos similares, se han convertido en metáforas de las relaciones entre*

> *México y Estados Unidos. El Halloween ha resultado, de hecho, un símbolo del imperial-*
> *ismo gringo* [Halloween and the Day of the Dead, celebrations with the same origin
> and similar features, have become metaphors between Mexico and the USA. Hallow-
> een is considered a symbol of gringo imperialism] (p. 18).

The Day of the Dead symbolizes Mexico for many and several Mexican muse-
ums demonstrate this celebration's importance. This festival is the foundation
of Mesoamerica, a cultural and geographic area from Central Mexico to Costa
Rica, which includes the Olmec, Aztec, and Mayan pre-Hispanic civiliza-
tions (Brandes, 2000). Although Spanish conquerors attempted to destroy
this pre-Columbian celebration, the Spaniards failed; instead, this tradition
became a fusion of Aztec and Catholic religions and cultures (Eakin, 2007).
For example, before the Spanish conquest of Mexico, the Day of the Dead
occurred at the summer's beginning, but the Spaniards moved the celebration
to the end of October, to coincide with *el Día de los Santos* [All Saints Day].
Although the Day of the Dead merged into a Western religious celebration,
the former presents a way for indigenous Mexicans to disassociate themselves
from U.S. Americans and Europeans and to claim a uniquely Mexican practice and tradition (Brandes).

Furthermore, hanging out in cemeteries for festivals may be taboo, mor-
bid, and scary in Western cultures, but many Mexican-origin people have celebrations in cemeteries for the Day of the Dead because they perceive death
as a continuation of life (Brandes, 2000). Thus, Mexican-origin people may
be fearless when they clean and decorate the graves of loved ones with food
and marigold-like flowers—and leave possessions for the departed. Some hold
vigil until dawn.

> *Quizás más que cualquier otro rito mexicano, el Día de Muertos ha adquirido la reputa-*
> *ción de ser ora un resabio indígena precolombino con un barniz católico europeo, ora una*
> *fusión de prácticas ceremoniales prehispánicas y católicas* [Perhaps more than any other
> Mexican rite, the Day of the Dead has the reputation of being a pre-Colombian
> indigenous aftertaste with European Catholic varnish, a fusion of pre-Hispanic and
> Catholic ceremonial practices] (Brandes, p. 11).

In contrast, Brenda, a Baptist Church member where Pastor Sabio ministers
(see Chapter 4), said her church does not celebrate the Day of the Dead or Halloween. This 15-year member explained Sabio has preached on the spiritual
aspects of Halloween, and the holiday's anti-Christian messages. However,
the colonia's Baptist and Catholic Churches celebrate Christian holidays,
such as Easter and Christmas, and other special days, such as Mother's Day.

The Three Kings

The Catholic Church celebrates and preserves other Mexican traditions, such as *Los Reyes Magos* [Three Wise Men] or Epiphany; both hail from Christianity. This January 6 event includes cutting and eating a *rosca*, a braided, sweet yeast bread in a wreath shape containing at least one plastic replica of the baby Jesus. To signify the importance of pan dulce [sweet bread] and culture on this day, *Corazón* residents refer to the Three Wise Men Day as *el Día de las Roscas*. Contributor Claudia said, "Religion … is the most important part of culture. The Epiphany, *el Día de las Roscas*, we don't celebrate those things without church. They [these religious celebrations] keep our culture."

In our geographic area, the people who get a slice of the *rosca* with the figurine would host a *tamalada* [tamale party]. Normally, the tradition includes placing one figurine in the *masa* [dough]. However, in economically-strapped areas, people may add several baby Jesus replicas to the dough so people can share the cost of hosting the ensuing *tamalada*. This is slantwise because the tradition changes for a socially accepted goal—people coming together to celebrate. Meat, cheese, fruit, and/or vegetables can fill the steamed corn-meal tamales. The *tamalada*, associated with the baby Jesus figurine, occurs on February 2 on *el Día de la Candelaria* [Candlemas Day].

Las Posadas

Corazón residents also anticipate *Las Posadas* [inns], in which people go from house to house, singing and then eating food in the home they are invited. The nine-day *Posadas* revolve around the story of Mary and Joseph finding no room in an inn, problematic because Mary needed to give birth to Jesus. Children busting a star-shaped piñata filled with candy is also part of *Corazón's Posadas*. Spaniards brought Chinese-origin *piñatas* to Mexico, but now these hollow, papier-mâché objects are rare at Spanish events. *Las Posadas* and *piñatas* exemplify hybrid Third Space because they started in Spain, but abound in Mesoamerica and the diasporic USA. Many Catholic Mexicans celebrate *Las Posadas*, which take place during Christmas time.

Although we have presented some diasporic celebrations, we believe culture does not equate to mere celebrations. To believe otherwise would be a suitcase or holiday approach to multiculturalism. Instead, we believe culture involves "ever-changing values, traditions, social and political relationships, and worldview created, shared, and transformed by a group of people bound together by a combination of factors" (Nieto & Bode, 2008, p. 129). Culture—dynamic and multidimensional—involves more than race and ethnicity. By presenting conflicts in the next section, we demonstrate the community, although unified, was not homogeneous.

Clashing Cultures

Cultural disagreements existed, even within a close-knit family and neighborhood. For Mexican-heritage people in a diasporic community, culture clashes may relate to gender; religious intolerance; conflicting goals between parents and children; and social class, language, and neighborhood stigma. See Chapter 6. Diasporas relate to practices, not just expatriates bound together.

Gender

One such clash became evident when María interviewed Luchadora, the widow of Luchador; elderly co-researchers said the latter fought for *Corazón's* basic services. Luchadora loved being a catechism teacher for *Corazón's* Catholic Church; she taught the younger children in Spanish, which empowered her. However, her husband forbade her to continue. "*Cuando llegamos, yo tuve un tiempo ayudando a los niños en la doctrina*" [When we arrived (to the colonia) I helped for a while with the children in religious formation classes]. "*Pero luego a mi esposo no le pareció eso y teníamos muchos problemas, entonces ya dejé de ir*" [But my husband didn't like this, and he and I had a lot of problems then, so I quit coming]. "*Me salí y nunca volví*" [I left and never returned (to give classes)].

We do not know details of Luchadora's and Luchador's problems, but disagreements between loved ones represent life. Unfortunately, some conflicts can turn into domestic violence for women of all races. Moraga and Anzaldúa (1983) discussed multifactor difficulties of diasporic women. For example, Mexican women in the diaspora may lack U.S. documentation and may not call the police in cases of domestic violence for fear of deportation or arrest; immigrant women may be unaware of the U Visa, a visa for immigrant victims reporting crimes (Zatz & Smith, 2012). They may be unable to return to their homeland to see their parents—and risk re-entering the USA. To commiserate matters, diasporic women may live in places that devalue their linguistic strengths. Luchadora attempted to exert her rights (to teach a class, to have a reprieve from the home, to garner power), but because of problems with Luchador over her newfound freedom and possibly her higher role as a teacher, she acquiesced. Although a bridge can represent women of color's burden, Moraga and Anzaldúa urged nondominant women to be brave and open paths for others.

Denominational Intolerance

Open communication teaches us about others and can prevent binaries and stereotypes. Moreover, we cannot dominate if we dialogue (Freire, 2000). Yet dialogue was missing in vandalism at *Corazón's* Catholic Church. Brother James said shortly after he and Tim (both Marists, from the Society of Mary) arrived in the colonia in 1996, they found the Virgin's statue smashed into shards at her shrine, about 100 feet or 30 meters from their office. Miraculously, her face remained intact. Tim kept it. The vandal had left a note in Spanish, stating colonia residents do not worship idols. Brother James said worshiping and adoring *la virgen de Guadalupe* are misperceptions. Instead, Guadalupans venerate, or regard with great respect, *la virgen.* He equated the violent act and scribbled note with religious intolerance, which has occurred for centuries among religions. Brother James said much healing could begin if Pope Francis would acknowledge and apologize in public for the Catholic Church's role in this intolerance throughout history.

Parents and Children

Sometimes paths parents take, such as leaving their homeland, involve risks to their children, but parents aim to provide a better life for their children. Ovando (1994) discussed his experiences as a voluntary immigrant. His father, a Protestant minister, fled to Texas from Nicaragua during the Somoza dictatorship with Ovando and his family. U.S. educators punished Ovando for not knowing English. Similarly, Anhelo, nine, who attended the Catholic-sponsored Tutorial Center, flunked a grade level because he lacked English proficiency. Anhelo was angry his parents brought him to America because he left behind friends and extended family. Anhelo cannot cross the border to see them; if he does, he cannot reenter the USA easily. He remains in an in-between spot in the borderlands.

Other cultural conflicts occur within families over religious and Mexican identities. Catholic co-researchers lamented some family members were non-believers. Centripetal forces, unifying and constraining, and centrifugal forces, darting from the center, collide (Holquist, 1996). Children may adapt U.S. culture, while parents want them to keep the *tierra madre* [motherland] culture. *Corazón* children felt pressed to become Anglo-like (as older residents said, *americanos)* from school settings and the media, but their parents pushed them to embrace their Mexican roots. According to Father John:

> Forty-four kids were confirmed on Saturday, but they have no fires in their guts. There is a passivity because they don't dominate either culture. The parents have a steady foot in Mexico. The parents want their children to embrace the Mexican culture.

We interpret Father John's statement in different ways. First, perhaps the children were impassionate about Catholicism because they perceived it as ritualistic and boring. This could represent the colonial, totalizing aspect of Spanish Catholicism in the Americas. The cultural aspects, such as the celebrations mentioned earlier, might be more fun for youth and more connected to Mexico. Second, perhaps Father John was alluding to youth's inadequate social and political activism.

Alternatively, Brother James said perhaps some *Corazón* youth are unattached to religion because they believe *Dios es una máquina* [God is a machine], e.g., "If I do this, then God will reward or punish me." This contrasts to perceiving God as relational. Brother James also said materialism hinders spirituality, as colonia youth may feel unworthy because they lack the possessions they see on television and among peers. Brother James said *Corazón* now has two Hummer vehicles, which he believed to be a social sin related to materialism.

However, many *Corazón* children perceive religion as vital. When we asked each child to draw a picture representing their neighborhood, many included the Catholic Church in their depictions. Although identities constantly shift through contexts and time, many adult co-researchers believed in religion's importance. Most adult residents mentioned attending church services and celebrations when we asked them about themselves.

Social Class, Language, and Neighborhood Stigma

We found social class differences and prejudice about the colonia related to religion. Father Lucas, the priest during María's dissertation fieldwork, said he wanted to attract people with more money to the *Corazón* Catholic Church by offering English services. Many parishioners disliked his English focus; see

Chapter 6. Social class and the colonia's stigma may relate to the Church's difficulty in enticing outsiders. Father John said:

> Why are the two neighboring parishes known for rich people …? Here, we're a simple Hispanic community and so … outsiders would see [*Corazón*] as a place where there's dirt on our shoes and bodies lying around that have gotten shot, that have been dumped from [another neighborhood]. Everyone's real poor and a lot of domestic violence and it's a dangerous place to go to. And it's just not true. Maybe it was at one point, but not anymore. And outsiders just haven't been too keen about crossing over those lines.

Similarly, a Church staff member said Catholics who live within a five-mile radius are supposed to attend this Church, but *Corazón* cannot attract many outsiders.

Some *Corazón* Catholics attend Church outside of the colonia, which exacerbates the problem. Father John said, "Those who speak English [from *Corazón*] go to an up-market parish. Those people like to wear their ties, their *corbatas*, to church. We're not about this [at this church]." We interpret Father John's statement to be a criticism of some *Corazón* Catholics who pretend to be rich by wearing neck ties and attending wealthy churches, and in so doing they appear to reject their neighborhood. Thus, identities consist of multiple factors, not just neighborhood. Social class matters when some seek a worship home. External appearances are unimportant to Father John, who said he welcomes teenagers attending mass in cut-off jeans and flip-flops. He wore tan tennis shoes and khaki's to the 2015 *quinceañera* Kathy attended, which he officiated. Kathy has never seen him wear dress shoes. Instead, this priest focused on a person's inner-workings and participation.

Last, as we began to ponder our involvement with this neighborhood, we thought about the genuineness and faith of many residents, mostly of low socio-economic status (SES). An American priest we know attended a cathedral mass in Saltillo, Mexico, along with people in fine attire. He said attendees in fancy clothes participated due to obligation and he sensed little life in the service. We wonder how social class might relate to faith. We can see stark contrasts in *Corazón's* many Christmas lights and sparse owner-strung lights in nearby wealthy, mostly Christian communities. Joshi, Hardy, and Hawkins (2009) found lower-SES youth and adults had higher levels of religious beliefs than their wealthier counterparts. Additionally, most undocumented Latino/a immigrants represent this low SES group, with less than a high school education (Passel & Cohn, 2009). Wealthy Mexicans may not need to ford the Rio

Grande and lurch in the brush to make a better life for their families in the USA, but poor people may. Undocumented immigrants in poverty risk their lives for their families. Their bridges called their backs weigh like iron (Moraga & Anzaldúa, 1983). They possess tremendous faith.

Religion and Colonialism

Separating religion from socio-cultural and political elements proves difficult because of Latino/a immigrants' complex, shifting identities (Ek, 2009). *Corazón* events in this chapter were in Spanish and mostly Mexican-origin people participated. Father John perceived religion intertwined with history, ethnicity, and language. He unearthed another element—colonialism in the Americas:

> Also, it's a culture thing. *Guadalupanos*, that's Mexican. Guadalupe, the Aztec princess, joins history and culture to religion. *Guadalupanos* is [sic] a popular religion, which in some parts of South America has been despised. And after some time it has been recognized and has helped people to come to a more enlightened sort of faith. It's not just popular religion based on folkloric things, which goes to the psyche of the Mexican or South American. All that language is in there. It's all Spanish.

To explain why he said some South Americans despise the Guadalupe faith, we loop back to the chapter's start and the apparition of *la virgen de Guadalupe*. Hardon (2003), a Jesuit Priest, stated indigenous people shot Juan Diego's uncle before Juan Diego had returned from the Hill of Tepeyac because they resented Juan Diego's conversion to Christianity, believing Juan Diego had colluded with the Spaniards. Juan Diego spent a day nursing his uncle's wounds. The next day, he tried to avoid *la virgen*, but she visited him lower on the Hill, telling him his uncle would live and she needed her church built. Hardon stated that some indigenous people in South America dislike *la virgen de Guadalupe* because they argue she caused countless indigenous Latin Americans to convert to Christianity and accept colonialism. However, many Latinos/as identify with the *la virgen*, Mother of the Americas.

Until the appearance of *la virgen* in 1531 (historical accounts point to the mid-1600s), Spanish priests had difficulty converting indigenous Mexicans, who had ancient religions and advanced societies, but were spiritually disenfranchised. The Spaniards burned every Mayan book, destroyed temples, committed human rights abuses and murders, and annihilated thousands of indigenous people with European diseases, as did other colonizers (Eakin, 2007). Many believe Spanish colonialism took root in the Americas after the apparition; millions of indigenous Americans have converted to Catholicism because of *Guadalupe* (Ahlstrom & Hall, 2004).

Religion can be complicated. Some feminists, such as Moraga and Anzaldúa (1983), disliked Christianity's paternalism, e.g., the Lord's Prayer begins with *"Padre nuestro"* [Our Father]. Actually, *patronismo* [patrimony] and padre [father] share Latin roots. Patrimony, a Middle-Ages concept, relates to royalty channeling resources to friends only. It continued until during Americas' conquest because Spanish monarchs resisted the European reformation (Eakin, 2007). With the New World conquest, Spaniards and others *en suite* have created paternalistic relationships with indigenous people. We see *patronismo* today when wealthy people take care of indigenous people (mostly in poverty) in exchange for loyalty and labor. This colonial system exists in eurocentrism and capitalism (Quijano, 2000) and hierarchical and racist systems (Eakin).

This colonialist system relates to the Catholic Church, also. Spaniards brought to Mexico a Christian denomination of persistent evangelists, people raised in hierarchical Spain, and a much-lighter race. Once firmly established after the apparition of *la virgen*, the Church wielded power and privilege in the Mexican government. For the most part, the Church leaders in Mexico sided with wealthy landowners, owned much property, and favored exploitative dictators who mistreated indigenous peasants (Ahlstrom & Hall, 2004); during the Mexican Revolution, most Catholic clergy fled the country and revolutionaries killed a few. The resultant socialist constitution diminished the Church's political and economic influences in Mexico (Eakin, 2007). Yet, violence continued. A year after the Mexican Revolution ended officially, a bomb disguised in flowers exploded right under *la virgen's* iconic apparition image at her shrine. The bomb damaged the cathedral and nearby homes, but not *la virgen's* fabric or image (Diamond, 2012). Metaphorically Juan Diego represented to some "an underling … a source of labor, a peon; and in the long run he was to respond with resentment, revolution, and anticlericalism" (Ahlstrom & Hall, p. 52).

However, *la virgen* has given many Mexicans national identity during and after the Spanish conquest (Anzaldúa, 2007). She helped Juan Diego, an indigenous peasant, to have a voice; he became a canonized saint in 2002. Furthermore, she and Juan Diego, both dark skinned, spoke Nahuatl and wore indigenous clothes. Kathy's Mexican-heritage friend said her brothers had teased her because of her dark skin, but this friend's father shushed them, saying, "*La virgen también es morena*" [The Virgin is also dark-skinned]. Skin color and internalized racism remain issues among Latinos/as (Valenzuela, 2008) and relate to social justice.

Religion and Social Justice

Some *Corazón* residents, volunteers, and Church employees may have believed, and continue to believe, in social justice. Campano, Ghiso, and Welch (2016) discussed the connection between religion and social justice, also. Tim (former priest), Brother James (retired clergy), and Father John (current priest) appeared to associate religion with political activism. These clergy, staff, and Catholic volunteers have fought against *patronismo*, colonialism, inequities, and abuses of power. At times their superiors agreed, depending on which higher-ups were in power. Only Brother James, now retired, mentioned he followed liberation theology, but we surmised many other *Corazón* Church leaders and laity embraced it, also.

Yet what is liberation theology? When and where did it originate? Vatican II in 1962 called for Church leaders' immersion into the poor's struggles. Shortly thereafter, Peruvian-born Gutiérrez created liberation theology; he believed European theology was irrelevant in Latin America, oppression (e.g., military dictatorship) was not God's will, and committed world actions determined orthropraxis, or correct conduct, as opposed to correct rituals and beliefs (G. Gutiérrez, 1973). Freire's praxis inspired Gutiérrez's Christian orthopraxis (Lange, 1998). Praxis means action and reflection to transform the world. Due to priest shortages, many South American Catholic churches formed Base Ecclesial Communities, in which laity held meetings in humble homes to apply liberation to biblical principles (Williams, 2000). During mass, priests may apply liberation theory when they ask parishioners to comment on homilies. Social justice connections become obvious in Lange's liberation theology explanation:

> The paradigm of liberation in theology rejects conceptions of God that colonize the mind and spirit and perpetuate the political and economic status quo ... God has historical agency in liberating the oppressed from their bondage in Egypt and God seeks justice through human prophecy and political action; and where, through Christ, God shows preferential love for the poor, marginalized, and oppressed (p. 82).

Liberation theologists influenced Freire, also. Continuum (n.d.), Freire's long-standing publisher, stated, "Freire began to embrace a non-orthodox form of what could be considered liberation theology" (back cover, para. 3). Freire, a Catholic, worked in Chile for five years for the Christian Democratic Agrarian Reform Movement. Freire (2000) believed in the Easter Experience; we must "'die' in order to be reborn through and with the oppressed" (p. 131). In this sense, the oppressed and oppressor transform, taking on new wineskin.

Pope Francis exemplifies aspects of liberation theology, also (Burke, 2015). "With the election of the first pope from Latin America, liberation theology can no longer" be ignored (McElwee, 2013, para. 4). Pope Francis had a private meeting with Gutiérrez, now a Notre Dame endowed professor. Liberation theology follows coherent religious ideas; it is not a political movement (Williams, 2000).

Brother James told Kathy helping people in poverty remains essential in liberation theology. He said conversion relates to a change in your gut (making a fist close to his stomach) to fight for the poor. This radical conversion does not allow ambiguity (Freire, 2000). Over lunch, Brother James asked Kathy, "What caused your conversion?" Kathy discussed the dead Honduran babies and toddlers she saw in her village when she served as a U.S. Peace Corps volunteer. As Kathy and Brother James were eating, she avoided mentioning children's corpses on kitchen tables, flies on cold open mouths, and stomachs bloated like soccer balls from amoebas.

Immediately transported back 30 years, Kathy exclaimed to Brother James, "Why?! Why does this have to be?!" Kathy blamed the structural inequality of poverty. The parents, if they could carry the children to the nearest clinic at least two hours by foot, might lack the money to pay for the consultation, medicine, and intravenous fluids (IVs). In that Honduran village, many people owned just one or two outfits, but they demonstrated spirituality and love. Kathy realized material possessions were unimportant; they would not bring her closer to God or people. Indeed, "conversion to the people requires a profound rebirth" (Freire, p. 61).

Certainly, not all who believe in social justice are religious and not all religious people are social justice proponents. From what many told us, Father Lucas did not seem to endorse liberation theology and appeared uninvolved in colonia life. According to some parishioners, Father Lucas would tell regular mass attendees he could not officiate their weddings or *quinceañeras* because they did not attend mass. Additionally, he appeared to have an English-only agenda. In his defense, perhaps he believed the best way for residents to prosper involved renouncing Spanish and adopting English, the language of commercialism and power. Father Lucas may have wanted the best for them; see

Chapter 6. Thus, it depends on those involved regarding whether Christianity relates to social justice.

However, the most religious Latinos/as are the most political, based on a study of 4,016 U.S. Latinos/as. Latinos/as who self-identify as Catholics are more likely to be Democrats (Martini, 2012). As we pondered why Latinos/as might be more drawn to *The Side of the Poor* (Gutiérrez & Müller, 2015), we turned to the Virgin of Guadalupe. The Virgin appeared to an indigenous Mexican in poverty; she represents poor, marginalized Mexicans (Eakin, 2007). In fact, Miguel Hidalgo, a parish priest born in Mexico, used *la virgen* for his rallying cry against the Spaniards *en el dieciséis de septiembre"* [September 16], 1810.

> His call to seize the property of Europeans, abolish Indian tribute, and to invoke the support of the Virgin of Guadalupe had enormous appeal to the poor masses. The Indians were especially devoted to the Virgin and she became the rallying symbol for the assertion of their own identity (Eakin, pp. 190–191).

Flash forward to 2015. Kathy sits at Poeta's and Esposo's kitchen table, asking questions about Luchador. Luchador was a devout Catholic who worked with César Chávez in California in 1965; see Chapter 3. Luchador, who moved to *Corazón* in 1974, asked, *"¿Por qué estamos así? Hay que empezar a luchar"* [Why are we like this? We have to begin to fight]. Poeta and Esposo, close friends of Luchador, who died in 2006, have yearly Catholic remembrance services for Luchador with his family. Luchador attended protests and rallies to fight for potable water and other basic services in *Corazón*. His favorite Bible verse, according to Poeta, was, "And the meek shall inherit the earth." Poeta said Luchador was a Guadalupan, *"El siempre llevaba la virgen de Guadalupe en frente* (waving her arm like she has a flag) *adonde íbamos"* [He waved the Virgin of Guadalupe flag in front of him always, wherever we went]. Poeta continued with the acrostic poem she wrote in his honor, *"Nunca luchaste sólo, porque siendo mexicano, nuestra virgen de Guadalupe te resucitó"* [You never fought alone, but you, being Mexican, the Virgin of Guadalupe, revived you].

Patriota confirmed this information about Luchador. Patriota and Patriot had lived about 25 minutes from *Corazón*, but helped the colonia to receive potable water and went on a Washington D.C. bus trip, in which Luchador participated; see Chapter 3. Patriota showed Kathy an endearing black-and-white photo of a dark-skinned, white-haired Luchador, walking in the rain, with a Mexican poncho and light-colored cowboy hat. Luchador was leading a rally, but was laughing and holding a Styrofoam cup of coffee (perhaps) with both hands. His left hand, visible to the viewer, was splotched from crop duster chemicals when he labored as a United Farm Worker (UFW) worker, according to a historical newspaper article. A laughing dark-skinned man to Luchador's right, also in a light cowboy hat, carried a flag. Perhaps Luchador turned to his friend and said, "Here, carry Her for a moment as I drink my coffee." The flag had an emblem on it, but Kathy could not distinguish the emblem because the flag wove between Luchador and the friend. We imagine *la virgen*, just as she appeared to Juan Diego centuries before.

Intrigued about social justice connections to *la virgen*, we sought *la virgen de Guadalupe* associations with rallies and immigrants. We found Chicago groups planned immigration rallies on *la virgen's* feast day; the rallies signified disapproval of the increased number of Latinos/as deported under President Obama (Hispanically Speaking News, 2013). Interdenominational churches and leaders, not just Catholics, held a 2006 rally in Indianapolis, Indiana:

> Scattered throughout the white t-shirts and posters pleading for comprehensive immigration reform were images of the Virgin of Guadalupe, a familiar image used to promote social justice. The Guadalupe banners present in Indianapolis echoed the civil rights-era images of United Farm Workers strikes (Vega, 2015, p. 89).

Vega (2015) juxtaposed the Guadalupe banners with the United Farm Workers (UFW), which surprised us because many U.S. priests and bishops sided with wealthy growers during UFW citrus strikes (M. Day, 1971). This reminds us of priests and bishops who supported wealthy landowners in Mexico before the Mexican revolution in the early 1900s (Eakin, 2007). Furthermore, equating hierarchical aspects of religion (e.g., human leadership) to spirituality and Christianity proves erroneous. Alas, *la virgen* is not male.

We began to understand the Virgin of Guadalupe and social justice connection more clearly in mid-September 2015, when Kathy noticed a framed print of César Chávez in the *Corazón* parish office. She had probably passed this art at least 30 times, but had never got close to listen to it. *Portrait of La Causa*, by Mexican surrealistic/folkloric painter Octavio Ocampo portrayed César Chávez and more. Dead farmworker families, including children, lay in the shapes of skulls beside Chávez's right shoulder. To Chávez's left, images and words depict the United Farm Workers' (UFW) strikes, pickets, and placards. The U.S. flag edges César Chávez's hairline, demonstrating his U.S. loyalty. Kathy noticed Virgin of Guadalupe images on Chávez's shirt. Dolores Huerta, co-founder of the UFW, said *la virgen* symbolizes leadership, which we interpret as taking a stand for the poor. We learned César Chávez and UFW supporters walked in protest because growers intentionally sprayed strikers with poison; protesters walked for 340 miles from Delano, California, to Sacramento during *Semana Santa* [Holy Week] in 1965. Strikers carried the Virgin of Guadalupe flag throughout the journey (Labor Archives and Research Center, 2007).

As we searched for scholarly articles about *la virgen* related to education, Baquedano-López's and Ochs's (2002) book chapter captured our attention. The chapter's title associated *la virgen* with social justice and hegemonic language policies: "The Politics of Language and Parish Storytelling: Nuestra Señora de Guadalupe Takes on English Only." A Catholic parish council voted to eliminate Spanish *doctrina* [religious education] classes in a Los Angeles church, but resistant Mexican-heritage teachers continued to teach Spanish *doctrina* unofficially. This exemplifies linguistic prejudice, yet *la virgen* champions for the oppressed and Mexican-origin people. Spanish Catholicism and the Aztec religion have meshed to create a strong sense of Mexican nationalism, and *la virgen* of Guadalupe has played a vital role. Religion, culture, and language overlap. Subaltern students' spiritual and religious practices can provide resistant language.

Baptist Religious Education

Certainly, religious traditions and politics vary, depending on context. One such variation exists within Christianity, as cultural differences between Catholic and Baptist churches in *Corazón* proved enormous. It appeared the Catholic Church focused on affirming Mexican traditions and Spanish to lead people to deeper faith. However, the Baptist Church communicated strong messages of unity, morality, and education. Pastor Sabio, *Corazón's* Baptist minister, equated education with culture, and culture with northern U.S. states:

> We have a great many intellectuals that come to the area that misunderstand this area. We have people come in from the north and they want to do bike-a-thons. And they want to turn a road into a bicycle this [sic], and I'm all for cultural. At the university we wanna teach culture ... People have no culture without education. But you cannot educate if I'm not able to meet my basic needs; I'm not interested in knowledge.

Thus, it appeared Sabio believed in a banking educational system in which northerners bestowed a gift on Rio Grande Valley (RGV) residents, similar to pouring knowledge into empty vessels (Freire, 2000). Perhaps this Mexican-heritage man believed local knowledge ranked low and that culture did not involve shared and contested beliefs; he said that culture was something university professors taught. However, we argue that local and global knowledge have value and that people without formal educations possess rich cultures. We do agree with Sabio regarding the impact of food insecurity and other poverty issues on people's motivation and ability to learn. Additionally, we believe informal education and knowledge of norms, values, beliefs, and traditions influence authentic cultural associations.

Pastor Sabio did recognize structural inequalities regarding local officials' treatment of his colonia and state and national officials' dismissal of the RGV:

> I worked 10 years in Corpus Christi. I've been to America. He (a reporter) said, "Sir, we're in America." I said, "No we're not. This is a militarized zone. It's been left without employment, without industry for a reason. We have what we call the domino theory. We do not have a federal highway like I-69. We do not have no [sic] factory, one industry that's down here."

Pastor Sabio was alluding to the 18-foot (5.5 meter) high U.S.-Mexico border wall, no major highway to escape hurricanes from the north, and inadequate state funding.

Church member Brenda said that Sabio treats the congregation as family, another cultural example. Brenda said members gather for socializing, including a New Year's pot-luck. Brenda linked family and church, as her boyfriend's mother invited Brenda to the church in 1997. Brenda married this boyfriend and the couple raised their children in the Baptist Church.

As mentioned in Chapter 4, Pastor Sabio frets over his flock's morality, especially the youth, because of the U.S. cultural milieu, which reaches *Corazón* through television, movies, popular culture, school, and the nearby shopping mall. Sunday school teachers preach against immoral behaviors, such as drug and alcohol experimentation. "In this world, trying to raise teenagers is hard, especially with technology and things like Facebook," Brenda said. "Once the kids reach the middle-school level, these teachers begin to expose them to all the things that are out there" with the intention of instilling greater resistance to bad influences. Sabio said this inoculation approach helps youth to realize the harmful effects of immoral behavior, provides a safe zone, and enables *Corazón* youth to talk about their experiences and learn from them.

Brenda takes care of her church's newborns. She has three children of her own, two of whom attend Baptist Sunday school regularly. She said the church focuses on anti-drug/alcohol and pro-education messages because of the community's high poverty level. Thus, we realize another connection between social class and religion. Pastor Sabio asserted, "We're not only going to teach [the] kids about the Bible; we want to teach [them] how to stay in school." Hence, Brenda and Sabio believed their Church needs to shape children's educational paths.

Summary

Vitality emanates from *Corazón* residents' religious identities. We asked this inquiry question: How does religion connect to colonialism, culture, gender, language, socio-economic factors, and social justice? Religion connects to colonialism as it can oppress or empower diasporic people. In the Americas the Spaniards used Catholicism to dominate and subjugate indigenous people, yet *la virgen de Guadalupe* symbolizes social justice for many Latinos/as. Ironically, colonialism and social justice intertwined with religion because of *Corazón* residents' Guadalupan faith and political activism.

Because religion relates to culture and language, the church can serve as a Third Space to bridge divides. Yet we found religion struggled in fording socioeconomic differences, as some *Corazón* residents preferred to bypass their neighborhood parish to attend upscale Catholic parishes. Regarding gender, Luchadora relished teaching religious education, but Luchador told her she needed to stay in the home. However, we found many female political activists in *Corazón*, which showed they were not dissuaded.

Last, the clashes presented in this chapter demonstrate *Corazón* is *not* little Mexico. *Corazón* occupies a place where U.S. and Mexican cultures collide, a place of blended identities where adults represent Mexico and Spanish, while the children represent Mexico, the USA, translanguaging, Spanish, and English. Transformed individual and collective identities emerge in *Corazón*. Clashes re-presented in this chapter clamor between new identities.

Questions to Ponder

1. Why might a suitcase approach be harmful to diverse learners? What common suitcase approaches to culture have you experienced as a child or adult (e.g., learning about Native Americans around Thanksgiving)?
2. What clashes related to religion could you identify with? How do they relate to in-between spots?
3. How do the chapter's clashes relate to a community of mainly recent immigrants?
4. What remnants of colonialism do you see in your context? How do these colonialist remnants relate to this chapter?

· 6 ·

LANGUAGE AND LITERACY

Meet Nieves and Itza

Nieves, 13, savored watching a Mexican *telenovela* [soap opera] with Itza, her mother. Nieves did not attend the Tutorial Center to be with friends until *La Rosa* finished, which demonstrated the importance of the Mexican culture, Spanish language, and mother-daughter relationship. Religious and cultural connections flowed when Nieves discussed the program: "*En La Rosa de Guadalupe* [the Rose of Guadalupe] the kids talk about problems and someone asks Guadalupe to help them and she helps them" (Bussert-Webb & Díaz, 2013, p. 29). *La virgen* is the Roman Catholic Patron Saint of the Americas and the Blessed Mary, Mother of Jesus. *Rosa,* in the show's title refers to rare roses spilling out of Juan Diego's cloak in front of a doubting bishop, proving *la virgen* appeared to Juan Diego. The Virgin's image became imprinted on Juan Diego's cloak, also. Our Lady of Guadalupe symbolizes Mexico, discussed in Chapter 5.

Introduction

This chapter highlights the luscious language and literacy practices of Nieves, Itza, and other *Corazón* participants. Since residents used Spanish, English, and combinations of both, we refer to bilingualism as speaking and understanding two languages and biliteracy as written communication in two or more languages within bilingual continua and contexts (Hornberger, 2014). Third Space perspectives related to hybridity, clashes, and hybrid language practices, while social justice related to language and education policies, access, and resistance (Freire, 2000). Since we also discuss literacy, we include New Literacy Studies (NLS) traditions; literacy and NLS involve ideological, social practices in everyday life (Barton & Hamilton, 2012). Although NLS includes literacy events, or occasions involving writing, we did not address this phenomenon. Because of its political nature, NLS relates to social justice; Luke (2005) discussed the NLS social justice commitment related to redistributing power and goods.

Finally, we incorporate Fishman's (2001) language shift to analyze Spanish language loss or maintenance in the colonia. Fishman argued cross-generational language transmission at home is fundamental for minority language maintenance. However, children's first language (L1) tends to shift to the dominant language when their L1 remains in low-power spheres, such as homes. Formal education and employment exemplify high-power spheres. We refer to the target language, English, as L2. Yet, we recognize many Mexican-heritage people in the USA may speak indigenous languages first, then Spanish, and later English. Approximately six million Mexican citizens speak indigenous languages. We have not encountered multilingualism among our *Corazón* co-researchers. Because of immigration issues, we did not want to pry.

We asked this inquiry question: What language and literacy practices and access occur in this community? Data sources were mostly: interviews, language use surveys, language logs, and a linguistic landscape analysis of *Corazón* through commercial and public outdoor signs (Landry & Bourhis, 1997). We base this chapter mostly on María's doctoral dissertation (Díaz, 2011), but we include our published and unpublished work, also. Primarily religious workers, parents, Tutorial Center youth, and adult residents participated. See the Book Introduction for more methods.

Themes related to assimilation pressures, language and linguistic resources and practices, and some residents' resistance. Parents' desired to learn English to assimilate, help their children, and get better jobs. Regarding resources, youth and adults language brokered (similar to translation services) to help each other (Orellana, 2009). Youth translanguaging became a resistance theme; translanguaging transcends code-switching—linguistically and politically. Translanguaging signifies a dynamic, purposeful, sense-making practice and using two languages interchangeably across domains and contexts

(García, 2009). For example, in December 2015 Kathy overheard a local college student talking to a *Corazón* male child about a face he was creating. The college student said, "*Y el otro* eye" [And the other eye]. Translanguaging is recursive because it goes backward to the L1 and forward to the L2. Moreover, translanguaging represents a language and an asset (García). We sandwich the No Child Left Behind Act in the chapter's middle for centripetal (centralizing) and centrifugal (decentralizing) forces to dialogue (Holquist, 1996). Assimilation would be centripetal, while translanguaging resistance would be centrifugal or fleeing.

Spanish Language Use

As with this chapter's beginning with Nieves, Spanish has immersed itself in *Corazón*'s culture. In the sixties, when this colonia began, "*habían pocas familias y todas hablaban español*" [The few families all spoke Spanish], Isabel, one of the first colonia settlers, commented. The 2015 language situation yielded similar results; 3.4% spoke only English (U.S. Census Bureau, 2010). Isabel said she has heard only Spanish in *Corazón*; thus, she believed if people say something in English, residents will not understand.

Although youth translanguaged among each other, we heard Spanish most often in *Corazón*. Residents believed the colonia's environment offered no threat to their first language (L1): "*Yo creo que es imposible perder el español, aquí, adonde vas te hablan en español*" [I believe it's impossible to lose the Spanish language here. Everywhere you go, people speak Spanish]; and "*No tengo problema cuando voy a las tiendas aquí; todos hablan español*" [I don't have any problem when I go to buy here; everybody speaks Spanish]. The surrounding city's 93.2% Latino population (U.S. Census Bureau, 2010) has helped to maintain *Corazón* residents' heritage language. Southwestern Mexican communities have served as havens where Mexican-heritage people could communicate in Spanish (D. Gutiérrez, 1999).

Additionally, we heard only Spanish during *Corazón* religious events and festivities, embedded in Mexican traditions; see Chapter 5. One Spanish-related example is *Las Posadas* [the inns], a nine-day celebration for many Catholic Mexicans, occurring at Christmas. An elderly resident described *Las Posadas* in *Corazón*: "*Cuando celebramos Las Posadas es como estar en México ... todo es en español*" [When we celebrate *Las Posadas* it's like being in Mexico ... everything is in Spanish]. Luchadora, a long-time resident featured in other chapters, remarked about the inns, "*La iglesia se llena y viene gente de afuera*" [The church gets full and outsiders attend].

Youth translanguaged among themselves during colonia religious and social events. These youth, who usually spoke in English in nearby schools, conversed in Spanish in the presence of *Corazón* adults. The spoken Spanish among youth was natural because most bilinguals in the USA are U.S.-born and L1 Spanish speakers (Suárez, 2007). For instance, a well-known Valley musical group played for parishioners at the Catholic Church and sang exclusively in Spanish, with mostly Mexican and other Latin American songs. Youth clamored, "*Otra, otra*" [Encore, encore]. This shows how language relates to culture, consisting, in part, of values and traditions, which many *Corazón* residents bring from Mexico.

Linguistic Landscape and Spanish Print Access

Worldviews and political relationships, part of culture, relate to language, literacy, and policies, also. When discussing the word and world, Freire (2000) asked us to consider interests served by policies and practices. For example, how do business signs in English and the paucity of Spanish books in a diasporic Mexico community relate to U.S. policies? Barton and Hamilton (2012) discovered global and local literacies intersected in people's access to printed materials. Indeed, local and global literacies inform each other, e.g., a U.S. English push may have motivated business signs in English yet few Spanish books. María walked and drove around *Corazón* and documented its linguistic landscape, or the language visibility on commercial and public signs in an area. A community's linguistic landscape represents language vitality in bilingual settings and people's informal communication and attitude toward the first language (L1) (Landry & Bourhis, 1997).

Corazón's linguistic landscape included a range of literacies. María observed signs related to political campaigning and commercial activities (e.g., food stores, auto repair shops, and home businesses). Most business names (e.g., grocery) were in English. Spanish-only signs included church announcements for services and events. María noticed bilingual signs, or English and Spanish combined in one poster, mostly outside of smaller businesses; the notices focused on community service and health. Although Spanish was evident, English's role in the linguistic landscape surprised us, since many *Corazón* residents lacked English proficiency. English signs for businesses could indicate

Corazón residents perceived English as the language of power (Fishman, 2001). Figure 6.1 represents a business sign in English. Notice the Spanish name of a Latino/a political candidate, as over 90% of Valley residents are Latino/a (U.S. Census Bureau, 2010).

Figure 6.1. Business Sign in English. Photo by Krystal A. Yanez.

Additionally, María examined other *Corazón* print literacy resources, such as newspapers, indoor bulletins, flyers, and books. No bookstores, kiosks, or newsstands exist in *Corazón*. However, mini-markets, which sell groceries, offer a small selection of daily newspapers. Three of four newspapers sold in the colonia were in Spanish—one published in the USA and two in Mexico. This greater representation of Spanish newspapers suggested the language in which *Corazón* adult residents choose to read. An employee in a mini-market said people mostly buy newspapers written in Spanish: "*Los de inglés ahí nos quedan, casi nadie los compra*" [Those written in English remain; almost nobody buys them].

We found children co-researchers experienced little access to books in English or Spanish at home. One fifth-grader owned many books, which she stored in a discarded deep freezer (Díaz & Bussert-Webb, 2013). The children did not visit school libraries much for various reasons; they felt unwelcome, they lost their IDs, or staff cancelled library hours. The closest public library to *Corazón* was at least three miles away; inadequate transportation made book access difficult. One mother reported, *"No tengo carro, y dependo de otros para que me lleven"* [I don't have a car and I depend on others to take me to the library]. Teacher Joy pondered why the city library would send a book mobile to Walmart, a congested commercial area in a middle-class neighborhood, versus providing a mobile library closer to *Corazón*.

A youth book source consisted of an informal Tutorial Center library, but until 2014, children could not check out books during the summer. Less than 10% of the Center's books were in Spanish, which Reese and Goldenberg (2006) observed in other Latino communities. Immigrants in poverty face obstacles because of inadequate book access. Few participating children mentioned owning or sharing Spanish books in their homes, but some owned Spanish magazines and newspapers (Díaz & Bussert-Webb, 2013).

Corazón families and other minority-language families in the USA with incomes below the poverty line may find few reading materials in their heritage language. Library and book inaccessibility, especially during summer, contribute to children's academic difficulties (Allington & McGill-Franzen, 2008). However, books in children's L1 build vocabulary and concepts of print (Goldenberg, Reese, & Rezaei, 2011). This remains a social justice issue related to access among diverse people in poverty. Granted, socio-cultural contexts, such as a dearth of Spanish books, can influence literacy practices, yet as New Literacy Studies scholars, we do not believe books represent the sole sinew to literacy.

Children's Spanish Literacy Practices and Language Policies

English-Only Schooling Policies

Acquiring language and literacy skills in two languages proved complex for participating children, who spoke and heard mainly Spanish with adult family, but read in English. A child demonstrated school influences on English shifts: "I can read only in English because, in school, they taught me to read in English." Another child said his school books and teacher notes were in English. These statements demonstrate the difficulty of becoming biliterate with insufficient instruction and materials in a child's first language (L1). A fifth grader, attending a transitional bilingual program, reported,

El español fue mi primer idioma, pero cuando comencé la escuela aprendí el inglés, y tenía todas las clases en inglés, y aprendí el inglés porque todas las maestras me acostumbraron a leer puros libros en inglés, porque la clase es de inglés y la maestra dice que leamos en inglés … Cuando vamos a la "library" sólo los niños que no más saben en español pueden sacar libros en español. Nosotros tenemos que sacarlos en inglés [Spanish was my L1, but I learned English when I entered school. All of my classes were in English. I learned English because all of my teachers made me read books in English. The teacher said we need to read in English because the classes were in English … When we go the library only those children who know only Spanish can check out books in Spanish. We need to check out books in English].

Transitional U.S. bilingual education focuses on preparing L1 children for a monolingual English world (Nieto & Bode, 2008).

Hermosa, narrated her adult child's (Mia's) U.S. school experience. Mia, who recently received a master's degree, was eight when she entered U.S. schools; Mia attended Mexican school previously. Hermosa, Mia's mother, said, "*La maestra* [in the USA] *la castigaba si hablaba en español. Tuvo que aprender a fuerzas*" [Her teacher punished her if she spoke Spanish. She learned by force]. Mia's fourth grade teacher isolated Mia and other Spanish-dominant youth in their own group, prohibited Spanish-speaking, and punished Mia because she thought Mia was speaking Spanish.

These subtractive practices exist throughout many U.S. schools. Proponents of such practices emphasize English-only instruction, rapid Americanization, and a monocultural assimilation approach. Additionally, bracketing Spanish and English by Mia's teacher demonstrates binary thinking, which may cause people to believe they must give up a language to learn another. This bracketing may influence the subaltern's negative L1 perceptions (García & Kleifgen, 2010). A native Spanish-speaking fourth grader referred to his peer, a recent Mexican immigrant, as dumb because his peer preferred to read in Spanish (Díaz & Bussert-Webb, 2013).

Tutorial Center

Unfortunately, the Tutorial Center extended hegemonic school practices and policies because the children brought mostly English homework. The Center endeavors to assist children with homework; see Chapter 4. A staff member said, "The instruction is in English … we help children in Spanish only if they bring homework in Spanish." The previous coordinator believed *Corazón* youth would triumph if they focused on English mastery. The Center's environmental print during her time demonstrated English promotion, as bulletin boards and posters were in English.

Parents

Parent co-researchers viewed the Tutorial Center as a school extension, where children could improve their English skills. Claudia, who had volunteered at the Center, said parents emphasized children learning English: "For the parents it is more important their children learn English rather than they maintain both languages. I believe they want to see fast results, that their children learn English fast." Some parents reported bilingual programs a waste because children needed to learn English quickly. They appeared unwilling for their children to develop Spanish literacy. Parents established a language separation between home and school, the opposite of hybrid Third Space.

A father accepted this bracketing: "*El español debe ser en la casa, y el inglés, la educación, eso lo vas a agarrar en la escuela*" [Spanish should be at home. English, education occur in school]. In Texas, some Spanish-speaking parents oppose additive bilingual education the most; they believe schools should focus on English because parents can teach Spanish at home. Additive and dynamic bilingual education value the first language (L1) (García, 2009). However, parents who spoke the L1 and encouraged its development supported L1 vitality. An adult resident believed language bracketing related to employment and outside forces, "*En este país uno tiene las opciones, habla inglés donde trabajas, donde se necesita, pero en tu casa habla español*" [In this country you have options, speak English at work where you need it, but you speak Spanish at home].

Staff members, who have worked with colonia residents for years, said children's Spanish literacy struggles are partly because parents have not mastered their own L1 literacy. Amiga explained, "I have come across several parents who can't even read their own language … their level of education gets in the way … Many migrate from rural areas [of Mexico]." Actually, English might be their L3 and Spanish their bridge language or L2, since many Mexicans speak Nahuatl and Yucatec Maya, and several indigenous languages.

Language and Literacy Practices at Home

However, participating parents and other adults reinforced the importance of oral Spanish at home. Even bilingual youth, who usually spoke in English in more structured contexts (e.g., school), reported communicating in Spanish at home; they said their parents, and sometimes grandparents, preferred for them to speak Spanish at home for better communication. Interactions with extended family, such as grandparents, are important for children's oral first language (L1) development. This influence relates to familism, or structural settings in which people with different activities and interests are bound together (Sparks & Reese, 2013). Durand (2010) found a positive literacy effect of home social practices on kindergarten students; 56 Latinas and their 56 children participated. Social practices included mothers teaching their children how to behave and relate to others.

In the family context, colonia mothers played an essential role in children's Spanish maintenance. As mentioned in this chapter's beginning, Nieves was so committed to watching a regularly scheduled telenovela [Mexican soap opera] with Itza, her mother, she kept her tutorial friends at bay, which demonstrated a shared family tradition involving the Spanish language (Bussert-Webb & Díaz, 2013). Home contributions, such as talking about a television show, playing video games together, and storytelling may help children to develop L1 and Latino/a identities. Close child-parent relationships relate to youth L1 use, proficiencies, and proclivities. Mexican parents in Ayón's and Villa's (2013) study believed teaching their children Spanish could help their children's ethnic identity development and family well-being, in light of Arizona's anti-immigrant law, Senate Bill 1070. The U.S. Supreme Court upheld this Arizona law. Thus, parent language policies, or language norms parents establish at home, are important in language maintenance in the Mexican diaspora.

Perhaps because of inadequate Spanish books, few *Corazón* mothers reported teaching their young children to read in Spanish. Those who taught their children to read used their linguistic strengths, which they brought from their own Mexican schooling. Hermosa reported, "*Cuando mi hija estaba chiquita yo le enseñé las letras, y también a juntar las sílabas ... Así es como aprendió a leer en español*" [When my daughter was little, I taught her the letters and how to put syllables together. This is how she learned to read in Spanish].

Bartolomé (2011) experienced similar literacy practices; Bartolomé learned English reading at school and Spanish reading at home. Her mother with limited schooling taught Bartolomé phonics and the alphabet. Once Bartolomé developed those skills, she could decode words in Spanish that held meaning for her. However, parents reading to children is nonessential, as alternative paths to print literacy exist. Smith and Murillo (2012) described how children learn Spanish by getting involved in financial literacies and family-owned businesses.

Families' English difficulties are not necessarily obstacles. Once children start school, Spanish-dominant parents use different resources to help their children with English homework. *Corazón* children brought books in English from primary school to be read at home (as per teachers' requests). Yet, mothers read the books in Spanish because the mothers and children could not read in English. One mother said, "*Cuando mis hijos eran chiquitos, y no sabían leer, entonces me basaba en los dibujos del cuento y les inventaba la historia*" [When my children were little, and they didn't know how to read, I invented the story, just focusing on the book's drawings]. This is rhizomic and imaginative because the mother circumvented language obstacles to help her children (Deleuze & Guattari, 1987). Furthermore, parents sent their children to the Tutorial Center or asked older children to assist younger ones. While language and literacy mingled in *Corazón* homes, we found some instances of collision between language, literacy, and religion, discussed in the next section.

Religion, Language, and Literacy

Prayers and Language

Children and parents merged Spanish-language and religion. One interviewee, a young adult Spanish speaker, said, "I was taught to pray in Spanish, so it is easy for me … Sometimes I asked myself if God understands all the languages, but since I know he does, I do not have to pray in English." Magnífico, an elderly *Corazón* activist, gave the same reasons: English was difficult for him and God understands all languages. One eight-year-old assumed most people learn Spanish prayers. He based his interpretation of language and religion on his experiences. Likewise, Itza (the mother of Nieves), mentioned her Bible is in Spanish, her first language (L1); she said she is literate in Spanish, especially in religious matters. As a Catholic layperson, Itza ministers to other L1 speakers.

English-proficient residents prayed in Spanish, also. Contributor Claudia, bilingual and biliterate, stated, "*Cuando me dirijo al Padre lo hago en español, quizás sea por la imagen de Padre religioso que tengo, pues las reglas de la iglesia yo siempre las he aprendido en el idioma español*" [I always address the priest in Spanish. Perhaps this is due to the image of priests I've had since I learned all church rules in Spanish]. Additionally, Brenda, a Baptist Church member, explained Mexican-heritage Sabio conducted most sermons in Spanish to accommodate members.

We found Spanish connected to adult Catholics' religious identities, which Father John confirmed. An Army veteran in his early thirties narrated his experience, "*Cuando hacíamos una misión en Irak, nos juntábamos y rezábamos el Padre Nuestro ... ellos lo decían en inglés y yo lo pronunciaba en español por dentro ... así es como me identifico más yo*" [When we served in Iraq, we got together and prayed Our Father ... They said it in English and I said it silently in Spanish ... This is the way I identify myself better]. This young man demonstrated he preferred Spanish for oral religious practices.

Families Teaching Their Children to Pray

Youth reported their parents or grandparents taught them to pray in Spanish as an oral tradition. One child, 11, said she prays in Spanish because "My grandma tells me to because she doesn't like English." Another child, 10, mentioned, "*Mi mamá me enseñó a decir los rezos en español y me los sé de memoria*" [My mother taught me how to pray in Spanish and I learned prayers by memorization]. Finally, a child, 12, said prayers in Spanish, "Well, my mom, she teaches, I think it's CCD [Confraternity of Christian Doctrine]. Since I was little, she teached [sic] us the prayers." This child mentioned his family only spoke Spanish.

Amiga said, "Parents are involved [with their children's religious education]. Parents must attend meetings and help with the involvement of their kids. They help them in memorizing prayers." Claudia, who taught CCD classes and lived in this colonia for over 20 years, corroborated Amiga's comments:

> The first or second immigrant generation of my students preferred to say their prayers in Spanish because that is what their parents taught them. My brothers and I learned the "Our Father" and the "Hail Mary" ... from my mom, and we learned them in Spanish.

Although the prayer booklets are in Spanish and English for CCD classes, Claudia said children in English-speaking houses feel more comfortable praying in English, but children in Spanish-speaking houses prefer Spanish prayers. Other studies among Mexican-immigrant families in Los Angeles and Chicago demonstrate religion relates to Spanish and Mexican cultural traditions (Baquedano-López & Ochs, 2002; Farr & Guerra, 1995). Our findings and others indicate oral language transmission can be a social practice, a literacy.

Fathers' Involvement

Fathers, in particular, played vital roles in children's Spanish and moral development. Kathy has witnessed *Corazón* men's Bible groups since she began teaching her *Corazón*-based course in 2006. The Catholic men, holding Bibles, sat in a small circle in a room adjoining the tutorial program. Amiga said the long-term Catholic men's group reads and discusses the Bible in Spanish.

Corazón fathers taught their children to read Spanish religious materials, also. Magnífico grew up in Mexico and learned to read and write there. "*Allá (México) es puro español*" [Everything there is only Spanish]. His first language (L1) foundation was deep. Magnífico served as a lector, or someone who reads scripture aloud during mass, for over 25 years. Magnífico motivated his son to read Spanish by having his son serve as a lector with him: "*Mi hijo leía conmigo. Lo llevé conmigo para hacer las lecturas durante la misa. Batallaba con algunas palabras en español*" [My son read scriptures with me. I took him to do the readings with me during mass. He struggled with some Spanish words], "*y me dijo, 'Sabes que, papi, yo voy a aprender el español para ser maestro de español.' Se perfeccionó*" [And so he told me, "You know what, dad? I'm going to learn Spanish and become a Spanish teacher." He perfected his Spanish]. A lector reads scripture aloud to the congregation during mass.

Magnífico's son taught Spanish, but is now a certified school counselor at a local middle school. Magnífico's account shows how religion can relate to L1 growth, because a Spanish teacher reads, writes, and teaches in Spanish, and knows subject-related literature, the arts, humanities, and social sciences. González (2011), a bilingual education professor, shared a similar story. González's father encouraged him to read the Bible in Spanish; the first reference book González read was a Bible Concordance.

School Policies Bleeding into Religion-Related Language and Literacy

Oral religious practices in *Corazón* homes were in Spanish mostly and many adults read the Bible in Spanish, which priests confirmed. Smith and Murillo (2012) corroborated our findings in two Texas colonias. When asked about the connection between religion and print literacy, a former priest said,

"Unfortunately, there were and are few written Spanish language resources." Despite obstacles, parishioners, like rhizomes, circumvented the paucity of Spanish materials. See Chapter 4 for the Church's informal lending library of religious books and movies.

Father John, current *Corazón* priest, said what we believe in our hearts and utter with our lips are connected through passion and sincerity. Thus, when praying, we use the language in which we feel most comfortable. However, because of local, state, and national educational policies, most colonia children experience less Spanish literacy instruction, so they feel more comfortable reading religious materials in English. Father John said catechism follows local schools' English-only curriculum:

Kathy:	How about reading and writing mixed with religion?
Father John:	Well, the catechists here are reading in English because that's what they [children] do in school. The catechesis is mostly classical and academic. But where they feel it, they probably feel it in Spanish more than they would in English because they haven't gotten to that stage yet [of English fluency].
Kathy:	What do you mean "feel it?"
Father John:	When you talk about something, when you're passionate about something. I don't think they [the children] can be passionate in English in their religion. Their parents are passionate about their religion; they're passionate about it in Spanish.

While the sentimentality of language (Kelman, 1971) might be rooted more deeply in Spanish for *Corazón* adults, Spanish has embedded itself into some children's hearts. Joy, who teaches many *Corazón* youth English, said her student wrote, "My heart beats in Spanish." Claudia, a certified bilingual education teacher, said children used Spanish if they learn something orally, yet they will use English to read: "But if they have to read to learn it, they will feel more comfortable in English because in school they teach you how to read in English." Claudia continued, "Some kids will say the 'Our Father' and Hail Mary' in Spanish, but the 10 Commandments, Sacraments, Act of Contrition, and Creed [Apostles' Creed] in English because of the wording." We interpreted English use based on these doctrines' complexity and length. When asked how she felt about colonia children not reading in Spanish, Claudia said, "It's not hard for them to read in Spanish." She taught all fourth grade students in her school (about a 10-minute drive from *Corazón*) a Spanish song; see Chapter 9.

Yet, Father John believed the Church could help children maintain their Spanish-language and Mexican identities. He said, "Having masses in Spanish can maintain their identity." Father John, like us, could not separate language from culture. He discussed the diasporic process for first, second, and even third generation immigrants, "English, it's a whole second generation thing that acts on a migrant notion." Referring to children's rejection of Spanish in diasporic Latino communities, he said, "*Hay un rechazo*" [A rejection transpires]. "The second generation migrant, the next generation down, is the English character. The next generation will come back to their roots." Father John's diasporic-process discussion relates to generational hybrid identities. His ideas about religion and language give us hope for heteroglossia, or competing utterances (Holquist, 1996).

Similarly, in a study of bilingual Mexican immigrant families in Chicago, Farr and Guerra (1995) found participants used Spanish language and literacy in the religious domain. Likewise, Ek (2009) discovered a Guatemalan Pentecostal woman's religious practices helped the woman to maintain high levels of Spanish literacy and she became a successful college student; her religious practices included advanced vocabulary, interpretation, and argumentation skills, which usually emergent bilinguals do not receive in their schools. Burrows-Goodwill (2009) focused on Spanish literacy church practices with high-poverty second graders. Six of the nine Mexican-heritage children received above-average standardized test scores in English, and four of six high achievers participated regularly in church-related Spanish literacy activities. Her study indicates that first language (L1) religious practices may help to reverse language shift.

Additionally, Rubinstein-Avila (2003) described Miguel, an eighth-grade ELL, who read the Bible in Spanish with this mother and his mother's adult friend. Miguel was a marginalized reader at school and disliked reading the Bible at home because he lacked L1 literacy. Miguel's caring mother attempted to teach him Spanish, but lacked pedagogical skills. Next, de la Piedra (2013) showed how a female Mexican-heritage restaurant owner organized a "rich and meaningful print literacy environment for others" by displaying Christian tracts, table messages, and posters (p. 345).

Some Church Leaders' Promotion of English, the Language of Power

Some Baptists and Catholics believed residents needed to master English. Amiga, who taught catechism classes, wanted colonia children to transition faster into English. This certified teacher, who migrated to the USA as a child, said:

> I try to talk to them in English. If they don't understand, I'll try to use mannerisms
> and slow down. If they really don't understand, then I try to talk to them in Spanish,
> but I try to force them to talk in English and listen to me in English.

Amiga said a fifth grade Tutorial Center attendee in May 2015 had experienced isolation from school peers the entire semester. A teacher placed the girl in front of a computer when the child arrived and told her to play discrete-skill video games in Spanish; the teacher spoke to the child only in Spanish the entire year. Amiga said she was not against bilingual education, but she believed children should also master English to succeed in school and in their careers:

> At home English it is not being practiced … It's a new country, it is new customs,
> and they have to survive here … It is not their native country anymore. And unless
> we want to break that cycle of, I wouldn't say "ignorance," but that lack of education
> in the new generations, they have to be pushed. We have a lot of very smart kids.
> But the lack of communication between the parents and them or the parents and the
> teachers, there is definitely a break that is not allowing them to push forward. They're
> content with what they have at the moment.

Others concurred that residents needed more English to escape poverty. A religious leader said he was against bilingual education. As a person outside of this academic field, this Mexican-heritage man may not have realized bilingual education focuses on learning both languages, hence the prefix, *bi-*. He did say, "I'm not against speaking Spanish. I am for people learning English. The more languages you speak the better off you are." He may have heard of others teaching bilingual education ineffectively. However, maintenance or developmental bilingual education proves effective (Thomas & Collier, 2003) and exemplifies additive bilingual education (Nieto & Bode, 2008). Furthermore, teaching first language (L1) learners to read in their L1 helps their second language (L2) reading achievement (Chuang, Joshi, & Dixon, 2012). García (2009) added recursive and dynamic bilingual models, which relate to multilingualism and translanguaging.

Although a church leader felt he needed to communicate with his congregation in their L1 to make his sermons comprehensible, he believed residents should transition fully to the L2 (English) and assimilate to U.S. culture. Poverty plays a crucial factor in language shift, as speakers tend to identify themselves with the most socio-economically prestigious language (Batibo, 2009). Some church leaders might perceive English as the language of power, as the English-only discourse connects to prestige, race, and language perceptions.

We observed a similar trend in language use in certain religious practices at *Corazón's* Catholic Church. Certain forces led Father Lucas to implement bilingual services a few years ago. Before that change, all services were in Spanish. Baquedano-López and Ochs (2002) reported a similar situation in a Catholic church in Los Angeles, where non-Mexican parishioners imposed an English-only policy in *doctrina* classes of immigrant Mexican children. *Corazón* residents disagreed with religious services in English. One claimed, "*La gente está inconforme…. porque algunos sólo hablan español … con esta nueva misa hay gente que viene de afuera, y habla puro inglés…*" [People are unpleased … because some only speak Spanish … Many people from outside come to this mass and they speak only English …]. A bilingual teenager said, "I do not like it, because he [the priest] says it in English … and I do not understand what he says … and then he says it in Spanish …" The latter quote demonstrated a Spanish preference for religious practices. The teen wanted María to interview him in English, which perplexed us because he did not comprehend the priest's English. Alternatively, choosing the interview in English may have related to the teen's desire to appear fluent in English.

Father Lucas's reasoning for implementing Spanish-English services related to introducing more English as a way to progress economically. Moreover, with the English services, he intended to bring more people from outside the colonia, who according to him, knew more English and therefore earned more money. Obviously, for this church leader and others, a way *Corazón* residents can escape poverty is by communicating more in English. Perhaps this former *Corazón* priest believed he could lead people from low-power spheres (e.g., home) to high-power spheres (e.g., business).

Adults' Motivation to Learn English

Organizations have offered free adult English classes at *Convivio*, *Afinidad*, and the Tutorial Center. Many mothers wanted to learn English to assist their children with English homework and be involved in school activities. One mother's motivation related to attending school meetings. She said, "*Yo quiero saber qué es lo que hablan los otros, así no me da pena o me siento sola cuando están hablando en inglés*" [I want to know what others are talking about, so I would not feel embarrassed or lonely when they are talking in English]. A *Convivio* employee, who taught *Corazón* adults English in 2010, said residents wanted to learn English "to get a job, to go into college, but mainly to help their children with their homework." He continued, "The majority of the students are females, with ages ranging between 25 and 40." Norton (2013) conceptualized different types of language investments related to psychological motivation. Although we appreciate Norton's move from simply discussing motivation, we refrain from using a capitalist metaphor for social justice scholarship.

Most fathers considered English important for job opportunities and integration into American society. A father commented, "*Si vives en México el idioma es el español, pero si vives aquí, en Estados Unidos, va a ser el inglés … Si tú sacas dinero mexicano acá, no tiene valor; tu lenguaje [español] tampoco tiene valor*" [If you live in Mexico the language is Spanish, but if you live here, in the USA, English will be the language … Neither the Mexican currency, nor your language has any value here]. Another father associated knowing English with better jobs: "*Por falta de inglés no agarro buenos trabajos*" [Due to my inadequate English, I cannot find a good job]. Thus, some co-researchers perceived English to be related, in part, to jobs and power.

Bridging Two Languages and Worlds

Brokering

So far, we have discussed findings related mostly to bracketing Spanish and English. This next section focuses on linguistic hybridity through brokering and translanguaging. Both practices relate to Third Space, transformation, and blended language and cultural identities (Gutiérrez, Baquedano-López, & Tejeda, 1999). Nieves, featured in the chapter's beginning, watched *La Rosa de Guadalupe* in Spanish with her mother; on other occasions she brokered when viewing U.S. English programs with her mother. Nieves translated words into Spanish for her mother and bridged linguistic and cultural divides.

Language brokering occurs when youth mediate language interaction and facilitate parents' access to dominant English environments in diverse settings. Although Anzaldúa (2002) related bridging to gender, race, and class, we include bridging languages. In our study and in Anzaldúa's analysis, people who bridge help people to another realm. Language brokering begins during the acculturation process, which indicates an individual's adjustment to a new environment. Brokering forms biculturalism. Youth may encounter American culture sooner and more intimately than their parents because of school. Children act as cultural brokers to older family members by using their knowledge of U.S. cultural traditions to accomplish social goals (Orellana,

2009). Thus, brokering as an everyday practice might indicate acculturation and bilingualism in *Corazón*.

Brokering functions as a social contribution, also. Children serve their families as societal institutions by providing services the government should provide, e.g., conversations between families and court personnel (Orellana, 2009). A bilingual teen in our study said, "I help my mother to translate, but sometimes also neighbors come to my house with letters from the Court … And they asked me what it says because they know I know English." Additionally, participating children helped their parents to translate school documents, medical forms, or bills, and documents from governmental offices.

Related to school, youth reported translating younger siblings' homework and interpreting for parents during school visits. Teacher Joy said, "Parents bring in older siblings to come talk with us." Parents emphasized the essential role their children played while translating during parent-teacher conferences and school events. Since elementary schools serving *Corazón* children had mostly bilingual personnel, first language (L1) and second language (L2) mediation between parents and teachers transpired mostly at the high-school level. One parent noticed high school teachers knew less Spanish:

> *Cuando iba a las escuelas primarias de mis hijos no había problema, pues las maestras hablan español, pero ahora es diferente pues muchos no saben. Son puro inglés, por eso voy a las "open house" con mis hijos, para que me expliquen lo que los maestros están diciendo* [I didn't have any problem when I went to my children's primary schools because the teachers knew Spanish. Now it's different because several teachers don't know (Spanish). They're all English, and that's why I go to Open House with my children, so they can explain what the teachers say].

Parents meet their children's teachers in the evening at school for "Open House."

Children translated for recent immigrant peers at school, also. A fifth grader explained, "*A veces vienen niños que no saben inglés … ellos me preguntaban que había dicho la maestra y yo les explico que dijo y se los digo en español*" [Sometimes children come to the classroom and they don't know English … They asked me what the teacher said, and I explain to them in Spanish]. Thus, *Corazón* children served as language brokers for each other.

However, brokering went beyond children explaining concepts to Spanish-dominant people. Sometimes adult neighbors translated and interpreted for parents who lacked academic Spanish skills and who were born in the USA. For example, the Garza children were third-generation immigrants and their mother was a second-generation immigrant. While taking Spanish as a foreign language requirement in high school, the Garza children needed to ask neighbors, L1 Spanish speakers, for homework assistance. Mrs. Garza reported, "I can speak Spanish, but I cannot help my children when they are taking Spanish courses. My children also struggle with Spanish, so I send them to my *comadre's* [Godmother's] house for help." Mrs. Garza used others' language brokering skills and valued neighbors' linguistic strengths to establish a bridge between home and school. Similarly, a Mexican-heritage teacher in Aquino-Sterling, Garrity, and Day (2015) learned Spanish by asking her grandmother questions about words when they watched Mexican television shows together.

Brokering related to rhizomic principles, also. *Corazón* residents created new paths, due to inadequate governmental translators and interpreters (U.S. Department of Labor, 2015c). Neighbors also made connections by helping others to achieve success, such as asking for items in far-away stores. Openness to modification and multiplicity were involved because diverse players brokered in diverse contexts. Furthermore, they translated and interpreted multiple texts (Deleuze & Guattari, 1987).

Translanguaging and Bilingual Youth Identities

Translanguaging appeared part of *Corazón* children's evolving identities and it helped them to communicate. We heard little translanguaging among elder *Corazón* adults. Besides contexts and identities, translanguaging may relate to skills because bilinguals rarely possess equal ability in both languages. Math and science teachers may translanguage for academic terms they may not know in the language of instruction; thus, translanguaging varies with the task. Herman, 11, discussed his translanguaging:

María:	"¿Qué piensas tú de las personas que mezclan los dos lenguajes? ¿Se te hace *curioso, o estás acostumbrado?*" [What do you think about mixing both languages? Do you find it unusual, or are you used to it?].
Herman:	"*No sé, pues yo hablo así*" [I don't know, because I speak like that].
María:	"¿Te das cuenta cuando lo haces?" [Do you realize when you are mixing both?].
Herman:	"*Sí, y lo hago, pues no sé cómo decir la palabra en español*" [Yes, and I do it when I don't know the word in Spanish] (Bussert-Webb & Díaz, 2013, pp. 17–18).

Herman switched between Spanish and English to fill linguistic gaps. He related translanguaging to his complex cultural and linguistic identities when he said, "I speak like that." Anzaldúa's (2007) statement, "I am my language" (p. 81) and Herman's utterance demonstrate evolving ontological language-world relationships, with inextricable murmurs and shouts in a Third Space. Language identities depend on time, space, and people. They represent yesterday, today, and tomorrow and connect to linguistic imagination (Norton, 2013). Cain, 14, enjoyed linguistic juxtapositioning, also:

María:	What do you think about the people who mix both languages? Do you think it is okay?
Cain:	Yes, we do it, too. It is cool.
María:	Why do you think it is cool? I would like to know how you feel when you are switching so easily from one language to the other.
Cain:	It feels weird. It's like, *Hola! ¿Qué onda?* What's up? (Bussert-Webb & Díaz, 2013, p. 18).

In "we do it, too," Cain associated cool-weird translanguaging with shared transnational youth identities. Herman's and Cain's translanguaging demonstrated centripetal and centrifugal tensions and worldviews. Centripetal discourses bracket or segment English and Spanish, while centrifugal discourses, such as translanguaging, resist normalization; this juxtaposition between and through languages resists closure (Bussert-Webb & Díaz, 2013). Sense-making for Herman, Cain, and other youth meant translanguaging. "After all, one's own language is never a single language: in it there are always survivals of the past and a potential for other-languagedness ..." (Holquist, 1996, p. 66). Languages collide and interact for heteroglossia. They resist monoglossia (García, 2009).

Thus, translanguaging represents a third language and a meaning-making practice (García, 2009). Translanguaging creates a discursive Third Space where actors negotiate identities and meanings. Translanguaging is also slant-wise. Practical communicatively and grassroots, translanguaging challenges bureaucracies and some societies (Campbell & Heyman, 2007). Last, translanguaging represents a transnational strength (Jiménez et al., 2009).

Summary

We posed this inquiry question: What are the language and literacy practices and access in *Corazón*? While school English-only language and discrete-skill literacy practices appeared subtractive, *Corazón* residents, including children, continued to rely on Spanish to communicate. However, *Corazón* youth have learned English and could bridge the two languages. Without a nearby public library, *Corazón* residents have little access to books. Regardless, they tapped into some books, magazines, and newspapers available through the Church, Tutorial Center, and local stores.

We heard Spanish most often in the colonia during our long-term study, but more residents, particularly youth, have learned English. Although *Corazón* youth moved fluidly between English and Spanish, most did not improve their Spanish literacy. Co-researchers perceived Spanish as useful to express passion, while English served as the language of power and mobility. As emerging Third Space theorists, we see no reason to bracket. Irene, a teacher candidate who worked with *Corazón* children, stated, "In the English language arts content, it is most important to value a student's first language as an asset." Similarly, Gutiérrez, Baquedano-López, and Turner (1997) argued for putting students' first language (L1) back into language arts courses. Those struggling for social change represent waves, creating crags to build language bridges (Anzaldúa, 2002).

Corazón children and adults played key broker roles, bridging two worlds. Bilingual brokering and translanguaging appeared connected to children's evolving cultural and language identities. Translanguaging and brokering are literacies, or socially-situated, ideological practices. Our findings demonstrate language and literacy are not neutral; instead, they knot-up in identities and contexts. Also, English-only education policies filtered into *Corazón* tutorials and religion. The English policy in No Child Left Behind exemplifies power and context and a "reaction to globalized economies, polyglot cultures, and mass-mediated childhoods" (Luke, 2005, p. xiii). In the next chapter, we will explore media related to digital literacy and language.

Questions to Ponder

1. Regarding language, how do colonias differ from other Latino communities?
2. How can poverty influence people's mother tongue maintenance?
3. How can poverty influence a community's shift into second language?
4. What kind of support do *Corazón* residents and residents in your community need to develop their literacy in two or more languages?
5. How could colonia parents be empowered to continue implementing mother tongue literacy practices with their children after the youth enter school?

· 7 ·

DIGITAL LITERACIES

Multimodal Pushback

Meet Joy

Joy and Kathy are finishing an interview when Joy adds, "I still have the rebellion in me. I still don't check out textbooks … and every year it [the administrative chastising] comes out: 'We're supposed to use the textbooks. Why aren't you?'" The planned 20-minute interview turns into two hours because Joy and Kathy are reconnecting, swapping stories and curricular ideas. Joy was a teacher candidate in Kathy's 2004 and 2005 methods classes. Joy, class members, and Kathy co-wrote a play, performed for the public and Joy was one of Kathy's first students who tutored *Corazón* Tutorial Center children; see Chapter 1. Since Joy received her educator's license in 2005, she has taught middle school English across the street from *Corazón*; about half of Joy's students have been from this colonia.

Joy, an accomplished artist, writer, and Facebook aficionado, takes her love of the arts, writing, and technology into the classroom. Joy's students use paints and brushes to describe stories and they create photo-story projects. Joy serves as the yearbook advisor, also. Because she uses no textbook, Joy searches constantly on Facebook and other Internet sites for authentic, generative multimodal activities and assignments; http://corbettharrison.com/ remains Joy's favorite. Modalities, or socioculturally-embedded resources related to power, can involve technology, sounds, visuals, print, and oral conversations.

Introduction

Chapter 7's inquiry question was: What are the digital language access and practices of children and Joy and Hermosa? In 2010 and 2011, 22 primary and six middle school youth completed literacy logs, documenting their reading, writing, and technology use in a 24-hour period. Youth participated in two sets of interviews, including cell phone and computer think alouds. We gathered youth data in *Corazón's* Tutorial Center (Bussert-Webb, 2014; Bussert-Webb & Díaz, 2012, 2013). We interviewed Hermosa and Joy at the Center, Hermosa's home, and restaurants in 2015. See the Book Introduction for more methodology.

Were we ever depressed before Joy's interview! From children and teacher candidate accounts at *Corazón's* Tutorial Center, we dreaded sharing dismal digital literacy findings. Before Joy, we could supply one counter-example in Frank, who engaged in authentic digital school experiences. However, other children, such as Nieves, 13, Pati, nine, had paltry digital experiences; Pati even wanted digital exam preparation to prepare for high-stakes tests (Bussert-Webb & Díaz, 2013). These exams bear enormous consequences for students and families if children cannot pass a grade level or graduate, and for educators who may lose their jobs, credibility, and school and program funding. Hermosa, a parent and grandparent, unlike Pati, was nervous about taking a computerized test, but Hermosa committed herself to passing the General Educational Development (GED) test electronically, the only format available, to demonstrate high school mastery.

Emerging themes related to co-researchers' digital access and practices in and out of school. Joy's classroom and the Tutorial Center served as transformative Third Spaces vis-a-vis education, literacy, and technology. We found digital translanguaging or hybrid meaning-making occupying this Third Space. Thus, in the second part of this chapter, we focus on children's digital English use (the children's L2) and Spanish (the children's L1). No *Corazón* resident informed us of speaking indigenous languages. We tell the stories of Joy, Frank, Nieves, Pati, and Hermosa and add a few more children's accounts.

Besides Third Space, this chapter relates to social justice because we discuss systemic inequities and Joy as a change agent. Digital literacies hail from New Literacy Studies (NLS) perspectives. Digital literacies are socially situated, multimodal practices related to skills, strategies, tools, and dispositions to make and share meaning (O'Brien & Scharber, 2008).

School-Related Access and Practices

Access

Joy fought for digital classroom tools; unfortunately no child co-researcher had Joy as a teacher. Frank, 13, experienced regular access to digital tools for authentic school purposes; 27 others did not. Before interviewing Joy, our findings about digital school experiences saddened us. Joy's district has improved student and teacher digital access in science, technology, engineering, and mathematics (STEM) fields recently. Joy said her school's homework quality and amount vary, but she has noticed science and history teachers have assigned many projects. The principal directed reading and math teachers to give daily test-prep homework. *Corazón* youth attend several elementary, middle, and high schools, so our findings from the children represent more than Joy's school.

Children co-researchers attended campuses offering free breakfast and lunch to all students under a U.S. Department of Agriculture (USDA) special provision. As per public domain data, 95% of the district enrollment is low-income; 99% are Latinos/as. About 87% of the district's teachers are Latinos/as, so the children's meager digital school experiences are not because Anglo teachers discriminated against Latinos/as. Joy, a culturally responsive Anglo teacher, creates a Third Space by providing authentic, rigorous multimodal experiences and assignments and incorporating her students' home experiences. While her Latina colleagues decorate their classroom doors with Anglo-related secular holiday themes, such as Van Allsburg's *Polar Express*, Joy adorns her door with Garza's *Charro Claus and the Tejas Kid*.

The children's poor school-related digital experiences are not because of mean, lazy educators either, as most teachers want the best for their students. In a survey of 20,200 U.S. teachers, 59% desired more student-centered technology (Scholastic & Bill and Melinda Gates Foundation, 2014). Instead, we believe the digital dearth relates to the No Child Left Behind Act (NCLB), international testing competition vis-à-vis the Organisation for Economic Co-operation and Development (OECD), and the opportunity gap for children in poorer school districts.

Joy's students create videos from their burning questions or passions. Most of her seventh graders focus on friends and family. Joy took a technology course in her district and received five Netbooks (small computers) so students could work in Netbook groups for this major inquiry project. Each August students will ask Joy, "Do we get to do that video project?" They will mention how much their older siblings enjoyed the project. Joy's approach reminds us of the digital storytelling of Darvin and Norton (2012) who discussed the Third Space possibility of students sharing their migration stories. This approach builds on children's evolving, intermingling transnational identities, languages, and literacies.

Joy's students also watch a YouTube research project about delayed gratification and Joy connects the video with marshmallows she had placed on students' desks previously. Joy said, "YouTube is not blocked for teachers, not now." When asked how she bypassed the district's previous website blocking, Joy, like a rhizome, stated, "I downloaded the video at home, saved it, and brought it to campus."

Joy fights for the computer lab and computers on wheels (COW), due to limited school resources. Only STEM and reading teachers appeared on the lab and COW schedules in fall 2014, so Joy asked, "Why am I not scheduled for the lab?" She won her case for technology inclusion as a non-STEM and non-reading teacher. Joy served on the STEM team and was on the computer schedules; her principal moved her to a non-STEM team in fall 2014 because the principal "needed someone stronger on the team." Joy's principal was correct because the best teachers should teach students who struggle the most (Haycock, 2001).

We perceive Joy as a change agent because she teaches in culturally responsive ways and she assists others in transforming practices for the benefit of nondominant children (Giroux, 2016). Furthermore, she recently presented to about 500 regional teachers about risk-taking in writing.

The STEM and reading preferences extend to U.S. educational policies and incentives (Fleischman, Hopstock, Pelczar, & Shelley, 2010). The USA ranked behind 31 countries in math, 22 countries in science, and 14 countries in reading on OECD's Programme for International Student Assessment (PISA) among 15-year-olds. International exams have resulted in a de facto global curriculum (Sparapani, Perez, Gould, Hillman, & Clark, 2014). Nationally, NCLB highlights reading and mathematics. Governmental literacy purposes tend to focus on economic development, not individuals' aesthetic and emotional fulfillment (Perry & Homan, 2014).

The Texas Education Agency appears to focus on reading over writing at the primary and middle school levels; youth take state-mandated reading tests in grades three to eight, but writing tests only in four and seven. Joy teaches English (e.g., writing and grammar), not reading; Joy's district made this demarcation. In February, the principal gave a directive, "No more writ-ing instruction. You will be testing on reading, not writing." Joy believes these policies are a disservice to children because they focus on testing and fail to prepare children for the rigors of college writing. However, Joy said the dis-trict's new superintendent is a writer and has supported writing instruction.

Practices

Frank, like Joy, was an anomaly. He had engaged in about 15 technology-re-lated projects by seventh grade. During his interview Frank effused about a current science project on respiratory systems, but he only mentioned copying and pasting interactions. No analysis. No creation. Moreover, Frank could play games in one class (technology), but only after work completion.

Other *Corazón* tutorial children used technology much less in school and for homework. When asked about school digital experiences, Nieves recalled one:

> I can't remember, but I do know we did a project. I had to look up information on the Internet in sixth grade. They made me use the computer for Christmas, like we had to make a list about what we wanted for Christmas. We sent it through the computer to the teacher. It was a technology class. I didn't do more than this in classes (Bussert-Webb & Díaz, 2012, pp. 5–6).

Nieves may have typed the wish list quickly because most lists lack recursive-ness. After students emailed their lists to the instructor during that period, no instructor or peer comments followed. Nieves' teachers did not emphasize dig-ital inquiry. Nieves could recall only calendars, vocabulary words, and finding stock prices for digital-related class activities. When asked how she felt about her digital use in school, Nieves became incensed:

> We haven't done projects. I get mad … In other schools they might do that and we don't … Like some other classes, they do PowerPoints about songs and in our class we don't do that, like write about a person you admire. I would stay after school and work on it, if it was a technology project, or go to the public library … At school I would like to use more technology. I would like to have a laptop and we would have to use it in every single period (Bussert-Webb & Díaz, 2012, p. 6).

Nieves desired rigorous, relevant, and authentic digital work and realized the inequities, not only in other schools, but in her own school. She longed to use a laptop in classes; however, no youth reported this use. Child co-researchers experienced little choice and ownership, which appears similar to the discrete-skills curriculum in many local public schools with mostly low socioeconomic status (SES) Latino/a pupils (Bussert-Webb, 2009). The curricular starvation contrasts with a hoity-toity banquet, enrichment, and critical thinking for high-SES white pupils (Oakes, 2005). These systemic opportunity gaps represent structural inequalities (Gorski, 2013). Technical- and ethos-related considerations can support and extend digital social practices; ethos relates to collaborative, participatory, distributed social practices, such as shared decision-making and problem-solving (Lankshear & Knobel, 2006). Thus, digital literacies encompass more than emailing lists, using computers for test-prep, clicking answers on a device, or keyboarding. The latter may become obsolete in 10 years anyway because of touch technology.

As a child on a roller-coaster ascent, Pati was bracing for the reading battery of the Texas Assessment of Academic Knowledge and Skills (TAKS), which morphed the State of Texas Assessments of Academic Readiness (STAAR). When we asked Pati, a third grader, what kind of digital experiences she preferred at school, she said she wanted worksheets on computers:

> Passages, like the stories for the TAKS test. I would like this so I could use the computer. I like the TAKS passages 'cause I don't have to get any homework. Like, when you take the TAKS, you don't get homework (Bussert-Webb & Díaz, 2013, p. 14).

Pati mentioned her homework focused on spelling, test passages, and writing sentences featuring memorized vocabulary. We interpreted her desire for digital test-prep as a reprieve from endless paperwork.

Teacher Joy provides students with authentic digital activities and homework. However, inadequate and inauthentic technology integration pervades schools serving mostly low-income (Henry, 2007) and Latino/a children for another reason: No Child Left Behind (NCLB). Texas leads the nation in accountability pressure (Nichols, Glass, & Berliner, 2012). Kathy lived this context as a local high-school teacher, succumbed to test-prep, and feels teachers' frustration (Bussert-Webb, 1999). Unfortunately, test-prep is shifting to digital formats. Joy shared an example of worksheets on computers. The teachers incorporated Fun Friday right before report cards, and Joy was thinking of quirky, but academic activities. A math teacher piped in, "I can bring in the COWs for CoolMath games!" This teacher internalized the NCLB testing focus—digitally.

As New Literacy Studies scholars, we believe authentic, generative practices and participatory new literacies are essential. Priming with video games may not improve test scores (Warschauer, 2011). Yet, Dennis, Bhagwatwar, and Minas (2013) advocated for this digital test priming, assuming power lied in the technology of literacy, that literacy was neutral (Street, 2003).

Before computers' proliferation, many low-income students completed countless worksheets and quizzes to pass a class. Although worksheets on computers and test-prep games substitute for low-level paperwork nowadays, systemic inequalities for this group remains. Switching tools, but keeping test-prep is akin to nicely packaged food that lacks nutrition. Instead of collaborating in creative ways with peers as most high-income students do, low-income students might sit at individual computers to replicate the factory model of learning (Kellinger, 2012).

The Texas Education Agency has offered end-of-course high school tests on paper and online since 2012, which does not mean students locate, synthesize, evaluate, and communicate online information for tests (Leu, O'Byrne, Zawilinski, McVerry, & Everett-Cacopardo, 2009). Digital tests unsettled Hermosa, who passed all General Educational Development (GED) tests on paper, except mathematics. However, she must retake all GED subjects on the computer, since the electronic GED is now the only local version. Hermosa said it might take months to prepare for the online test: "*Ya termino el GED esta semana. Ya me puse como meta graduarme este año ... Pero necesito práctica en la computadora ... El GED ya no es más a mano*" [I finish my GED this week. I have made a goal to graduate this year ... But I need practice on the computer. The GED is now electronic]. Hermosa is trying to catch up. As a *promotora* [health promoter], she has learned to research health topics on the Internet, prepare PowerPoints, and present them.

In some U.S. states, the attempt and pass rates for the new GED have significantly dropped. Many older adults prefer to take pencil and paper versions, but Pearson's electronic GED in several states relates to costs and digital workplace shifts (Turner & Kamenetz, 2015). Perry and Homan (2014) critiqued this capitalistic drive related to adult education. While we support technology, we also wish to question underlying purposes for it in different contexts.

Out-of-School Access and Practices

Access

Most children accessed out-of-school digital tools, but for consumption mostly. Besides Frank, Nieves, and Pati, we discuss Prima, 10, Cada, 12, and Lulu, 13.

About 69% of 28 respondents owned computers and 62% used the Internet at home in 2010; 83% had both in 2011. Children's literacy logs corroborated usage; 59% engaged in out-of-school Internet practices, mostly with laptops. Two families had no functioning computers and Internet in 2010, but had both in 2011. Around 89% of teens with family incomes of less than $30,000 used the Internet; 99% of upper-class teens do so (Madden, Lenhart, Duggan, Cortesi, & Gasser, 2013).

Those without digital tools behaved like rhizomes, circumventing limited access by tapping into colonia resources. Most teens in poverty go online with cell phones. The children used *Corazón's* Tutorial Center for technology more than the public libraries, which were over two miles from *Corazón*. Prima, 10, had no Internet at home, so she visited the Tutorial Center to use the Internet. She said her family did have Internet at one time, but could no longer afford the monthly payments. Lulu owned a home computer, but accessed the Center's, also. Lulu shared a laptop with siblings: *"La comparto con mi hermana y con mi hermano. No nos peleamos porque cada uno tiene una hora para usarla. Mi mamá pone la hora"* [I share it with my sister and brother. We don't argue, since everyone has a time to use it. My mother sets the schedule] (Bussert-Webb & Díaz, 2012, p. 6).

Children collaborated to gain digital access. Only Frank owned a cell phone, but others reported borrowing the devices of friends, neighbors, and families. We posit more youth would own cell phones now, as data were from 2010 and 2011. Prima asked Kathy to take Prima's photo and to send it to Prima's email so the youth could put it on her Facebook profile; her mother did not possess a digital camera or cell phone camera. Prima accessed someone with more power, Kathy. Thus, Prima engaged in rhizomic principles of connecting and regrowing (Deleuze & Guattari, 1987). Unified residents excelled in helping and teaching others. Slantwise resource sharing (Campbell & Heyman, 2007) takes place throughout the colonia, where we may see power cords between homes so neighbors can split electric bills (Bussert-Webb & Díaz, 2012).

Similar to sharing resources to save money, children circumvented costly video games. Pati explained: "They're for free where it's in the normal games. When you click here [going to the start button], it's going to say games" (Bussert-Webb & Díaz, 2012, p. 7). Cada clicked on www.friv.com, with over 50 free games, including Mario and SpongeBob. Kathy asked, "But don't they ask you to start paying, like $3.00?" However, Cada explained she had to google "free" before "game." When Kathy told some local educators *Corazón* children had out-of-school computer and Internet access, the educators expressed doubt. Perhaps many teachers believe low-income children lack digital access. Thus, they do not want to penalize them for incomplete digital homework. Other teacher respondents in high-need schools hesitated to assign digital work, perhaps due to this assumption (Warschauer & Matuchniak, 2010). Furthermore, poorer schools tend to possess less technology and related staff development. This plays out in educators' digital knowledge. For example, teachers from high-income districts scored significantly higher on online reading comprehension than teachers from low-income districts; this necessitates more digital staff development in the latter (Henry, 2007).

Practices

Yet, what did the youth do with this access? Most used computers and hand-held devices to call and text friends, play games, listen to music, and participate in social media sites. Prima thought aloud as she explored Kathy's cell phone: "First I check if it has Internet. I will go to Myspace or Facebook. I will put a picture" (Bussert-Webb & Díaz, 2012, p. 9).

All *Corazón* children played video games, mostly low-level, and about half played daily on hand-held devices, mostly DS, DSi, PS3, and PSP. Frank used an Xbox 360 and PS3 many hours daily. Elementary children played 16 games, including Bejeweled, Cake Mania, Poptropica, billiards, and chess. When asked which games were the hardest, Pati responded: "Plants vs. Zombies, 'cause some buckethead zombies and football player zombies. They're hard to kill. You have to use the repeater in order to kill them" (Bussert-Webb & Díaz, 2012, p. 8).

Middle schoolers played at least 27 games, including Crash, Crime-City, Hello Kitty, Littlest PetShop, Pirates Ahoy!, Sonic, SpongeBob, and ZombieFarm. Chess may prompt more imagination and complex thinking, yet this depends on one's gaming decisions and collaboration. Frank played the complex and collaborative World of Warcraft (Bussert-Webb & Díaz, 2012), which follows 36 language and learning principles, such as interaction and distributed knowledge among players (Gee, 2007).

Granted, continuous aesthetic stances in stories help people to become proficient and engaged. However, complex reading skills coincide with complex video games and other ICTs. Gaming involves diverse semiotic domains, such as images, graphs, sounds, symbols, and words, and gamers can discover internal design grammar important in critical thinking (Gee, 2007).

Although Frank played video games in free moments, no child mentioned gamer collaboration, Internet help, or cheats, to which other gamers contribute. Thus, none appeared to have experienced language socialization for sophisticated communicative practices or online affinity spaces). Complexity relates to imagination and interest-driven digital experiences (Warschauer & Matuchniak, 2010). Besides video games, Nieves visited websites for entertainment:

> I go to Google and I look for pictures of Wisin y Yandel [a Puerto Rican Reggaeton duo]. And look for other famous people. [She clicks on another site on Kathy's computer]. When I used to have Internet at home, I'd go and play dress up … I would go to *Converse* and create. Something will pop up and I will click on it and I would design a shoe (Bussert-Webb & Díaz, 2012, p. 9).

All three sites (Winsin y Yandel, animals in costumes, and tennis shoes) focused on entertainment and consumption. Nieves' older sister mentioned these sites, which demonstrated siblings can reproduce consumption.

In their logs, only a third and a fifth grader used computers for academic projects outside of school. Lulu said: "*La uso para hacer trabajo, también para Myspace, y a veces texteo con mi prima. Tengo email y mando email a mis friends, cousins, y a mi tía*" [I use it to do work, also for Myspace, and sometimes I chat with my cousin. I have email and I send email to my friends, cousins, and aunt] (Bussert-Webb & Díaz, 2012, p. 9). We assumed Lulu meant school when she mentioned work. None mentioned searching the Internet for current events. This may relate to the youths' ages because popular websites among U.S. Latinos/as during data gathering were *Televisa*, *Univisión*, and *Yahoo en Español*.

Our results are similar to Warschauer's and Matuchniak's (2010), who found young Latinos/as in poverty use digital literacies mostly for more friendship (versus interest-driven) purposes. Few *Corazón* youth mentioned searching the Internet for topics of their choice. Similarly, Latino/a youth spend more time using technology for recreation than white children do (Rideout, Foehr, & Roberts, 2010), which we believe relates to inadequate digital mentoring of Latinos/as.

The Tutorial Center as Potential Third Space

The Tutorial Center possessed transformative Third Space potential. It went from being a caterpillar to a butterfly. In 2010, only the coordinator's office offered Internet access, so the children engaged only in video games installed in the Center's computers. By 2011, the Center had embraced technology. Free Wi-Fi became available throughout the Center, many college tutors brought computers and engaged children in Internet-related tutoring and tailored lessons, and working computers has expanded, thanks to donations. Moreover, grade five and older children engaged in journal prompts connecting global and local issues. Staff read and discussed responses with youth. We overheard staff commenting on a youth's response to the 2011 Japanese nuclear disaster, with a focus on the child's complex reasoning and empathy. Perhaps staff believed younger children were incapable, but even toddlers are intentional writers. As with Nieves and her older sister, many young children learn to use digital devices by watching older siblings. Nevertheless, with electronic journals, older tutorial youth could express themselves digitally sans test-prep (Bussert-Webb & Díaz, 2012).

Connecting global and local issues, such as *Corazón* children's reactions to the Japanese nuclear disaster, demonstrates how Third Space breaks binaries. The global and local should inform each other. Thus, when children and staff connected both spaces through electronic journal prompts, they created a transformative Third Space vis-à-vis education, technology, and literacy, which moved from mere homework help to enrichment and connections. Furthermore, the Center existed as a safe space in which staff did not judge youth by lower order concerns, such as spelling and grammar (Bussert-Webb & Díaz, 2012).

To transform practices, sophisticated digital users of all ages mentor others. The teacher candidates in Kathy's May program do this, but it only lasts for three weeks; see Chapter 8. When Claudia volunteered at the Center, she helped children with technology-related homework and assisted Alma (former Center coordinator) in creating and responding to digital journal prompts. However, tutorial children mostly bring basic-skills paperwork to complete at the Center, thus reproducing inequalities, as little opportunity exists for higher-order digital exploration. Upper-class students rarely engage in test-prep (Gorski, 2013). Perhaps Claudia's digital influence was limited, as she was not staff. Recently, tutorial staff refrained from giving children the Internet password because some youth had accessed inappropriate sites. We understand the Church must protect children, but for life-changing Third Space, youth must become digital agents who construct meaning through on-going challenging digital practices. Otherwise, children complete assignments adults tell them to do (Bussert-Webb & Díaz, 2012).

Digital Language Practices

Language and Digital Practices in School

We continue with Frank, Nieves, Pati, Prima, Cada, and Lulu, and add Herman, 11, and Ana, 12. These findings build upon previous ones in this chapter, but now relate to Spanish and English. As with the dearth in school-related digital literacies, youth reported little first language (L1) instruction and materials; hence, they lacked confidence and skills in written Spanish, even in informal contexts. Herman said, "Like the word 'because,' is it *porque* or *por qué?*" After logging into Facebook during his think aloud, he said, "See who's connected. Email them. Write them in English because it's better for me to spell." Lulu noted, "*Para mí, es más fácil hacerlo en inglés porque las palabras están más cortas*" [For me texting is easier in English because the words are shorter] (Bussert-Webb & Díaz, 2013, p. 14).

Many language-minority parents try to teach their children L1 reading and writing, but this remains challenging when the children learn teachers value English literacy more. Language and identity are related, contextualized, evolving, and power-laden. Those rejecting their L1 identities might reject themselves (Anzaldúa, 2007). Moreover, for 21st century success, children need to plurilingual, collaborative, and critical thinkers and readers (Gee, 2007). Children's school language experiences may influence shift into English, the language of power, which relates to the structural inequality in poverty (Batibo, 2009).

L1.4Word

Yet digital use in homes (low-powered spheres) may help to move the first language (L1) forward. Thus, we coined the word L1.4Word, which signifies the role of digital literacy in language revitalization. Revitalization may occur in the diaspora, or when people live away from their homeland; the subaltern may perceive Standard English as hegemonic in high-powered spheres, such as schools, and may wish to speak their L1. Local schools serve predominately low-income Latinos/as who use their L1 in their neighborhoods, or low-powered spheres (Fishman, 2001). Some local educators may no longer value Spanish, the children's L1, because of No Child Left Behind's relationship to English-only policies (Bussert-Webb & Díaz, 2013).

Translanguaging and Bridging

Language should not signify dualisms. Instead, language constantly evolves, evident when youth reported digital hybrid language use. *Corazón* children bridged constantly by translanguaging and by being sensitive to interlocutors, or receivers, of their digital messages. Youth emailed or texted based on the preferred language of the receiver, or communication accommodation. Herman stated, "When I'm texting to friends that don't know Spanish, I text to them in English" (Bussert-Webb & Díaz, 2013, p. 21). This context-driven language practice is essential for oral and written continuity between interlocutors, also.

To bridge can mean to translanguage between and through languages, to open up a new language for making and sharing meaning. Digital bridging can be transformative. It escapes place and time boundaries. Bridging related to reading came from Frank's think aloud when he went to *"Solicitudes de amistad"* [friend requests]. Frank began reading aloud. *"La Sadgirl,"* he uttered, smiling widely at a photo of a petite, pouty girl about Frank's age, with waist-length black hair and chestnut eyes. In his hybridized world, the juxtaposition of *La Sadgirl* was a smart use of Spanish-English translanguaging, a digital collapsing of words and worlds, and visual and verbal irony; *La Sadgirl* looked more sulky than sad. Frank's response demonstrated he reacted aesthetically to a Latina youth's blended Spanish and English digital practices (Bussert-Webb & Díaz, 2013). If he were responding only to her beauty, he would not have read *La Sadgirl* aloud.

Translanguaging such as this represents centrifugal language forces (Holquist, 1996), which cause utterances to branch in rhizomic ways (Deleuze & Guattari, 1987). When bilinguals and polyglots make the word their own in digital socio-ideological contexts, they become agents in a hybrid Third Space. This space, resisting compartmentalization, can occur in public school English classrooms, such as Joy's through face-to-face interactions and even in writing. Written translanguaging online resembles face-to-face and print media translanguaging (Hinrichs, 2006).

Family Influences

Interlocutor digital contexts also applied to family, particularly mothers, who helped children to maintain some first language (L1) One youth said she texted her mother in Spanish because the latter did not know English. Youth reported texting their mothers in Spanish to convey information regarding their where-abouts and schedules. While Prima texted her mother in Spanish, she got confused because Prima only texted in English to her friends: "*Me confundo en español porque mis amigas casi no hablan español*" [I get confused in Spanish because my friends hardly speak Spanish] (Bussert-Webb & Díaz, p. 22).

Parents and older siblings can influence children's ever-changing cultural and linguistic identities. Additionally, parents' positive attitudes and their close relationships with their children help children to maintain their L1. Nieves' older sister recommended Spanish game websites, such as *Videojuegos*, and sites of Latino/a entertainers who sung in Spanish. The older sibling by four years bridged cultures and languages and motivated Nieves' Spanish reading (Bussert-Webb & Díaz, 2013).

Next, digital technologies appeared to help some children to maintain family ties in Mexico. No youth discussed writing paper cards or letters to families in Mexico, perhaps because digital correspondence affords quick responses. However, the youth did mention they emailed their cousins and aunts in Mexico. Nowadays Latino/a youth can instant message (IM) families, can see their loved ones' faces and hear them online inexpensively through Facetime, Skype, Snapchat, and Zoom, with less time lag than the paper postal system. Digital tools and practices are contextualized, ever changing, immediate, and interactive.

Phone calls and visits to Mexico, especially during summers and holidays, also spurred some *Corazón* youth to maintain Spanish (Bussert-Webb & Díaz, 2013). Diasporic participants in Cho's (2000) study expressed discomfort in speaking during travel to their homeland, which motivated them to improve their L1. R. T. Jiménez, Smith, and Teague (2009) argued these transnational literacies, spanning national borders, demonstrate users' complex and evolving linguistic and socio-cultural strengths; educators can tap into youth's digital transnational literacies, also.

Digital Secrets and Youth Culture

Siblings and peers influenced *Corazón* children's English language practices, which related to youth cultures and identities. *Corazón* youth preferred texting peers, perhaps to escape censure. Based on California and national data of Mexican-heritage speakers, Hurtado and Vega (2004) found youth spoke English more with peers than family. Prima texted Latino/a friends in English to hide particular information and words from her Spanish-dominant mother:

"I text friends in *inglés porque mi mamá no sabe leer el inglés*" [English because my mother doesn't know how to read in English] (Bussert-Webb & Díaz, 2013, p. 25). Perhaps Prima's mother may have objected to the content in Spanish.

An oral example of bypassing parental authority came from teacher Joy, who visited a student's *Corazón* home for homebound tutoring. Younger siblings kept exchanges curse words during Joy's visit. Although the mother was around, she did not understand English. However, the younger children did not completely circumvent authority, as Joy's student was bilingual and the children's elder. Joy said her student "was taking the place of a mom and kept reprimanding them." Yet adolescents, linguistic leaders, bring new words into popular language use (Thelwall, 2008).

Digital Use in High-Powered and Low-Powered Spheres

Some *Corazón* youth mentioned the location from where they typed digital messages was important. Herman preferred texting in Spanish at home: "*Es que hago 'texting' desde mi casa, y como en casa hablo más español, entonces me siento más cómodo con el español*" [This is because I text from home. At home I speak more Spanish, so I feel more comfortable in this language] (Bussert-Webb & Díaz, 2013, p. 25).

Similarly, other youth demarcated language use in high-powered spheres (e.g., English for school) and in low-powered spheres (Spanish and translanguaging to communicate with friends) (Fishman, 2001). Frank used English for school and Spanish for Facebook and other social purposes. Additionally, the youth wrote peers in Spanish when the topics related to personal matters and in English for school-related concerns.

Digital Features to Improve L1 Reading and Writing

Some *Corazón* children used graphics to assist them in first language (L1) reading comprehension. During her think aloud, Nieves showed Kathy a Spanish-language website; she used pictures to comprehend the text. Nieves was learning L1 reading from the Internet. Similarly, Cada searched for her previous home in Nuevo León, Mexico during her think aloud: "Ca-der-ey-ta, that's where I lived. I can't spell it." (She attempted another spelling and the Internet performed an autocorrect.) "Ah, here it is!" (Bussert-Webb & Díaz, 2013, p. 26). Thus, through auto-correct features and visual cues, the Internet can teach people their L1. Why? We learn to read and write by reading and writing; thus, digital tools for authentic contexts can help. Yet people must know how to use these resources for language transformation.

Some, like Frank, switched cell phone, game, and social media settings to Spanish: "XBOX 360, English. PS3 Spanish. Call of Duty Black Ops in Spanish and English. I play it in English and I put it for my brother in Spanish." Frank showed Kathy where he changed Facebook to Spanish and then *notificaciones* [notifications] appeared. Similarly, Ana changed Kathy's cell phone settings to Spanish during her think aloud: *"Toco aquí. Busco mis contactos. Le pongo así. Y luego empiezo a escribir en español"* [I touch here. I look for my contacts. I put it like this. And then I begin to write in Spanish] (Bussert-Webb & Díaz, 2013, p. 27). Others may not know this option or how to create diacritic marks, such as: ñ; ¿, and ¡. They may receive constant auto-correction. Texting in Spanish can be time-consuming and frustrating with English-only settings. Digital tools do not hide class, ethnic, gender, and racial differences because many Americans suspect the bilingualism of low-income diverse populations (R. T. Jiménez, 2003). Technology is not neutral. Freire (2000) believed oppressors used technology to exert power over others. Yet as we found with Frank and Ana, power can be good.

Switching social media and cell phone settings to one's L1 can represent resistance to online English language hegemony (Bussert-Webb & Díaz, 2013). Although languages abound electronically, perhaps scant Internet use in Punjabi related to users typing Punjabi in Roman characters (Paolillo, 1996). Why? Initial Internet planners demonstrated a monolingual U.S. perspective. The American Standard Code for Information Interchange (ASCII) from the sixties employed the Roman alphabet and English language sounds. However, designers created Unicode 4.1.0 with 50 scripts in 2004 to invite more languages; before then, non-Roman-based language users employed numbers to signify tone (Danet & Herring, 2007). Less than one percent of the world experienced Internet access in 1995; nowadays Asia has 48% of Internet users and the Americas have only 22%; China is the highest user (Internet Live Stats, 2015).

Summary

We raised this inquiry question: What are the digital language access and practices of Joy, Hermosa, and *Corazón* children? Joy acted as a rhizome to offer multimodal resources and she and her students engaged in a multimodal, transformative Third Space. Joy rhizomed around No Child Left Behind, her school's math, science, and reading preferences, and unequal technology resources. Next, Hermosa's desire to get formally educated in the USA required computer competence. Although the electronic General Educational Development (GED) was an obstacle for Hermosa, she realized 21st century digital purposes for the GED, her job, and personal fulfillment.

While limited school resources resulted in limited digital language access for *Corazón* children in school, they accessed digital tools for social purposes. Children without home access to digital tools behaved like rhizomes and found access. However, they possessed little higher-order digital experience. We recognize dichotomies between home and school domains are unproductive, as both contexts can overlap. While most *Corazón* youth possessed great digital out-of-school access, they engaged in few authentic, creation-based generative digital practices, perhaps because teachers assumed the youth lacked access. Next, the Tutorial Center promised transformative Third Space to push the children's first language (L1) forward in authentic, generative ways. For L1.4Word, however, youth must continue to use the WiFi at the Center and engage in authentic digital literacies with each other and adults regularly in the mother tongue and target language.

Finally, we discussed *Corazón* children's digital English preferences, which related to their limited L1 literacy instruction in schools. We theorized high- and low-power spheres in the youths' language choices and interlocutor contexts, such as Spanish-dominant mothers and English-dominant friends. We found digital tools and contexts can help L1 speakers revalue and reappropriate their L1 as pushback against hegemonic language policies. Indeed, language revitalization implies advancing a language, not just maintaining it (Hornberger, 2006). Groups that have shifted to the dominant language tend to recover some "ancestral language practices as they develop a bilingualism that continuously reaches back in order to move forward" (García & Kleifgen, 2010, pp. 42–43). This L1.4Word reminds us of multi-generational Monarch butterflies heading to Michoacán from Canada and the Midwest, and vice-versa. The fourth generation migrant Monarch never forgets its destiny. The Monarch's tongue is its compass, as this butterfly must taste nectar plants to guide it. Alas, multiple tongues bring diversity.

Furthermore, digital hybridity and bridging may help heritage languages to move their language 4Word to resist monoglossia, a single utterance. These digital translanguaging and bridging practices represent literacies. When we frame technology-related bilingual practices as literacies, we increase their political power (Leu et al., 2009).

Questions to Ponder

1. Programme for International Student Assessment (PISA):
   A. Click on the Organisation for Economic Co-operation and Development (OECD) PISA assessment link: http://www.oecd.org/pisa/pisaproducts/48852548.pdf Shanghai, a wealthy industrial Chinese city, tops the list, yet only countries appear otherwise. Discuss why OECD might allow Shanghai's scores.
   B. Using the same link, find any country's test results in reading, math, and science. Discuss if a country should participate in PISA, and if results indicate a country's future.
   C. Google information about Norway's socio-economic factors (food insecurity, poverty, etc.). How would a country's socio-economic factors relate to PISA test scores?
2. Discuss whether technology in your geographic area and in other places represents the great equalizer for people of all ages.
3. Based on this chapter, why is using digital tools for creation, interest-based research, and collaboration important in school and in out-of-school settings?
4. How did participating children use their first language for in- and out-of-school digital practices? Explain what you have observed about culturally diverse children in poverty, non-standard dialect speakers, and bilinguals regarding digital practices.

SECTION III

EDUCATION

$$\cdot\ 8\ \cdot$$

TUTORING AND GARDENING

Towards Liberatory Literacy Space

Meet Rosa

May 14, 2015. 9:02 p.m. Rosa and Kathy are standing in the parking lot next to *Corazón's* Tutorial Center. Rosa, who helped to remove Kathy's teaching carts before the Center's security alarm sounds, tells Kathy what the community service learning (CSL) program means to Rosa. Wreaths of years teaching at this site encircle Kathy's mind. "I mean, I used to live here. One of the moms [who helped to prepare snacks] was my Holy Communion teacher," Rosa said. "I recognized her face the moment I walked in and she asked me, 'Are you [Juana's] daughter?'" Rosa, who left *Corazón* at age 18, is majoring in English and minoring in Mexican-American Studies. Soon she will teach high school English. Rosa mentions disliking the gardening part of our CSL, but adds, "I did it for my tutees."

Three weeks pass. Rosa is discussing the transformative nature of the CSL for her and Anhelo, nine. Kathy realizes Rosa understands social justice and the importance of a wider literacy definition. Yet during the focus group, Rosa mentions CSL involves more than a course and CSL can make a difference in the life of a child: "To hear her [the mother's] feedback, it's something that's short and simple and something that we might think, 'It's a grade for my class.' It's very impactful for people like that. She was just incredibly thankful."

Introduction

Kathy remembers her irritation when the discussion parts of our course were to begin at 6:15 p.m., but Rosa would arrive at that time from another room without her journal even started. Rosa would take every opportunity to talk with parent volunteers, tutorial staff, and children. Later, Kathy realized Rosa was reconnecting with *Corazón*, Rosa's former community. This chapter unpacks an ongoing community service learning (CSL) project with teacher candidates (TCs), such as Rosa, and children they tutored. We describe the history (see Chapter 4), purpose, organization, and reciprocal CSL impact. This pedagogy involves TCs' service in non-school sites and their connections to course concepts through oral and written reflections, essential in deep, liberatory learning (Maynes et al., 2013). Both those served and those serving benefit in CSL. This reciprocal CSL pedagogy differs from a deficit model. Just because people want to work *in* community does not mean they possess a deficit model. Moraga and Anzaldúa (1983) stated, "And those of us who have more of anything: brain, physical strength, political power, spiritual energies are learning to share them with those who don't" (iv).

Chapter 8's inquiry question was: "How does CSL help TCs and children?" Besides methodology in our Book Introduction, children used disciplinary logs to document their subject-area engagement in a 24-hour period. Although we summarize our longitudinal study, we base most of this chapter on unpublished May 2015 data. Yearly CSL co-researchers include: 13–17 TCs (mostly Latino/a and native-Spanish speakers), two staff, 10–12 parents, and 25–33 children (all Latino/a and native Spanish-speakers). Many youth return yearly. One parent might enroll four children at once.

Themes related to CSL include impact on TCs and children regarding literacy and *conscientização* [critical consciousness]. Conscientization occurs when people realize and take action against systemic inequalities, such as policies negatively affecting culturally diverse families in poverty. Literacy signifies socially embedded, ideological practices (Gee, 2012). Thus, gardening is a literacy. In addition, science and language arts, discussed in this chapter, possess distinct literacies; disciplinary literacy involves (de)constructing academic texts (Moje, 2007). Language and literacy are not neutral; they relate to power, identities, and contexts. Some may argue that studies focusing on beliefs are inessential. However, beliefs, biases, and prejudices regarding children impact how and what we teach (Gorski, 2013).

History, Purpose, and Organization

History and Purpose

In 2004, Kathy began requiring her education students to complete community service learning (CSL) in local agencies, including the Center. Kathy's literacy methods course represents one of the few offered in a neighborhood setting with the instructor constantly present. A course goal is advocacy for nondominant learners. In 2005, Kathy and Alma began planning this May 2006 CSL project. Kathy has taught the course and has planned and supervised tutoring and gardening with Alma until 2013. Kathy began working with Rita, Alma's replacement, in May 2015.

This neighborhood-based social justice model focuses on teacher candidate (TC) social justice preparation in neighborhoods. CSL—intellectual, pedagogical, and political—counters hegemonic or controlling, schooling practices related to national and state mandates. The latter presents major consequences for families and schools. We combined gardening with tutoring so TCs could make subject-area connections. The CSL purposes for children involved enriching disciplinary experiences and bridging academics and life, as children worked alongside successful college students. We aimed to provide a unifying project and ecological service. Self-righteousness and racism may relate to some CSL, but this was not our intent.

Believing *Corazón* possessed many attributes and that children were teachers, Kathy and Alma designed reciprocal CSL. About 95% of TCs over the years have been of Mexican descent, but some were uncomfortable speaking Spanish. The children helped TCs to embrace Spanish. Children also taught TCs about their unified community, which helped TCs to plan lessons honoring children's organic experiences. This equal footing differs from a banking concept, which focuses on knowledge as a "gift bestowed by those who consider themselves knowledgeable upon those whom they consider to know nothing" (Freire, 2000, p. 72).

Organization

English majors must take this course, but other teacher candidates (TCs) may enroll. Each session transpires at the Tutorial Center, Monday through Thursday. Kathy, tutorial staff, and parents supervise and assist daily. Additionally, university staff give a presentation in Spanish to *Corazón* children and adults about college opportunities. Each teacher candidate tutors one to three children and creates gardening and community-strengths lessons. Gardening lessons relate to: calculating hole sizes, area, and perimeter for math TCs; ecology, flora, and fauna for science TCs; and reading and writing for English TCs. Community-related math lessons may involve determining prices for family barbeques, science lessons on car engine combustion, and English lessons on family stories or Mexican song lyrics.

After tutoring and lesson sessions, we plant native flora. During snack time, each TC and child complete journals about their time together. From yearly institutional $500 grants, we have bought garden equipment, plants, and other supplies. Companies have donated to the project and the College of Education Dean's Office has paid for research assistants.

Impact on Tutors

Conscientization

Rejecting Stereotypes

Stereotypes can marginalize neighborhoods. Less than 2% of participating teacher candidates (TCs) have grown up or lived in *Corazón*. Although most TCs were Latinos/as and grew up close to *Corazón*, they did not necessarily understand *Corazón's* context or want to help initially. In fact, most had not entered *Corazón* before beginning this course. Many expressed fear because of rumors they heard, e.g., "High in crime, bad reputation, dangerous and ghetto, and portrayed to be one of those places to avoid at all costs." TCs soon realized these rumors ostracized *Corazón*. This marginalization occurs in layers. Many local and regional officials ignore *Corazón*. However, state and national officials ostracize the border region, falsely claiming its danger (Solomon, 2015).

These misperceptions relate to media stereotypes, which prevent outsiders from seeing a community's strengths and obstacles. After all, liberatory learning cannot occur without contact (Maynes et al., 2013). Some TCs expressed shock at *Corazón's* conditions, admitting they felt oblivious to poverty before the project. Others realized systemic inequities in housing and infrastructure, such as street drainage. A TC wrote about rain flooding her tutee's tiny home: "It made me wonder how a neighborhood in the United States could be so poor if supposedly the United States is so rich. People should not have to live in these kinds of situations." Seeing a tutee's home upset another TC:

> I got to … pick up Garfield. He lives just down the block from the tutoring center. When we pulled up into his driveway, I could not believe my eyes … His house was literally a small shack attached to an old, beat-up mobile home. In my head I was thinking, "My God, this can't be where he actually lives." (Bussert-Webb, 2008, p. 7)

Retrieving or returning tutees stopped after 2006, but TCs still saw the conditions by driving to and from the Center. The TCs critiqued disparities between the colonia, and nearby gated communities; TCs also discussed local school gentrification. English major Irene believed that she and others in power should work for change:

> It [education] differs depending on their neighborhood and that really defeats the purpose of education as the great equalizer … Like Tony Morrison said, it's not a "grab bag" … Once you get a little bit of power, it's your job to go help someone and empower them.

Some stereotype Latinos/as and assume homogeneity; the former might believe TCs identified easily with *Corazón* contexts. For example, one in three non-Latinos/as believe all Latinos/as in the USA are undocumented, but only 18% are (Lilley, 2012). Additionally, many Latinos/as do not believe they share the same culture. The school district, where most TCs and children had attended, consists of about 87% Latino/a educators. However, cultural differences between *Corazón* youth, local educators, and TCs existed. Many TCs said local educators discriminated against *Corazón* children, expecting less after discovering the children's neighborhood. Although most TCs were of Mexican heritage, the majority were U.S.-born children of white-collar professionals. Some, like Gloria, mentioned toward the chapter's beginning, spoke no Spanish. Constantly evolving, culture includes neighborhood status, social class, language, and beliefs. Moreover, diverse perspectives expand dialogue (Anzaldúa, 2002).

Connecting and Revaluing

Despite differences, teacher candidates (TCs) made connections with the children to bridge inequalities. Rita, Tutorial Center coordinator, wrote:

> The May program gives our children the opportunity to interact with college students that share their experiences and knowledge. This year one of the [college] students [Rosa] had lived here when she was young and her tutees were very impressed to know that. This instills in them the idea that they too are able to pursue a career.

In this Third Space, child and adult learn, grow, and share power. Although TCs were college juniors and seniors, they did not enjoy perfect childhoods. In fact, their desire to bridge for their tutees helped them to heal. Ella had crossed the bridge physically and metaphorically as a child; she quit looking back to Mexico because she had faced much linguistic discrimination. Showstack (2012) found Spanish-English bilingual college students in central Texas expressed dualistic language perceptions, based partly on hegemonic discourse about U.S. Spanish speakers. Yet Ella's tutee continued crisscrossing the bridge, helping Ella to remember Ella's roots and to re-value transnational practices and languages. When people bridge they connect and take risks by revealing their inner selves (Anzaldúa, 2002). On the metaphorical bridge, English major Mabel and Spider Woman confided in each other: "My tutee does not know her father. I told her I did not know my father, neither, and she felt better. I know this because she smiled at me."

Since they participated at the Center for many hours daily, TCs realized abounding child and family strengths and the TCs became attached to the children. Thus, TCs may have associated the colonia's disenfranchisement with their young friends. The children were no longer the other, but the loved. English major Rachel wrote:

> Some people find it easier to blame the people in poverty for their problems and fail to see the issues with our own society that brings socioeconomically disadvantaged people down. … I know my tutee is a valuable person who will bring joy in my life.

The TCs may not have made such heart-felt, socially just connections by listening to lectures; instead, they learned from the children. Why? Dialogue is a loving process, not a method (Freire, 2000). For transformative education, teachers and students must form these relationships. For example, Mona stated, "Ultimately, what I have come to learn from [the May project] is love … Wolverine is my tutee; we have built a close bond that is intellectual as well as spiritual." The city and county mistreatment of *Corazón* angered Mona and propelled her to activism. Mona saw marginalization's effect on 10-year-old tutee, who had flunked fourth grade and who experienced low teacher expectations. Additionally, Mona drew a connection to the Civil Rights era and explained educators' roles involved helping students to understand social injustices. To connect education and poverty, we must realize the inequities and biases youth in poverty face (Gorski, 2013).

Besides making connections, TCs bridged in another sense. They carried the burden of racism and xenophobia on their backs (Moraga & Anzaldúa,

1983). Oral and written reflections helped TCs with internal conscientization, so they, in turn, could adopt external liberatory beliefs and pedagogies. Indeed, a teacher cannot be a change agent without reflecting on her/his positioning in the world (Giroux, 2016). By revaluing her experience as a migrant worker, Irene remembered how she worked around inequities: "Structural inequalities did not seem like a road block so much as an obstacle to go around." Rosa (portrayed in the chapter's beginning) crossed the Rio Grande from Mexico as a young child, but was embarrassed to tell others:

> I was especially ashamed to say that I was born in Matamoros and not [city]. I hid something so insignificant, yet for me, it was quite relevant. I felt if I stood proud to my nationality, I would be labeled as the typical "wetback" and that was definitely something I was not looking forward to. I also thought there was no way "true Mexicans" had any talent or reading/writing/skills; I was wrong.

Perhaps hearing parents, children, staff, and Kathy speak Spanish helped some TCs to re-value their mother tongue, to loosen English's hegemonic hold. Many TCs said teachers made them ashamed to speak Spanish and to translanguage (García, 2009). This shame demonstrates the coloniality of power, designed to lower the subaltern (Quijano, 2000). English major Lorena experienced detention as punishment in first grade for speaking Spanish. She problematized English-only policies: "I believe the schools don't offer adequate support. It is important for students to become fluent in their native language before going full blast into Spanish."

Theorizing

The teacher candidates (TCs) built theory by connecting their childhood experiences with community service learning (CSL), class discussions, and readings. Kathy had explained the children's rhizomic behavior of vis-à-vis digital literacies; however, Ella changed Kathy's description of a behavior into an intentional, resistant move. Hence, we coin the word to rhizome to signify an action of conscious resistance. Ella wanted to teach future students how to rhizome around systemic inequalities:

"It is the job of the wealthy to empower the poor. As teachers we must teach our students the importance of being rhizomes ... They need to know how to branch out whenever they are faced with an obstacle." Immediately, another TC said she (herself) needed to rhizome around inadequate classroom resources as a teacher. She was building on Ella's theory. This

CSL and authentic experience afforded TCs with opportunities to create educational theories. Ella built theory when she took Deleuze's and Guattari's (1987) notion and made rhizoming purposeful resistance. Kathy had not considered using a social justice framework to teach children how to rhizome. Ella and others demonstrated they were becoming theoretical change agents, vowing to show students how to rhizome around inequities. Educators who possess equity literacy believe in resiliency instead of deficits (Gorski, 2013).

Seeing Colonia Strengths

Yet, what strengths did teacher candidates (TCs) see in *Corazón* families? Some may use the musty discourse of no parent and child effort when explaining why many subaltern children do not graduate college and may erroneously believe in a culture of poverty (Gorski, 2013). However, TCs noticed parent volunteers, parent attendees at the college information sessions, and parent education passions. TCs, such as Rachel, realized the tutees tried in school: "They are thirsty for knowledge and care about their education. Every day they walk to the center to get that extra help when they could be playing or watching TV at home." The TCs were astounded by each child's "eagerness to impress the tutors. They tried really hard to do their best on the garden to make us happy."

The children would stand by the windows, anticipating their tutors' arrivals. English major Gloria wrote about Raspa, a fifth grader, whose teacher cast her aside: "She's so loveable and she wants to learn, but her problem is she doesn't know English." Low teacher expectations toward this Mexican-heritage student angered Gloria, who expected much, essential in student achievement and every student's right. Low expectations represent discrimination.

Future Plans

Teacher candidates (TCs) planned to continue making a difference as socially-just educators, essential in liberatory learning. Many intended to engage future students in community service learning (CSL) vis-à-vis tutoring, gardening, and performing plays at homeless shelters. Irene planned to use her car for a *Corazón* library. Others wanted future students and families to write books on family strengths and experiences.

The TCs believed this CSL project helped to shape them as transformative educators, who see their profession as much more than preparing students for high-stakes exams. Although few experienced CSL, some had read to children in pediatric clinics for CSL experiences. However, educators must experience an empowering curriculum as learners to teach in a life-changing way. English major Jesusa wrote, "This motivated me to invest in my community and take part in other service learning projects" (Bussert-Webb, 2008, p. 8). Through solidarity with children, TCs recognized the need to fight for change, which relates to praxis (Freire, 2000).

Liberatory Literacy

Broadening Definitions, Inviting Diversity

So, what does a justice orientation mean in the context of literacy? It becomes easier to realize literacy involves more than reading and writing when connecting tutoring and lesson plans to an outdoor project in a marginalized community. Here we focus on teacher candidate (TC) shifts because beliefs are essential in equity literacy (Gorski, 2013). At the course's commencement, Kathy asked TC pairs to read the first few pages of an article she had published, with key words, such as literacy, highlighted, because she wanted them to see how she was defining terms. Ella, English major, and Marisa, science major, reported to the class that Kathy had defined literacy as reading and writing, which was incorrect. Kathy realized Ella and Marisa could not fathom literacy as socially situated and ideological without more community service learning (CSL). A week of experiences, readings, and class discussions passed. Finally, after reading Cline and Necochea (2003), Ella opened her viewpoint:

> It's funny. I had always attributed my love for reading to my kindergarten teacher … Now I'm thinking that passion could have been planted way before with all the stories my family and me [sic] shared. All in all, the art of storytelling has been very present in my life, through the spoken language and through the pages of wonderful books.

Ella realized informal teachers (her family) and non-print texts (stories), helped her to become literate. These open conceptualizations can invite people with limited formal education into print literacy. Confining literacy to printed texts hails from a white, middle class perspective, as some perceive literacy as orality (White-Kaulaity, 2007). If children who struggle in a discipline can experience family stories and multimodal curricula, they may be inspired in that subject. Conversely, narrow definitions of literacy can prevent diverse people from entering a gallery. For example, Irene wrote about her lesson with the tutees:

> Usually, reading and writing is difficult for them to do on decontextualized work-sheets, like the ones they get for homework. However, they felt like they were playing a game, and didn't notice they were utilizing their English language arts skills.

Rejecting a wider definition of literacy may relate to perennialism (emphasizing the classics from a white, Western perspective), essentialism (focusing on basic and discrete skills), and a misunderstanding of diverse, 21st century learners. Essentialists and perennialists believe children come to school with little relevant knowledge. These Eurocentric, child-as-empty-vessel philosophies may have been why teachers said two colonia boys lacked experiences and referred the children to special education (Hernández, 2003). Inspired by Rubenstein-Ávila's (2003–2004) account of a marginalized reader, Diana, a future elementary teacher, wrote: "Every student has their unique needs and ways of learning. It is important as an educator to view literacy broadly."

Undoubtedly, our literacy stances influence our methods and how we define struggling readers (Rubenstein-Ávila, 2003–2004). If we substitute *marginalized* for *struggling*, however, we shift the onus from an individual child to social structures, such as schools (Moje, Young, Readence, & Moore, 2000). Rosa entered the CSL course believing teaching English meant correcting a child's spoken and written English. Yet Rosa's tutees helped her to realize teaching English involved making and sharing meaning and motivating youth to love reading and writing.

The CSL experience helped TCs to break free of mechanistic curricula, which may represent hegemony and colonialism for diverse learners. Mabel experienced difficulty interesting Spider Woman in grammar: "When I would ask her questions, all she would say is, 'I don't know' and smile. I thought, 'Oh God, this is going to be tough.'" Thus, Mabel used spiders as a hook: "We touched soil, picked up rocks, felt leaves, etc., and that is one way I applied verbs and adjectives." The next day Mabel and Spider Woman made a "Nasty Critter" dessert, a lesson reinforcement. They discussed crumbling crackers and squishing gummy worms. "At that moment," Mabel wrote, "I realized a student learns best if they see, touch, taste, smell, and hear things (the use of realia)." Similarly, Lorena realized the effectiveness of a hands-on approach on synthesis: "When you're outside you can tell them, 'Oh, remember what I was telling you in class? … What is this? The stem, right?'" These realizations demonstrate TCs' *conscientização* and their broader literacy notions. TCs honored children's existential experiences and nudged the youth toward critical consciousness.

Impact on the Children

Conscientization

A Spark

Some children made conscientization inroads by realizing that outsider negative perceptions' of *Corazón* were unfounded and that their families and neighbors possessed many attributes. Additionally, English major Gloria provided greater views of Raspa's ability. Gloria helped Raspa to realize Raspa was smart and that she should aspire to attend college. Initially, Raspa thought her only option was to join the U.S. Army. Gloria, a military spouse, said military service should not be one's highest accomplishment. Raspa adored Gloria, so we hope Gloria's words were kindle.

A Paucity of School Science and Outdoor Experiences

The children experienced educational gaps that shocked some of their tutors. We believe these curricular gaps related to No Child Left Behind (NCLB) and Texas testing policies, which started before NCLB. Texas functions as the U.S. pressure-cooker for testing (Nichols, Glass, & Berliner, 2012). For example, science does not count for grade-level promotion in Texas primary and middle schools, which might explain why Flo, a fifth grader, did not realize plants were alive and Leona started crying during a science lesson. Leona had never heard of the concepts, although her tutor followed the Texas Essential Knowledge and Skills (TEKS) for Leona's fifth grade level.

Although schools offering environmental education do experience better student test scores, NCLB and test-prep relate to fewer recesses (outdoor play), especially in schools serving predominately low-income students; these students represent the most sedentary student population (Strife & Downey, 2009). Exercise and movement are essential in culturally responsive instruction (Gorski, 2013) and relate to experiential disciplinary learning.

However, Joy provided a counter-example. She said an educator, who teaches behavior management at her middle school, has organized a school garden with hydroponic gardening, using no soil. The teacher invites all students; many participate after school. One child brought minerals and mashed them with a mortar and pestle and explained the pH concept to Joy; the youth possessed complex science knowledge.

Figure 8.1. Flash with Plant. Photo by Krystal A. Yanez.

Ecology and Conscientization

Perhaps the dearth of science instruction and outdoor experiences in school motivated children to progress in ecological conscientization. Some might believe science bears no relationship to social justice, but Brazilian ethnoscientist and ecologist Campos helped Freire to realize First World (developed) and Third World (developing) ideologies and the ethnocentricism and colonialism inherent in northern scientific orientations (Freire, 1994). Although most teacher candidates (TCs) were not science majors, they taught the youth planting native flora could help insects and animals and could conserve water in our drought-stricken region. A Mexican-heritage naturalist gave an outdoor lesson on these topics, also. Flash, in Figure 8.1, expressed pride in knowing plant names in Spanish and their medicinal purposes. Others were proud of their families' ecological contributions; many grew native plants in their yards. Children mentioned plants' importance for oxygen and soil conservation.

Science major Tesla involved Victor, 14, in a water pollution experiment connected to *Corazón's resaca*. Victor, agitated, fired off questions: "This made an impression on him because he realized how fragile life is if it is not taken care of." Victor made connections to the *resaca* bordering *Corazón* and realized he could affect change in his colonia by not polluting and by discouraging others to pollute. *Corazón's resaca* and banks contained litter, related to environmental racism (Peña, 1999). Tesla bridged scientific and local knowledge, creating a Third Space related to ecology with Victor (Bussert-Webb, 2011). Victor's epistemological curiosity resulted from Tesla's apprenticeship.

Other children mentioned the *resaca's* pollution during a focus group discussion: "*Pero el agua está muy sucia*" [But the water is really dirty] and "*Y nadie se puede bañar allí*" [No one can bathe there]. Alma, former Center coordinator, stated, "The children learn to appreciate nature and learn about caring for the environment." Most asked continuously when they were going out to plant and they wanted to show their families the fruits of their labor. Juan, 11, stated, "I like the things we planted. I can show my mom what we did." The children's motivation to beautify their neighborhood disproved the notion of Latinos/as as ignorant land and water abusers (Peña, 1999).

The children's passion for caring about their earth was evident in our May project. Yet environmentalism does not happen without the body. To foster equity, children can critique their circumstances and work together to improve them (Boyle-Baise, 2002). After all, why cannot disciplinary literacy involve physical labor and public dialogue vis-à-vis social and environmental factors (Yore, Pimm, & Tuan, 2007)? From our longitudinal research, we found children co-researchers lacked social-justice oriented science. Although our May program has helped the children in science, we must do more to invite *Corazón* youth to explore this discipline from a critical lens—in *Corazón* and school. Quigley (2011) argued we need diverse people's participation to improve a discipline.

Repositioning Themselves and the Disciplines

Authentic disciplinary experiences from equity-oriented Latinos/as in a Third Space—not quite school, not quite home—may have helped the youth to reconceptualize themselves and their disciplinary positioning. These authentic experiences may relate to whether a child sees her/himself worthy of the discipline. Perhaps a nondominant child tests the disciplinary waters before jumping in, asking "Can people like me swim here?" Flo corrected herself constantly to the point of interrupting comprehension because she feared censure. Lorena told Flo to focus on making and sharing meaning instead: "She thanked me during the ceremony for believing in her and giving her the confidence she lacked."

Rosa wrote that Anhelo, mentioned in this chapter's beginning, was "coming out of his nutshell" as a distraught recent immigrant in an English-only classroom. See Chapter 9. Rosa found ways to make this third grader more confident in academic English and to express his pain and joy. Rosa realized how much she helped Anhelo after talking to his mother at the program's end. Anhelo's mother said Rosa helped to transform Anhelo's identities as a learner, reader, and writer and that Anhelo was putting more *empeño* [effort] into school. Rosa stated:

> But the one thing she really poured her heart out on was this program and it was just mind-blowing for me because she was like, "Man, I wish it was just a little bit longer because just in a couple of days, he's totally different."

Kathy's soul flew when she read Anhelo's end-of-program essay: "*Aprendí a rimar el mundo es hermoso y tan marabilloso [sic]*" [I learned to rhyme the beautiful and marvelous world]. Anhelo awoke from his despair. We like to think that Rosa, as well as the gardening—the touching, seeing, and smelling of soil and flora—helped.

One way that educators, such as Rosa, can help children to believe in their disciplinary worthiness includes sharing children's progress with parents; parents then relay the positive messages to their children. This helps youth and parents, who want the best for their children. If youth struggle academically, educators' helpful words can give parents hope, helping them to see their offspring in new ways. Rosa bragged on Anhelo and Rey (Rosa's second tutee) to their mothers. Rosa sensed the conversation helped Rey's mother to believe in Rey, the poet:

> But I also talked to the other one, the poet, and the mom too she was very surprised … What the other mom told me was she just knows he's a bad kid in school. He doesn't wanna try. He doesn't wanna do the homework. He finds it boring. When I told her, "Yes, all of that is true. He doesn't like it. He sees no purpose in it, but aside from that, let me show you what he's done." And that kind of put a spark back into the mom. She kind of looked at him, her son, and it was kind of a belief, like, as much as he complains, he is also a good student if he tries very hard.

Rey had practiced slantwise crisscrossing between Mexican and Texan schools, but said his schooling experiences in Spanish and Mexico were positive. Rey found his Texas education boring and irrelevant, which relates to a banking curriculum or depositing information on learners (Freire, 2000). We believe Rey's negative experiences related to No Child Left Behind (NCLB) and subsequent teach-to-the test curricula. Despite stepping close to a liberatory stance, Rey did not ponder systemic reasons for this banking education. However, Rey enjoyed his conversations with Rosa. He mentioned he especially liked "the time she gives me to think," which relates to dialogue, or drawing out and honoring learners' knowledge. Yet in a banking system, children lack time to exchange ideas with teachers. During the disciplinary log experience, Rosa talked with Rey about how reading related to her everyday life and how literacy involved more than reading and writing. Rey made a literacy connection to his mother, a gifted storyteller with a fourth grade education. Rosa continued, "He mentioned she would have been great in reading and writing stories … He treasures his mother's intelligence." Rosa suggested Rey write his mother's stories.

Although Rey said English was not his strength, he discovered he was a poet, a colossal realization for this disenfranchised student. Rey wanted to keep writing poems and showed Rosa poems he wrote at home since he met her. Rosa stated, "He reflected a sense of breakthrough in his new-found talent," demonstrated in his *Amazing Moment*:

> From the moment
> I got outside
> Hot and sweating
> I got surrounded by the infested heat
> When I was planting
> My fingers were muddy
> My face was sweating

> And my muscles were tired
> It was worthless
> Not interesting
> It was a chaos
> With all that work
> Although towards the beginning
> It was boring and tired
> But at the end
> I realized it was all worthwhile

Sonrisa, featured in the book's Forward, also realized her poetic talent, but this took much scaffolding from her tutor, Rachel. Rachel and Sonrisa read a poem about a garden. Next, Rachel showed Sonrisa flower and bee pictures and asked Sonrisa questions about how she felt, what she smelled, and so forth, based on a strategy we discussed in class. Next, Rachel had Sonrisa draw in response to the poem, another course strategy. Last, Sonrisa spoke in a stream of consciousness and dictated to Rosa, similar to the Language Experience Approach, which Rosa learned in our course:

> *Smelling Love*
> I am a flower in my garden with every kind of flower and tree—bushes, palm trees, smelling their beautiful smells and seeing the sun. I hear the bees buzzing and the leaves rustling. I feel tranquil. I see other flowers as beautiful as me. We are all friends. Seeing the beauty makes me happy.

Interestingly, no competition between beings existed in Sonrisa's flower world, which demonstrated Sonrisa's collaborative essence. Inspired by her newfound ability, she wrote that day in her journal, "Today I learned that I'm good at writing." Sonrisa disliked reading and writing at the May project's onset, yet Rachel hooked her on both. From their dialogue over the disciplinary log, Sonrisa broadened her definition of reading and realized its importance: "I learned reading is everywere [sic] and it is important life." Toward the end of the program, Sonrisa wrote, "Today I learned that John Grisham is an awesome writer. I like that I got to read John Grisham book, *The Innocent Man*." Some might not attempt such a thick, difficult book with a fifth grader, such as Sonrisa, but Rachel knew Sonrisa liked mystery shows and attempted to hook her young charge in mystery books. Additionally, Rachel demonstrated high expectations, but built background for the child by reading the outside cover and the first few pages to Sonrisa.

Although some children disliked reading, they realized it involved more than test passages or worksheets. Perhaps teacher candidates' broader definitions of literacy may have helped the children to re-value reading. English major Lea stated, "She realized she reads every day. I told her reading does not have to be strictly books." In schools with high-stakes testing pressure, children erroneously learn hidden curricula or unintended lessons (Giroux, 2016)—reading equals test passages and school bores children. Youth in these contexts lack freedom to explore and inquire. After all, freedom involves creativity (Freire, 2000).

Summary

We posed this inquiry question: How does community service learning (CSL) help teacher candidates (TCs) and children? This project has helped TCs to move beyond surface-level pedagogical and instructional practices, towards a learner- and community-centered teaching philosophy. Beyond access to TCs as teachers, children benefited from the newly formed TC relationships and college-student role models.

What TCs and children learned had yielded more than expected in social justice and literacy. They composted, dug, mulched, planted, and watered flora together, which broke down barriers and created conditions conducive to dialogue. Many tutors had an Easter Experience, which requires a profound equity rebirth (Freire, 2000). Likewise, gardening created a Third Space and allowed new participation, which changed individuals, practices, and relationships. Hopefully, this gardening project will inspire more formal and informal educators, at all levels and disciplines, to create a Third Space to propel the field of education. This chapter begins and ends with Rosa, a former *Corazón* resident who had been embarrassed about her roots:

> I actually thought [it would be like] the service learning I did for other classes; that's what I expected from this. Just go do a couple of hours, read to the children, but nothing major that actually impacted you … I went in with a mentality of, "I'm going to impact a child's life and give them my time," but it was the other way around.

Questions to Ponder

1. Describe a future community service learning (CSL) project appropriate in your community. How would it be similar to and different from the one in this chapter?

2. From this chapter, explain why a CSL course would be more beneficial for primary, secondary, and tertiary students (including teacher candidates) than a course taught on campus. Which of your course objectives would complement a CSL experience?

3. We mentioned social justice concepts. Describe how you could use one of our social justice concepts in your locale.

4. In this CSL project, tutors' ethnicity generally matched that of the tutees. How might the program results be different for tutors and tutees who do not share the same ethnicity?

· 9 ·

EDUCATION IN *CORAZÓN*

Meet Ana and Olivia

Brother James, long-term *Corazón* resident and retired clergy, and Tim, *Corazón* priest at the time, had met young Ana and Olivia, sisters. Ana, the older sister, displayed enormous talents, according to Brother James. She was a "wiz at computers" and made them scrumptious Sunday meals. "She was a natural," Brother James added. Ana graduated with two bachelor's degrees in nursing and Spanish from our local university and with a master's in translation at a university in Guadalajara, Mexico. Tim gave Ana's younger sister, Olivia, a *Harry Potter* book, transforming Olivia into a voracious reader; Olivia received her bachelor's degree in psychology. Brother James explained,

> What gets me is how these two girls [were] living in this little house. It's a trailer, a travel trailer, for uh, for vacations. It only has two beds in it. They didn't have a desk to study on, no hot running water. And they were able to go through college, both of them cum laude. And the second one had only one "B" in all her college career. And it's just amazing how they could do it.

Introduction

Chapter 9's inquiry question was: What are the educational opportunities and practices of *Corazón* children and adults? Most data sources consisted of interviews and surveys; see the Book Introduction regarding methodology. Co-researchers were mostly: Tutorial Center youth, teacher candidates, adult staff and volunteers, and parents. Emerging youth themes were school readiness, children's dreams and family influences, obstacles, two outstanding public school educators, teacher quality, school gentrification, and the impact of out-of-school factors, such as socio-economic status and immigration on secondary and college attainment. We return to Ana and Olivia in this higher education section. College and adult education themes centered on *Corazón* residents' obstacles, motivations, and successes. We discuss the aesthetic potential of adult education for individuals and communities.

Educating *Corazón* Youth

Educational Opportunities

We highlight youth, 18 and younger, who represent about 2,800 (40%) of *Corazón* (U.S. Census Bureau, 2010). Various educational institutions are available, from pre-school to high school levels. Regarding young children, a federally-funded Head Start program operated in *Corazón* from 1998 to 2014 for low-income infants, toddlers, and pre-school children. However, it moved to a location about a mile away due to inadequate space issues. Private day-cares operate nearby.

Corazón children attend nearby non-charter public elementary, middle, and high schools, rated recognized and exemplary, due to above average attendance and state test scores. A middle school borders *Corazón's* west side, while two elementary schools border the east. *Corazón* children may attend two additional elementary schools, less than a mile north and a mile south from *Corazón's* core, and another middle school about three miles away. Thus, *Corazón* child may attend four district primary schools and two middle schools, depending on a child's physical address. High school students may choose between campuses, depending on their career interests, yet most *Corazón* youth attend a campus about three miles away.

Additionally, colonia children with reliable transportation may attend private and charter public schools, which abound in our area. *Corazón's* Tutorial Center, which has thrived for over 12 years, represents another educational opportunity; see Chapter 4. Besides sports and other extracurricular activities, pupils in most local schools can participate in nationally ranked chess teams. Although these activities can internalize youth's sense of school belonging, obstacles for nondominant youth include transportation and perceptions of club exclusivity. Schools could incorporate these activities sometimes into part of the day (Gándara, 2010).

School Readiness: Coming Out on Top

Corazón children scored toward the top (the highest quartile) of many neighborhoods on multiple kindergarten readiness skills, including basic literacy. Rio Grande Valley (RGV) kindergarten teachers tested their children using the Early Development Instrument (EDI); report writers categorized the results by children's neighborhoods. *Corazón* children placed behind country clubs, but above middle-income neighborhoods. Brother James said the results testify to *Afinidad's* outreach programs (see Chapter 4) and parent involvement. Brother James also mentioned the at-risk myth: "There is a misperception that poorer areas are not preparing children adequately." We cannot cite the 2012 report because it will give away the research site, but the EDI is valid and reliable (Janus & Offord, 2007). A California university created the report for a RGV service agency.

Corazón's early childhood results contrast with results from the Early Childhood Longitudinal Study, in which Latinos/as and Native Americans scored at the bottom quartile of racial groups (Gándara, 2010). However, over 90% of RGV residents and about 99% of *Corazón* residents are Latino/a (U.S. Census Bureau, 2010). See Chapter 4 regarding *Afinidad's* mother-child school readiness program. If *Corazón* families and organizations prepare these five-year-olds so well, then something else relates to the colonia's low college attainment rates; we return to this later.

Academic Dreams and Family Influences

While conducting interviews during the May 2015 program, Krystal met children with great academic goals and an understanding of how to achieve them. Angel, a confident and sweet 12-year-old, dreamed of joining Special Weapons and Tactics (SWAT) forces. Krystal asked him, "Why do you want to go to college?" Angel said, "I've seen people that are old and they dropped out of school when they were little. I wouldn't like to be in their position right now." Dulce, 13, shy, but articulate, lived with her aunt and attended a nearby middle school, while her parents resided in Mexico. This is slantwise (Campbell & Heyman, 2007) because receiving a quality education represents a socially acceptable goal. Although Dulce felt uncomfortable with English and disliked reading every day, she wanted to be a lawyer and knew she must be organized and diligent for college success.

Payne (2005), a self-proclaimed poverty expert, believed some youth and parents possess a poverty culture and lack academic motivation. However, nondominant families aspire to succeed academically and Gorski (2013) demonstrated a culture of poverty does not exist. May 2015 teacher candidates (TCs) argued against Payne's assertions. Jorge said, "A lot of these students want to go to college and their parents encourage them to continue studying" and Ella explained, "Payne's ideas could not be more wrong. The students … have an appreciation for learning. The girl I'm mentoring wishes to improve her skills in the English language and is willing to work hard in her studies." Mabel wrote:

> The children have big hearts and long to be someone in life! … They are eager to learn and gain knowledge. They might not have the resources upper-class students have, but I can assure you they have hearts of warriors. These students and parents might have faced struggles in their lives, but they are still standing strong.

Joy started tutoring colonia youth as part of community service learning (CSL) in 2004; see Chapter 1. She now teaches English across the street from *Corazón*. Joy provides her students with the lifetime earning difference between high school and college graduates and encourages them to pursue college. Joy fears students, including those from *Corazón*, will trade their higher education dreams for a paycheck, a conundrum for low-income youth who wish to help their families. Many Latino/a youth take an early school exit for several reasons, including working to support family (Coronado, 2003). Construction and service jobs appear the most popular, as they require no advanced degrees. This becomes cyclical because the more formal education a person possesses, the higher her/his salary (U.S. Department of Labor, 2015a).

Involved Parents and Barriers

Some educators believe colonia parents are uninvolved and uninterested in their children's education. Hernández (2003) surveyed teachers and parents in an elementary school serving a Rio Grande Valley (RGV) colonia; 10% of surveyed teachers felt the school's parents desired involvement in their children's education, but 92% of surveyed parents reinforced school's importance to their children. Many parents (with little English background) reported they could not assist their children with English homework or read to them in English. Similarly, Coronado (2003) interviewed a colonia mother who could not help her high-achieving son in English. Other barriers prevent direct involvement, such as inadequate child-care and inflexible work schedules. Additionally, *Corazón* parents might be unaware of the academic opportunities available for their children and may lack the skills, knowledge, or information to help. They may lack social networks related to college, compared to white middle-class parents (Nora & Crisp, 2009).

We have found *Corazón* families to be involved and committed to their children's education. Contributor Claudia said, "My mom was my first teacher. She taught me how to read and write, add, subtract, before any other teachers." Joy, who teaches many *Corazón* children English, knows an administrator who grew up and still lives in *Corazón*. The administrator, a migrant, had performed poorly in school, but was to get a school award, for the first time, in third grade. "Either they didn't have a car or the car wasn't working," Joy said. The administrator walked with her mom to the school for a long distance to attend the evening ceremony because the administrator's mother realized its importance.

Based on May 2015 parent surveys we conducted, many mothers wanted their children to attend college. Some mothers even wanted to attend college to motivate their children (Bussert-Webb, 2015). Rita, current Tutorial Center coordinator, stated parents attend school-district parenting classes and monitor their children's grades through the online grading system; as mentioned in Chapter 7, most participating children possess high-speed Internet and functioning computers.

High School Rates

Parental monitoring and support become apparent when we examine U.S. Census Bureau data (2000, 2010) regarding *Corazón's* high school improvement data. Among *Corazón* residents, 25 years and older, 10% in 2000 and 31% in 2010 completed high school or the equivalent, a 210% increase. However, this means only one in three graduated high school in 2010. In 2000, 46% completed less than ninth grade, compared to 34% in 2010. Although this represents a 26% reduction in ninth grade dropouts, it signifies almost one in three did not finish ninth grade. If students can make it past ninth grade, they are more likely to graduate high school (Allensworth & Easton, 2005). Although most youth who regularly attended the Tutorial Center graduate high school, we estimate less than 4% of *Corazón* youth attend the Center. See Chapter 4.

Despite *Corazón* children's high school gains, many struggle academically. Some educators and leaders are helping colonia youth through mentoring and raising up leaders and activists. Community engagement, when connected to the curriculum through service learning, can be crucial in graduation rates (Lockeman & Pelco, 2013).

The Harmful Effects of *NCLB* and Teacher Resistance

Mandates and Banking Education

The No Child Left Behind Act (NCLB) has intensified test-prep, especially in schools serving predominately low-income Latino/a children (Palmer & Rangel, 2011). High-stakes testing presents an especially tenuous situation for fifth and eighth grade Texas public school students who must pass state-level reading and mathematics tests for clear advancement to the next grade level. Participating *Corazón* children have mentioned over the years mostly teach-to-the test curricula, discrete skills instruction, and a pedagogy devoid of local context. However, much of this relates to state and national policies.

NCLB accomplished federal mandates and reports about schools, districts, and students. NCLB's biggest failure relates to negative consequences on children and educators (Nichols et al., 2012). The pressure imposed on students exemplifies social injustices, with anti-democratic, bureaucratizing, and predetermined academic experiences. With so many potentially negative influences, students may fall prey to the banking concept of education, in which they accept passive, imposed roles (Freire, 2000). Youth may believe they cannot achieve social justice. The revision of NCLB, Every Student Succeeds Act (ESSA), may decrease pressure on teachers and youth, but not on university-based teacher preparation programs.

Joy, Eusebio, Failure, and Segmentation

Local youth begin taking developmentally inappropriate, day-long State of Texas Assessments of Academic Readiness (STAAR) benchmarks in the fall of first grade to determine remediation needs. Despite the constant weigh-ins, some children fail, especially recent immigrants with no prior English language exposure (Palmer & Lynch, 2008). Imagine taking an academic test in Hungarian after living in Hungary for a few months. Indeed, the Spanish language lacks value in many U.S. public schools due to federal English-only education policies and racism.

When asked about the impact No Child Left Behind (NCLB) on her students from *Corazón*, Joy explained those who fail the STAAR perceive themselves as failures. Joy mentioned two of her former middle school students, Rogelio and Eusebio, which school staff identified as limited English proficient (LEP) level ones. Rogelio learned English in Mexican schools and passed the STAAR. However, Eusebio had no English instruction prior to moving from Mexico; Eusebio took the same test, but failed, which devastated Eusebio and Joy. All middle and high school students must take the STAAR in English; eligible students can get a one-year extension and linguistic accommodations.

Additionally, Joy said high-stakes testing diminishes the way many of her students see themselves as whole persons, as they learn subjects unequally. Her school administrators emphasize reading and math, STAAR subjects that determine student retention. Therefore, youth may devalue a piecemeal education and may be unprepared adequately for college. A segmented curriculum can result in segmented teachers and youth, cut and parceled in curricular coffins, devoid of life. English. Math. Science. Many subaltern youth shuffle from one classroom to another with no interdisciplinary connections. Yet from open-system and Third Space perspectives, curriculum should mingle between fissures.

Rosa, Anhelo, and Bilingual Education

Despite colonia children's Spanish dominance and research supporting recursive and dynamic bilingual education (García, 2009), participating children have mentioned receiving English-only curricula or subtractive bilingual education to prepare for the English STAAR. A child's L1 constitutes a strength in additive bilingual education, yet a scar in the subtractive model (Nieto & Bode, 2008).

Rosa, a passionate teacher candidate in the May 2015 program, told the story of Anhelo, her third grader tutee and a recent immigrant; see Chapter 8. Anhelo was in an English-only program, despite his obvious language barrier. Rosa said Anhelo and his family suffered dramatically: "It's kind of like they leave it up to him at home and the mother to do pretty much everything else and it was just having a huge toll on all of them." Anhelo's mother told Rosa Anhelo had been struggling with suicidal thoughts; she and her husband had considered returning to Mexico to save their son. The parents pondered the irony of doing so much to bring their son to America if he committed suicide. Thus, Anhelo's mother tried to get him into a bilingual program. She talked with the school counselor and principal to no avail. Next, she visited the district office; district staff immediately placed Anhelo into the bilingual program.

Although Anhelo is doing better now, depression and suicidal thoughts and plans are highest among Latino/a high school students (Eaton et al., 2008). We ponder relationships between Latino/a youth's socioemotional health and the national English-only, anti-immigration, and high-stakes testing milieu. Some do not realize the emotional impact of living in a new country. Isolation, exhaustion, and loneliness can take over. Anhelo could not rhizome in an English-only environment. "They kept on BREAKING HIS RHIZOME and BLOTCHING HIS MAP, setting it straight for him, blocking his every way out until he began to desire his own shame and guilt" (Deleuze & Guattari, 1987, p. 14, original emphasis).

Joy, Claudia, and Teacher Efforts

To help create a passion for knowledge, Joy and Claudia engage students in collaborative, culturally relevant literacy and language experiences. Joy described a typical mandated assignment in which students were to write summaries of Twain's Tom Sawyer. Joy did not believe "the kids could relate to it," so, she had them discuss and write about Garza's *Creepy Creatures and Other Cucuys.* While Joy does require students to read some classics to teach youth about the global, she searches for accompanying local texts to invite her students to make intertextual links. "Here I am busted," she recalled, when a district administrator turned to Joy, in front of everyone at a meeting, and asked if Joy used a certain textbook. Diplomatic, and calm on the exterior, Joy replied, "I find things from everywhere." The administrator liked the answer and said good teachers do not focus on textbook instruction. Joy's keen understanding of how to engage diverse learners with texts and each other has allowed her to create a Third Space (Gutiérrez et al., 1999).

Student inquiry remains problematic in high-stakes environments where teachers feel pressured to prepare students for the spring onslaught of test batteries. Paugh and Moran (2013) discussed how Moran, a third grade teacher in a kill-and-drill urban school, created raised bed gardens with students so they could read, write, and talk about the team project, difficult to attain in commercial, decontextualized, scripted lessons. Moran, like our co-researchers,

Joy and Claudia, dealt with a district-mandated, paced curriculum unrelated to the local context. Many teachers struggle with similar pressures. We, María and Kathy, experienced high-stakes testing as former local teachers. María taught elementary and Kathy taught high school students. Because we lived these experiences, we empathize with teachers in similar or worse environments.

High-stakes testing vis-à-vis No Child Left Behind (NCLB) collided with Joy's desire to help students make connections to texts and to each other. This collision represented a centripetal, pushing in, and centrifugal, pushing out, tit-for-tat (Holquist, 1996) as students and Joy attempt to make sense of the school system. NCLB policies are subtractive because children and families are deemed unworthy (Valenzuela, 2008). Fortunately, educators, such as Joy and Claudia, recognize the potential of culturally-responsive teaching and include youth and family cultures, languages, and literacies.

Additionally, Claudia, certified in bilingual education, promoted her fourth-grade children's Latino culture and mother tongue. Although she does not teach *Corazón* children anymore, she lived in this colonia for over 20 years, volunteered at the Tutorial Center, and many of Claudia's family members live in *Corazón*. She taught the entire fourth grade a Spanish song, entitled *Señora Señora* [Mrs. Mrs.]. The children sang it to their mothers at a school-wide Mother's Day event. Claudia taught them with YouTube Karaoke, which she used regularly in San Antonio for first graders. Seeing the words while singing with others helped the youth to read in Spanish because they kept up with the music and were not singled out. Claudia explicitly taught students Spanish vocabulary, syntax, and fluency. Moreover, she explained a song was another form of poetry to hook them into reading and writing poetry.

Claudia said, "When I first told them we were going to learn a song in Spanish, many of them kept complaining, 'Ma'am, I don't know how to read in Spanish.' I told them, 'I had first graders who learned to read in Spanish.'" Claudia said most of the fourth graders spoke Spanish as a first language (L1); however, since their schooling focused on English acquisition, they did not know how to read Spanish. Claudia resisted the hegemonic language forces of English-only when she purposefully taught her students to revalue their mother tongue and Mother's Day, important in the Mexican culture.

Furthermore, Claudia challenges fourth grade students in collaborative math investigations. Each person provides input; the note taker writes the understanding and planning part, the illustrator draws out the problem in the checking part, the editor solves the problem with help from the group, and the speaker explains each step to the class. Claudia rotates students' roles, also.

Teacher Quality and Gentrification

Fourth grade teacher Claudia and seventh grade teacher Joy exude competence. They are certified in the fields they teach. They participated in university-based teacher educator programs and passed their licensure tests the first time. Joy has taught for 11 years and Claudia for four. They also appear to be school leaders. Joy's principal placed her in a new interdisciplinary team to improve it and sent Joy to a district-level leadership meeting focused on writing. Claudia teaches more difficult content areas (math and science) because they come easy to her. Moreover, she had garnered enough power to teach a song in Spanish to the entire fourth grade, an accomplishment because by fourth grade many schools tend to focus on English-only instruction. Claudia completed a 54-hour M.Ed. in counseling, also. Joy and Claudia teach in high-poverty schools.

However, some of Joy's and Claudia's colleagues may not possess similar qualifications, which relates to neighborhood and school gentrification. Some teacher candidates (TCs) mentioned gated communities and rich and poor schools in a district. Neighborhood segregation may result in school segregation, e.g., School X has mostly low-income students and School Y, mostly high-income students (Gándara, 2010). A few TCs posited officials built schools on *Corazón's* boundaries because personnel from the farther-away schools did not want *Corazón* children. Perhaps personnel worried Spanish-dominant children in poverty would pull down test scores. We return to the top literacy rankings of *Corazón* five-year olds. We believe *Corazón* does not fail schools, but rather the educational system fails these high-poverty Latino/a children.

Teacher quality and gentrification relate to a study by Goldhaber, Lavery, and Theobald (2015), who examined elementary, middle, and high schools in all Washington State districts. They found every measure of teacher quality (licensure exam scores, years of experience, and other measures of effectiveness) "inequitably distributed across every indicator of student disadvantage, e.g., student academic performance, free- and reduced lunch, and minority status" (p. 304). Goldhaber et al. related teacher quality to educators transferring to higher-socioeconomic status (SES) schools. Goldhaber et al. mentioned effective solutions, e.g., educator bonuses for teaching in low-performing schools and limiting within-district transfers. Indeed, instead of discussing the achievement gap, we could focus on the opportunity gap related to low-SES culturally diverse children, who possess unequal access to highly quality teachers, curricula, and resources (Gorski, 2013). Besides teacher quality and school gentrification, out-of-school factors related to *Corazón* children's academic achievement.

Out-of-School Factors

Corazón children's academic outcomes related to out-of-school factors (OSFs) (Berliner, 2009), including the home-school disconnect, poverty, food insecurity, and inadequate healthcare (Bomer & Maloch, 2013). We add immigration to OSFs. Amiga, a catechism teacher, mentioned children new to *Corazón* are vulnerable to negative influences as they struggle through the transition of moving to a new country and school. A gang was recruiting a seventh grade boy she knew; Amiga attributed his gang recruitment to his school alienation. *Corazón* and the Rio Grande Valley (RGV) are safe (Solomon, 2015). Over a million people live in the RGV and some gangs exist, e.g., the Texas Sindicate. However, we know of no *Corazón* gang.

Although we disagree with Berliner's pathologization of neighborhoods in his discussion of OSFs, we do agree many low-income youth do not identify with school. Yet this attachment is crucial for Latino/a academic success. Although devastating statistics demonstrate needed support for children of low-income communities, schools servicing these areas have struggled to create strong family involvement. Hernández (2003) discussed the home-school disconnect in a RGV colonia; teachers referred two colonia boys to special education and said the two pupils lacked experiences. This perplexes us. We perceive colonia youth possess rich experiences. For example, why do some teachers magnify children's tourist trips, but diminish the wealth in children's migrant trips and family visits to Mexico?

Kathy told Joy how the U.S. government competes constantly with other countries for high test scores on the Programme for International Student Assessment (PISA) in mathematics, science, and reading (see Chapter 7). Joy discussed her students' out-of-school factors and said comparing countries' test scores is folly. Joy said, "If I hear about Finland one more time, I will vomit." Contemplating Finland and the positive press about its educational system, we wondered what types of OSFs its students faced. Finland has the lowest food insecurity in the world; any child in Finland receives free dental care and only 5% of children in Finland live in poverty, compared to 23% in the USA (Bomer & Maloch, 2013).

How do these OSFs affect families' educational dreams? Gloria, a teacher candidate (TC) in the May 2015 tutoring program (see Chapter 8), mentioned her tutee's father pressured the fifth grader to join the military. Gloria attributed this to parents' inadequate knowledge of other possibilities, due to the desperate need for a guaranteed living. While the military exists as a possibility, this military-only push might be attributed to the father's misunderstanding of how college can help his daughter.

Berliner (2009) found low-income students face the greatest disadvantage in public schools; our outcome-oriented educational system ignores the effects of academically detrimental inputs associated with poverty. Poeta, an elderly activist, described the relationship between SES, marginalization, and bullying. She said *Corazón* school children tied plastic bags around their feet when the unpaved roads became muddy from rain. These plastic bags became ways to identify and harass *Corazón* children, which hurt their self-esteem deeply:

> *Y les decían: "Ay, vives ahí en ese mugrero, ahí en [Corazón], que feo". Pero eran buenos niños, su único defecto era haber nacido pobres* [And they said, "Oh, you live in that dump, over there in *Corazón*! How ugly!" But they were good youth. Their only defect is they were born poor].

Another possible OSF relates to consumption and youth's quest for *El Dorado*, a land loaded with gold and spices (Eakin, 2007). A *Corazón* female student expressed glee her boyfriend quit school and got a job to buy her school clothes, according to teacher Joy. The girl's admiration for this boy's behavior could be explained by formal schooling resistance and machismo. However, dropping out can be detrimental to one's academic dreams. Machismo obligates males to be responsible for their families' honor and well-being (Hyde & Else-Quest, 2013). Alternatively, machismo may relate to some indigenous people's internalization of Western culture, whereby the subaltern take on values and practices from colonizers (Anzaldúa, 1990).

Additionally, foreign-born students tend to have idealized cultural views of America, associated with materialism: "Media images of the U.S. prior to arrival and the materialism they see after arrival creates an unrealistic view of America" (Hadaway, Vardell, & Young, 2009, p. 9). Poeta connected this phenomenon to *Corazón*, whereby youth compared their living conditions and material goods with those seen on American television or in peers' homes:

Y estas familias entraban a una cultura y a un modo de vivir muy diferente. Y yo creo causa efecto en su estima pues ellos piensan "ay, donde vivo" o "mi casa está muy fea" porque este país es muy materialista, y los padres no podían darle a sus hijos lo que querían [These families enter into a different culture, a way of living distinct from Mexico when they come to the USA. I believe this affects their self-esteem because they are thinking, "Oh my! Where do I live?" or "My house is really ugly." Because this country is materialistic, and parents haven't been able to give their children what they've wanted].

Perhaps Poeta meant materialism obscures a people's struggle. The colonia children may begin to think about external conditions and materialism instead of pursuing an education or social activism. This greed relates to capitalism, commercialism, and colonialism, the antithesis of social justice. The latter focuses on conscientization and helping to change unjust societal structures (Freire, 2000). TCs also discussed the ways in which some tutorial children compared their shoes with other tutorial children. However, when Chicanos/as criticize and compare themselves to each other, they perpetuate colonialism internally and in their relationships; when this happens, they internalize Western cultural values and modes of production, e.g., competition, materialism, and social stratification (Anzaldúa, 1990).

The College Experience

At least three community colleges (technical institutes) and a university of nearly 30,000 students are within an hour's drive of *Corazón*. Other universities offer satellite programs in the Rio Grande Valley, also.

Low College Attainment and Structural Inequalities

When examining *Corazón's* university endeavors, we explain contextual factors, which include socioeconomic status, race, immigration, and residence.

Socioeconomic Status (SES)

We extend out-of-school factors to college students' SES. Strick's (2012) analysis of data from a college preparatory charter school on college access depressed us; 73% of students in families with a combined income of $100,000 or more are enrolling at four-year colleges within two years of high school graduation, compared to 23% of students in families with a combined income of $20,000 or less. Few low-SES students achieve success at the highest academic levels; they leave the high-achieving group disproportionately during secondary school and few graduate college or attend graduate school (Wyner, Bridgeland, & DiIulio, 2007).

We paint a scene of some *Corazón* families' financial needs. In June 2015, Kathy saw Rita giving prizes to children who brought in their report cards, as the coordinator tracks the children's educational progress. One mother arrived, but could not get a prize for her daughter (Libra) because Libra's school would not release her grades; Libra had lost three library books. Granted, Libra should have been more careful. Yet here is the clincher: Libra's mom arranged to pay the school in three installments, beginning with $10 that week, after she got paid. For many, $30 would not be a big budget issue. Rita had Libra pick out a prize and promised she would hold it for Libra. We believe Rita would have given Libra the prize right then out of compassion, but Rita would have had to contend with the others in line, who may have lacked report cards. When teacher Joy reviewed our book manuscript and read this story, Joy exclaimed, "That's horrible. They [district staff] can't do that for financial reasons." Joy thought if someone would have challenged the administrator, the staff member would have backed down. However, the *Corazón* mother may have felt disempowered to contest the administrator's decision.

Neighborhood

Where children live and attend school relates to their college graduation because they may have less access to qualified teachers and opportunities, a civil rights issue (Orfield, 2014). *Corazón's* college graduation rates depress us. Among residents 25 and up, 2.7% received a bachelor's degree or higher in 2000, versus 1.3% in 2010, a drop of 52%. This means only one in 10 residents over 25 held a bachelor's or higher. The surrounding city's rate was 16%, 12.3 times higher than *Corazón*, although both locations share similar Hispanic demographics. Texas' college graduation rate is 27% (U.S. Census Bureau, 2000, 2010). The 2010 differences between *Corazón*, city, and state rates indicate the role residence plays in academic achievement, which represents a systemic inequality (Orfield, 2014). Rita, tutorial coordinator, stated, "My dream for [*Corazón*] is that every child has the opportunity to obtain a high quality education and life." Yet few *Corazón* residents finish college. Why do so many *Corazón* children score high on the Early Development Instrument (EDI), but do not graduate college?

Brother James said the Census statistics are unfair because many college graduates leave *Corazón*, and the Census only measures *Corazón* residents. While some *Corazón* youth complete degree programs and find success in launching professional careers, most leave *Corazón*. As researchers, we heard this over and again, but as subjective beings and activists so committed to this community, we wanted to wear earplugs! We wanted to hear the youth were graduating college and staying in *Corazón* to give back to their community. Leaving meant their college graduation rates would not count in the Census, which measures residents. Thus, regarding college attainment, *Corazón* appears stagnant to outsiders.

Race and Immigration

Educational achievement relates to race and immigration, also. Although Latino/a undergraduate enrollment has increased, in 2012–2013 Latinos/as represent 16% of U.S. undergraduates (National Center for Education Statistics, 2013). The national gap between Latinos/as and other groups who obtained a degree remains vast, as 20% of adult Latinos/as possess college degrees versus 36% of U.S. adults. In Texas, only 16% of adult Latinos/as compared to 32% of Texas adults have college degrees (Lilley, 2014). Race influences students' educational attainment. Gándara (2010) reported these percentages by race for bachelor degree completion: 37% white, 21% black, and 12% Latino/a. Only 4% of Latinos/as possess master's degrees, 3% doctorates, and 5% professional degrees (Nora & Crisp, 2009).

Many Latinos/as' inadequate college progress may relate to immigration issues, also. Texans without official U.S. documentation can attend college and can receive local and state financial aid, providing they meet certain criteria, as per Senate Bill 1819, which the Senate upheld in May 2015 (Rangel, 2015). Those attending the free college information sessions at the Tutorial Center were surprised this 14-year-old law existed. According to some co-researchers, youth fear that officials will deport the youth or undocumented family members, so they do not enroll. However, university staff do not report immigration status to authorities. In 2009, we began inviting our university's financial aid and recruitment staff to the Center, but a small proportion of colonia residents have attended. A tutorial staff member explained why she believed *Corazón's* graduation rates appeared so low:

> *Falta de conocimiento/información, estatus migratorio, temor, falta del idioma, piensan que entrar a la universidad es algo muy difícil … Tienen miedo. Una presentación no es*

suficiente para quitar el miedo … No son documentados [It's a lack of knowledge and information, the migratory status, fear, lack of knowledge of the English language. They think that entering the university is onerous. A presentation is insufficient for them to lose their fear. They are undocumented].

King and Punti (2012) interviewed and observed 15 high school students and young adults about their everyday experiences related to legality; their participants' low self-image, self-development, fear, and anxiety related to their undocumented status. Moreover, their undocumented status dissuaded some from college coursework. Certainly, obstacles to higher education can create an immigrant underclass related to being stuck in low-paying jobs.

Additionally, skin color relates to undocumented college students' marginalization. King's and Punti's (2012) interviewees believed their marginalization and prejudice related to race. Some felt that their liminal status stood out more if their skin was darker, as light-skinned undocumented people escaped scrutiny. Furthermore, Ortiz and Telles (2012) conducted an intergenerational study spanning 50 years and found discrimination related to darker skin color among Mexican-heritage people. Darker, more educated Mexican-heritage participants with more more white people contact experienced more stereotyping and discrimination than their less educated counterparts.

College Motivations and Obligations

Claudia and her best friend, Mireya, grew up in *Corazón* and lived down the street from each other. Although they graduated from high school together and enrolled at a nearby university together, Mireya was taking it slower than Claudia. Mireya withdrew from some classes and dropped out for three semesters. During that time, Mireya married and became a mother. Mireya confided in Claudia, saying, "I should have listened to you and taken advantage when I had more time." However, Mireya has recently returned to college to finish. This relates to many local university students, who may take longer to complete college because of family situations. Some *Corazón* youth stated they wanted to graduate college to help their families. Latinos/as from low-income families enroll in college for various reasons, including: not wanting to repeat other family members' mistakes and family support (Nora & Crisp, 2009). Santos (2004) found knowledge acquisition to be the top motivator of Latino/a community college students, then self-enrichment, career advancement, social status, and improved social life.

Many Latinos/as place a strong emphasis on assisting their families financially, which also relates to valuing academic achievement and going to college. However, the same motivation may cause some Latino/a college students to quit. Family obligations, discrimination, and finances may burden youth. Frank, the technology wiz we interviewed years ago (see Chapter 7), is now a high school student. Frank was motivated enough to attend the local university's college financial aid and admissions presentation at the Tutorial Center in 2015, but he left early to work at McDonald's. Frank told Kathy he wants to pursue a doctoral degree in criminology and he talked to the college recruiters and obtained their brochures. Frank attended the Center for years and participated with teacher candidates in Kathy's May programs.

While *Corazón* participating children were motivated, Rita, tutorial coordinator, asserted, "Many families do not feel college is something that is available for them. There are so many misconceptions about the admission requirements and the financial opportunities." However, Rita mentioned *Corazón* residents lose their fear, ask questions, and gain insights when college recruiters present at the Tutorial Center as part of Kathy's May program. Thus, attendees possess an advantage once they receive correct information about opportunities; as the first generation in their families to attend college, they realize why they must succeed.

Rhizoming

Never Giving Up

Our interviewees repudiated the numbers others used to define *Corazón's* future; many students and leaders have worked diligently to change the children's educational outcomes. At the chapter's beginning, we told the story of Ana and Olivia, two sisters living in a travel trailer. Ana, the older sister, started studying nursing. Yet to get her certification, she needed to go to Corpus Christi to take the state exam. The State did not offer the test locally. Unfortunately, Ana lacked U.S. documentation and could not cross the Border Patrol checkpoint in Saritas, Texas. Thus, she could not become a licensed Texas nurse. Instead of being defeated, Ana, like a rhizome, returned to school to get another bachelor's, but this time in Spanish. Ana completed all requirements to be a certified Spanish teacher, but again, Ana could not obtain the necessary State of Texas license due to her immigration status.

Broken-hearted, Ana left America and crossed the U.S.-Mexico border years ago. Brother James said, "I knew she would never come back, never see her family again." Ana needed a visa to return to America, although she had lived in the USA for over 10 years and possessed a spotless record. The USA selected 38 countries for non-immigrant visa waivers, but most Mexican citizens need a visa to enter (U.S. Customs and Border Protection, n.d.). However, some can enter through the Deferred Action for Childhood Arrivals (DACA) and Deferred Action for Parents of Americans and Lawful Permanent Residents (DAPA). Ana graduated with her master's degree in translation in Guadalajara, Mexico, eventually. Texas and America lost a high-achieving, caring person because of immigration and professional licensure policies.

Pastor Sabio, the Baptist Church founder (see Chapter 4), had happier stories to share. He jumped out of his seat to brag about church youth who have become successful academically:

> I know a lady here, that … has 10 kids that all went to the university. All her children graduated from the university. All of them went. Some went for two years. Some got an associate's degree. One became an engineer… a lot of teachers. One is going back to school to become a nurse. That's just one family. There's another family, the [López] family, all their kids are professionals today.

The Military

Additionally, Sabio said *he* sent a young girl, Leticia, to the Navy: "She had no money at all, but had her heart set on becoming a nurse. I said, 'Join the Navy!'" "Guess what?" he asked Krystal, grinning slyly, "She's in the Navy, and she's already studying to be a nurse." Sabio continued before Krystal could squeeze in a vowel:

> I have a young man stationed right now in Hawaii. His problem is his dad made too much money, so he couldn't get no grants. And the dad was one of those that wasn't going to invest in the boy's education. I sent him to the Navy and he was going to be a pharmacist, but in the Navy he got re-directed. And now he's going to be a physician's assistant.

As a maintenance worker at a local high school, Magnífico, an elderly *Corazón* activist, noticed boys in fancy Reserve Officers' Training Corps' (ROTC) uniforms. He said ROTC students looked clean-cut and respectable, but other students appeared as hippies. Magnífico persuaded his two sons to join ROTC.

Now both sons have received bachelor and master degrees, as the military helped with tuition. Magnífico said their officer ranks kept them from being foot soldiers in the Middle East. One son served in Iraq, but sat behind a desk.

Corazón residents rhizomed, appearing undaunted by systemic inequalities, such as inadequate finances. They found alternative paths to obtain a college education. *Corazón* families, staff, and volunteers push the youth and guide their paths, demonstrating Anzaldúa's (2002) bridge metaphor. Tim bridged Olivia's academic success by gifting the Harry Potter book, Pastor Sabio mentored youth, and Magnífico convinced his sons to join the ROTC. And although the military provided some colonia youth with educational opportunities, we are not recommending all non-dominant students join the military to receive financial support for college. Instead, we argue *Corazón* youth rhizomed by moving in other directions.

Community Colleges

Although many Latinos/as may not complete four-year college degrees, they are enrolling more frequently in community colleges (O'Connor, 2009). About 66% of Latino/a students attended community colleges, versus 45% whites (Nora & Crisp, 2009). However, only 0.5% of *Corazón* residents possess associate's degrees, while 12% have attended college without obtaining a degree (U.S. Census Bureau, 2010). We know of no *Corazón* residents attending a community college, but again, we base findings only on our participants. Junior colleges may perpetuate coloniality related to lower divisions of labor (Mignolo, 2011). The median income of a high school graduate is $668, an associate's $792, and a bachelor's $1,101. Indeed, neutral schooling is nonexistent (Freire, 2000).

Adult Education in *Corazón*

While the higher education landscape for some *Corazón* youth has improved, we cannot ignore some adults, who might be left behind. Thus, we turn our attention to adult education. Although Krystal missed much of the conversation from the language barrier, an undeniable passion in the dialogue transpired between Hermosa, Itza, Claudia, and Krystal. Book contributor Claudia sat closest to Krystal and the audio-recorder, translating for Hermosa and Itza, family friends; Claudia acted as an additional interviewee and added to the conversation. Both Hermosa and Itza are *promotoras de salud* [health promoters] for *Afinidad*; see Chapter 4. Krystal looked over at Claudia as she read the next question she needed translated, "What impact has adult education had on your life?" At this point, both Hermosa and Itza began to outline their recent educational experiences, which included formal and informal education.

Often when we discuss educational attainment for culturally diverse people, such as *Corazón* residents, we focus on the youth, and rightly so, as they can change Census results through their academic successes. Adults desire a formal education, also. Hermosa, middle-aged, mentioned on her survey a "100% possibility she will go" to college. She has earned a high school diploma from Mexico, but will take the General Educational Development (GED) test on the computer soon. See Chapter 7.

Hermosa has worked hard for a GED. Hermosa and other women expressed interest in studying business, clerical work, nursing, and teaching. The GED content presents more difficulty, especially the mathematics section; the pass rate has plummeted nationwide (Turner & Kamenetz, 2015). Public school accountability pressures leak into adult education with career and college readiness versus finding voice (Perry & Homan, 2014). We interpret the increased GED test rigor and electronic version as ways to suppress the subaltern and to wield the coloniality of power. Furthermore, we connect GED changes to ubiquitous, fear-inspiring, bureaucratic testing machineries. Panopticism exemplifies a surveillant culture (Bhabha, 2004). However, adult education programs should involve a learner's psychological and spiritual fulfillment and evolving, situated identities.

Although Texas possesses the most elementary and secondary school accountability pressure of any U.S. state (Nichols et al., 2012), it has the highest number of adult immigrants who have not completed high school (Camarota, 2012). This is not because Texas has the most immigrants. In fact, California has the highest immigrant population (25.4%), then New York (10.8%), and Texas (10.4%) (U.S. Census Bureau, 2012a).

Influence and Impact

In the previous paragraph, we use the word "adult" to include both men and women, but it seemed women were pursuing educational opportunities more than men. Pastor Sabio explained some men were unwilling to get educated because it implied assimilating to the American culture, a process during which immigrants tend to lose their ethnic identities. We believe in blended identities, not dichotomies (Bhabha, 2004). People should not have to yank their homeland from their hearts. Sabio said, "I know people that are my age, a couple of men in this church that they get $700 worth of social security, and they're content. At one time, they were young. I told them, 'learn English. Get your [General Educational Development] (GED), even if it's in Spanish.'"

However, Fuerza, an employee at *Convivio*, a service organization mentioned in Chapter 4, said some men signed up for a computer class she taught:

> I had some unemployed men that felt like, "I have to learn computers because my children, my grandchildren, our neighbors, people know how to use computers, and I'm scared of it. I don't even know where the turn-on switch is, and I don't even know the first thing about email. I don't know the first thing about Facebook." And they're scared. And let me tell you everyone that signed up, stuck it out, they loved it, and it gave them a sense of freedom … and some of them signed up for English. And you see how opening one door led to another.

Conversely, *Corazón* women realized education's value and sought learning opportunities. Education was not always Hermosa's and Itza's priority, however. Machismo [strong masculine pride] is a code men from many cultures follow, calling for a man to provide for and protect his family. This Spanish and Portuguese term from, *macho* [male], demonstrates colonialism's influence. Although machismo is Iberian-born, the concept has spread due to the coloniality of power and the subjugation of women worldwide (Mignolo, 2011). *Marianismo* refers the Catholic veneration of "the Virgin Mary who is both a virgin and a madonna" (Mays & Comas-Díaz, 1988, p. 235). According to this code, Latinas may deny themselves in favor of their family, which can decrease the importance of mothers' education. Hermosa's and Itza'a experiences are part of a national trend. About 41% of Latina mothers possess less than a high school diploma, versus about 18% black and 6% white mothers; less than 10% of Latina mothers have earned a bachelor's, versus about 15% black and 32% white mothers (Gándara, 2010).

"We did study and go to school," Hermosa explained, "but because of our culture, once we got married, we just dedicated ourselves to our kids and family." Familism, or structural settings in which people with different activities and interests are bound together, can be positive phenomenon for Latina mothers (Zinn, 1982). However, Juarbe, Turok, and Pérez-Stable (2002) found familism might keep Latina mothers in the home. While Hermosa and Itza put aside their academic dreams earlier for their families, they eventually sought after the education and symbolized females' shifting consciousness (Anzaldúa, 2002).

Hermosa's and Itza's educational experiences have improved their families' lives. The women discussed how, in their *promotora* training, they learned how to get healthy by cooking nutritious meals and serving appropriate portions. As Itza explained how she transformed her buying and cooking habits, Claudia chimed in,

> I was telling my mom the other day [that] I remember we used to eat a lot but now [she] limits portions. She learned from education, and she tells us it's never too late to learn because once we have our kids, we'll be able to learn and show them.

Additionally, Hermosa and Itza learned much about child development and psychology from the training they received. Subsequently, they taught their children how to get along with peers. Krystal asked how Itza's and Hermosa's education had helped their families. Itza explained she is finally doing what she could not accomplish when she was younger – get educated, advice she gives to those she loves." Hermosa added, "When I graduated as a promotora, all of my children were there." Hermosa looked at Claudia and Itza and said, "I was happy to see the support of my family and to see I was making my kids proud."

Hermosa and Itza received few educational opportunities before, so they believe in seizing any educational opportunity. Both began volunteering at AVANCE, a nonprofit organization providing support to Latino/a families through services and education. They then heard from other women about a Parent Teacher Association (PTA) at a nearby elementary school. Hermosa explained, "We went there because we heard the person in charge was teaching other women in the group how to make jewelry." *Afinidad's* PTA has no public school affiliation and Hermosa serves as an *Afinidad* PTA officer. See Chapter 4 regarding how Hermosa informs parents of the hidden effects of Texas House Bill 5 (Texas Education Agency, n.d.).

Hermosa continued as Claudia translated, "From there, we would slowly become aware of even more opportunities." Itza added, "We started going to [*Convivio*] (see Chapter 4) and there we would each teach each other whatever we knew." Hermosa and Itza hungered for more educational opportunities; they are taking GED classes at *Afinidad*, another community organization (see Chapter 4). Sister Joan, who leads this organization, described ways people can keep advancing in their education, starting with the GED, taught by local school district personnel: "We have step-up programs: GED, [English as a second language] (ESL), citizenship. After people pass their GED tests (in Spanish or English), they go on to ESL classes. After that, they take the citizenship classes. All of these are for people to get better jobs."

Receiving an associate's degree proves difficult if one has not earned a high school diploma or equivalent. Thus, the GED becomes a college pathway and income for many adult colonia residents. Sister Joan said it takes one to two years for a person to get a GED; a waiting list exists. *Afinidad* has made the GED program available to people inside and outside of *Corazón*. Hermosa and Itza explained the GED classes occur once weekly at the Tutoring Center. GED classes follow the same schedule as the local public school district, since the district pays for the GED teacher. Staff divide classes equally between two subjects from August to May. Once students finish a semester, they can take electronic subject exams. If they pass, they can take two new subjects the following semester.

A friend introduced Itza and Hermosa to the Tutorial Center and these mothers began to help *Corazón* youth. While Hermosa and Itza might have started out volunteering, they have now extended their rhizomes to affect community health and education and are working towards professional growth. "What do you hope to do with your GED?" Krystal asked the women. They beamed with confidence and excitement, "We expect to be able to work and, if possible, continue getting a technical education or something" Itza shared, "There's even a possibility for a substitute teacher job." As Krystal typed furiously, the women kept talking, now more to each other and Claudia. "I sometimes think I'm doing now what I didn't do when I was younger," Itza explained, "but when I was younger, I didn't have these opportunities." The women kept smiling at each other encouragingly. Hermosa chimed in, "Now that we're older, we see the opportunity; we can't let it go because it doesn't come twice."

Summary

We inquired: What are the educational opportunities and practices of *Corazón* children and adults? We explored answers for pre-school, primary, secondary, college, and adult education learners. Low educational opportunities have worked against residents' intense desire to get educated, but neighbors and families provided educational support. Specifically, we discussed youth and adult academic goals, family influences, obstacles, effective teachers, and the ways residents have rhizomed around barriers.

Nobody expects for primary and secondary teachers to solve multi-faceted systemic issues related to ethnicity, gender, neighborhood status, and social class. However, we can support families in educational endeavors. Ideas include conducting family needs surveys, collaborating in inquiry communities and activist parent coalitions, creating welcoming school environments, hosting bi/polylingual family nights, and partnering with families for school and community events (Rubin, Abrego, & Sutterby, 2012). Classroom-level ideas involve: teaching families and students to articulate their needs; providing tutoring, mentoring, and effective bilingual programs; and educating more Spanish-speaking teachers (Gorski, 2013). Students lower their affective filters and learn more readily when their classrooms and schools honor their languages and lived experiences (Freire, 2000). Above all, we aspire to provide a collective Third Space for students to reconceptualize who they are and what they may accomplish in and out of school (Gutiérrez, 2008).

We cannot encourage students to explore this transformation with us until we ask ourselves some hard questions, such as "What kind of politics am I doing in the classroom?" As educators, we work always for and against something because all curricula, all pedagogies are political (Shor & Freire, 1987). However, we can reflect on our own positioning to help students to find their context-driven identities amid issues of power. Power, enveloping our lives, relates to many education mechanisms, such as No Child Left Behind. As Kathy found as a former local high school teacher, fighting against a testing panopticon proves difficulty. Through collaboration, we can find ways to help youth to achieve their dreams. Many *Corazón* residents do just that—toil to pursue their education and labor to help others.

Questions to Ponder

1. How has No Child Left Behind (NCLB) affected people in your community? What other school policies have impacted students' educational experiences in your community?
2. How can educators get more involved outside of the classroom to create a stronger home-school connection for their students?
3. The devastating *Corazón* college statistics did not align with our observations. What is your community's college attainment rate? Do the statistics represent your observations?
4. What factors influence youth in your community to drop out? How do these factors relate to our chapter?
5. What cultural factors in your community encourage adults to continue their education?

· 1 0 ·

CONCLUSIONS AND IMPLICATIONS
Poeta's Dream

As Kathy concluded conversing with Poeta, Kathy asked the elderly *Corazón* activist her dream for *Corazón*. Poeta said *Corazón's* struggle is now internal and relates to education. Poeta alluded to past and present civil rights struggles of U.S. Latinos/as and the Latino education crisis (Gándara, 2010):

> … *En cuestión de educación, yo pienso que es lo más importante porque es el futuro, y no más de [Corazón], es el futuro de aquí de este país, ahora porque los hispanos tienen derechos igual que otra persona, los mismos derechos, y están batallando mucho ahorita … por la cuestión de entrar a las universidades* [Education is essential because it's the future, not for just *Corazón*, but for the future of this country. Now Hispanics have the same rights as other people, but they're struggling right now in entering universities].

In the next statement, Poeta mentioned the USA needs healthy Latino/a professionals, which relates to Latino healthcare and education disparities. Poeta's heart ached to see discouraged *Corazón* youth:

> *Me gustaría ver en este país lleno de hispanos buenos, sanos, con carreras, que sean buenos ciudadanos. Eso lo que lo quisiera de aquí. ¿Cómo sabemos si tienen capacidad para ser ingenieros, arquitectos, doctores? Claro que los hay. Que les den conferencias, que les digan que valen, que les digan que pueden ser grandes gente en el futuro, muchachas y muchachos. Que les inyecten ese ánino* [almost touching her short hair with both sets of

fingers spread out, as if her head is alit], *esas ganas de superarse. Eso es lo que veo más aquí porque es muy triste ver los muchachos ociosos, con sus mentes sin ideas, sin proyectos. Con ese desánimo de que, "¿Para qué estudio? ¿Para qué? De nada me va a servir"* (almost touching her shoulders with both hands) [I'd like to see in this country full of good Hispanics, healthy, with careers, who are good citizens. That's what I want here. How do we know if they have the capacity to be engineers, architects, doctors? Of course they have the capacity. We need youth conferences here so people can tell the male and female youth that they're worthwhile, that they can be grand people. These people need to inject the youth with motivation to overcome obstacles. That's what I see here because it's sad to see idle boys, their minds without ideas, without projects. With the discouragement that studying isn't worth it].

David Gutiérrez (1999) connected Mexican-heritage youth's immobility and marginalization to the gangs, drugs, and incarceration of this group. Next, Poeta defined herself not by material possessions, but by her values:

¿Sabe por qué lo digo con tanta pasión? Porque yo no tuve eso de joven ... A mí no me asusta ser pobre, al contrario, me siento bien orgullosa de ser pobre porque soy una persona buena, trabajadora, honrada, y cristiana. Eso para mí son los valores ... Pues mucho materialismo ... Aunque estés rodeado de lujos, de dinero ... esa no es la riqueza del ser humano, son sus valores [Do you know why I have so much passion? I didn't have these opportunities when I was young. I am not afraid to be poor. On the contrary, I feel proud of being poor because I am a good person, hardworking, honest, and Christian. Those are values to me. Much materialism exists. Although a person might be surrounded with luxury, money, this isn't what makes a human wealthy. Wealth is from a person's ideas].

As in Chapter 9, Poeta declared a person's values, or internal issues, trump materialism, or external issues. Colonialism lingers in people's minds and relates to the subaltern taking on Western values, such as materialism (Anzaldúa, 2007). Next, Poeta wanted *Corazón* youth to be activists. She appeared to associate activism with civic engagement and fighting for *Corazón*:

Por eso digo yo que la lucha de esta colonia, bueno yo así pienso, se luchó mucho pero si tú no luchas por algo, no lo vas a apreciar ni a querer. Y por es yo estoy muy contenta de vivir aquí, por la lucha que tuvimos [For this reason I say the struggle of this colonia, well, this is what I think. This colonia fought, but if you don't fight for something, you won't appreciate it or care. And I'm thrilled to live here, for the fight we had].

Introduction

Poeta's remarks and this book testify that *Corazón* residents fight for every millimeter of justice, despite prejudice and exclusion. In our collaboration with *Corazón* residents, residents have astounded us in their struggle for liberation and their care for others. After all, caring and social justice overlap (Campano, Ghiso, & Welch, 2016). Some *Corazón* residents have overcome barriers through slantwise activities and have acted as rhizomes to achieve their goals. Others have found sanctuary and power in Third Space. However, even some who work across the street misunderstand *Corazón*. It is not enough for colonia residents to "unveil the world of oppression … [and] commit themselves to its transformation" (Freire, 2000, p. 54), which is why we sought to begin honest, purposeful dialogue and myth busting.

In this final chapter, we draw conclusions and reflect on our experiences by discussing research dilemmas throughout the data gathering process. We mention these instances related to power dynamics inherent in research. Next, we highlight three major implications that resurfaced continuously: Third Space, community service learning impact, and academic disparities. Finally, we review our purpose for this book, return to questions posed in the Book Introduction, and allow our theoretical framework to prompt additional questions for future research.

Section and Chapter Summaries

In the Book Introduction, we explained our theoretical frameworks of social justice and Third Space related to education, language, literacy, and technology, and the analytical tools of bridge, power, rhizome, and slantwise. We also discussed our research methodology, including limitations. We explained why we believe colonias exist and why their marginalization continues, e.g., colonialism and the coloniality of power (Quijano, 2000).

Section I

Section I built background. In Chapter 1, we explained our life experiences, privilege, and disciplinary socialization (Caelli et al., 2003). Additionally, we discussed our subjectivity and articulated our epistemic beliefs, or theory of knowledge, which influenced every research and writing decision. Our epistemological beliefs relate to knowing through dialogue, experience, risk-taking, and specificity of time, place, and people. For this reason, we avoided the present tense to discuss what co-researchers said or did, as we attempt no generalizations about the entire colonia or about all colonias. Next, we explained our ontological views, or how we relate to others, which included respecting co-researchers and realizing our subjectivity and privilege. Our ontological beliefs affected our connections with community members, data gathering and interpretation, and this collaborative writing process.

Chapter 1 included Kathy's venture into community service learning (CSL) in *Corazón*. She discussed building *confianza* [trust] with residents through community engagement and the decolonial perspective of researchers giving back (Paris & Winn, 2014). María's story outlined her initial involvement with *Corazón* as a tutor, volunteer, and researcher. Krystal highlighted her *Corazón* experiences and explained her interest in, and disposition towards, the research project. Claudia, contributor and inspirer, explained how she grew up in *Corazón* and how her childhood experiences influenced her pro-bilingual stances. Contributor Irma revealed her contributions and interests as a researcher by discussing her role in building *confianza* with Rita, current Tutorial Center coordinator, and making social justice connections.

We described some aspects of Texas colonias in Chapter 2 vis-à-vis key Rio Grande Valley (RGV) characteristics. We discussed how most colonia characterizations relate to deficits, not strengths (Dolhinow, 2010). We drew attention to the history and laws concerning Texas colonias. Specifically, we highlighted alarming and belittling practices that entrap colonia residents, which include sellers who confiscate land from colonia lot buyers if the latter miss one payment after paying religiously for years. While Texas lawmakers have passed laws to improve conditions in colonias, unethical developers persist, encountering little resistance from those in power. To debunk the myth that colonia residents burden state or national economies, we asserted colonia residents pay sales taxes on goods, pay county taxes, and rarely take advantage of social welfare programs for fear of receiving unwanted attention from immigration services. Conversely, these are neoliberal ideas because governments can wash their hands and not help (Duménil & Lévy, 2013). Finally, we described how colonias serve as unique research sites. We discussed how transnational, borderlands contexts can serve as a Third Space, teeming with potential and conflict related to culture, education, language, literacy, and technology.

In Chapter 3, we focused on *Corazón* and highlighted its similarities to other colonias, including residents' neighborliness. We described *Corazón's* demographics, emphasizing the Latino presence and immigration laws. We outlined various aspects of *Corazón's* past and present marginalization, including potable water and sewage services; homes; streets, sidewalks, and walking paths; electricity; police services; and public transportation. These services are lacking in at least 442 colonias (Federal Reserve Bank of Dallas, 2015). However, we concluded by reiterating the strengths of *Corazón*, including the strong presence of community activists, who have been working for decades to improve *Corazón*. We also highlighted residents' positive perceptions of *Corazón*, the thriving businesses driven by savvy entrepreneurs, and the freedom in a community unrestricted by city ordinances.

Chapter 4 explored *Corazón's* Third Spaces, including *Afinidad*, devoted to health promotion and community empowerment. *Afinidad* works vigorously to teach residents to become politically active. *Afinidad's promotoras* combine health and political activism in a Third Space. *Afinidad's* Parent Teacher Association (PTA) members inform other residents about influential laws, such as Texas House Bill 5 (HB 5), and the impact if parents sign the forms from the schools. *Corazón's* PTA is slantwise because PTAs function usually in schools. As an extension of *Afinidad*, the Civic Organization improves voter turnout, political activism, and community involvement.

Next, we outlined another extension of *Afinidad*, the Tutorial Center, which provides a space for homework, projects, enrichment, and Mexican-diasporic practices associated with food and celebrations. The Center has helped participating children and families immensely. Youth explore their academic identities through enrichment programs and teacher candidate (TC) mentoring. The Center receives some funding from Catholic religious organizations.

We explicated the impact of *Corazón* religious organizations, including Catholic and Baptist churches; both have had a strong presence in *Corazón's* educational and civic landscapes. The Catholic Church rhizomed and created a small religious book and DVD lending library. Parishioners also engaged in slantwise practices by conducting their own door-to-door census to determine registered voters and Catholics. The current priest is helping the youth to carry justice torches. Next, the Baptist Church empowers *Corazón* youth through a leadership club and supports many youth in educational endeavors.

Convivio, on *Corazón's* outskirts, appears to have made the most educational impact on adults, as residents have learned trade skills, such as health promotion, and computer basics, and have taken classes for personal fulfillment, such as jewelry making. *Convivio* hosts monthly meetings with leaders from the colonia organizations. At least two residents accompany each leader; outside officials address colonia problems. The slantwise meetings are grass roots and unorthodox, but they achieve socially accepted aims—to empower colonia residents (Campbell & Heyman, 2007). We found most organizations presented in this chapter promoted political activism, not neoliberalism. Thus, our findings differ from Dolhinow's (2010) New Mexico colonia findings.

Section II

Section II focused on sociocultural contexts of religion, language, and literacy. We highlight religion in Chapter 5 as it connects to culture, denominational intolerance, gender, language, social class, and neighborhood. We discussed Catholic hybrid or Third Space celebrations, which blend Catholicism and indigenous Mexican religions and cultures. Next, we outlined various religious clashes, including parents' and children's conflicting attitudes towards Catholicism. While parents genuinely embrace the culture and religion of the *tierra madre* [motherland], some children in Father John's congregation lack religious passion. They might be battling with Mexican and U.S. identities. Certainly, identities evolve and blend with language, immigration status, and race (Ortiz & Telles, 2012).

Additionally, we explained the beautiful history of the Lady of Guadalupe and acknowledged her divine connections to the subaltern and social justice. Finally, we opened our discussion to include the Baptist Church. Sabio conducted sermons in Spanish and empowered church members by pushing strong messages of self-accountability, morality, and education. We included the Baptist Church as a contrast to indigenous beliefs and practices, as this Christian denomination does not support *el Día de los Muertos*.

In Chapter 6, we moved into critical aspects of *Corazón*—language and literacy. Spanish and translanguaging dominated oral communication. When looking at the linguistic landscape of *Corazón*, most commercial signs existed in English, odd considering most residents were Spanish-dominant. However, inside of mini-markets, printed newspapers in Spanish sold more than English ones. While most adults preferred Spanish literacy, most residents possessed few print *literacy* materials in Spanish. We found residents maintained their mother tongue at home through family interactions.

Next, we explained how some mothers, such as Hermosa, taught their children to read in Spanish; many sent their children to the Tutorial Center for homework assistance and English reading and writing tutoring. In this chapter, we also explicated the intersection of religion, language, and literacy. Most *Corazón* residents prayed in Spanish and parents taught their children prayers in Spanish. However, some Catholic and Baptist staff believed English was the language of power for success and they encouraged youth to embrace

English. Bracketing can oppress Spanish-dominant pupils (García & Kleifgen, 2010). Some parents condoned bracketing because they felt Spanish was for the home, while English was for school.

Regardless, some parents expressed motivation to learn English to help their children academically and to find better jobs. Furthermore, we found many *Corazón* children acted as rhizomic language brokers by translating for interlocutors (Orellana, 2009). Youth engaged in translanguaging, especially with each other. They behaved as rhizomes because they worked around language obstacles, made connections with interlocutors, and employed linguistic and social strategies. The children created maps, not tracings, and prevailed between worlds and languages in a Third Space (Deleuze & Guattari, 1987).

Chapter 7 focused on *Corazón* children's digital literacy, with an emphasis on limited authentic digital experiences during school and for homework. We gave a counter-example by describing Joy's digital and multimodal activities and projects. Joy teaches many *Corazón* students; this middle school English teacher has engaged students in authentic, generative digital experiences. When Claudia volunteered at the Tutorial Center, she helped children with technology and co-developed electronic journal prompts. Out-of-school-digital access and practices of *Corazón* children focused on entertainment and friendship. These youth lacked digital literacy guidance or instruction involving critical thinking, collaboration, and complex reading and writing skills. On the positive side, the children bypassed digital obstacles, perhaps for Spanish maintenance and revitalization.

Section III

Section III involved education. Chapter 8 outlined the history, purpose, and organization of the reciprocal CSL, and social justice and literacy impact. The TCs connected to tutees and *Corazón*'s plight. These relationships helped TCs to reevaluate rumors. Additionally, TCs learned to build on theories, as Ella did when she coined "to rhizome." Ella aimed to teach students to circumvent structural barriers. By broadening their literacy definitions and affirming *Corazón*'s strengths, TCs realized they could become profoundly better educators who gave back to the community in meaningful ways. *Corazón* children also benefited from CSL. They learned they and their families possessed strengths. Youth began to enjoy the disciplines and drew connections between disciplinary literacy and their neighborhood. Anhelo's and others newfound love of poetry created pathways to express pain and joy; thus, children learned to reposition themselves within disciplines.

Chapter 9 highlighted *Corazón's* educational landscape. First, we explained education opportunities and issues relevant to *Corazón* pre-school, primary, secondary, and tertiary learners. We discussed Joy and Claudia, two remarkable teachers who attempted to push back hegemonic education and language policies. Despite increasing high school graduation rates, *Corazón* had a college graduation rate of 1.3% in 2010. Some outsiders might believe parents are not helping the children. However, why did the five-year-olds score in the top in the region for academic readiness? Indeed, participating youth and parents were impassioned about formal education. Thus, instead of taking an individual level approach, we looked to governmental policies and out-of-school factors. We believe OSFs, such as poverty and the home-school disconnect, might relate to the youth's dismal high school and college attainment. We shared stories about *Corazón* college students' motivations to complete college, family obligations, and rhizomic practices, such as joining the military. Last, we demonstrated adult education's role by telling Hermosa's and Itza's stories, cultural influences, and education's impact on family members.

In this next section, we discuss a few misunderstandings we had during data gathering because we would be disingenuous to pretend that over 10 years of data gathering were perfect. We want to make our research process come to life and to erase any romanticized images in your mind of our work.

The Researchers' Experiences

Humans interact in messy ways, making research dilemmas inevitable. We experienced challenges during our journey, also. Mentioning these dilemmas coincides with our beliefs in humanizing research that explores power issues. This section focuses on our experiences conducting research by highlighting research lessons learned. We theorize power and perception in these processes.

Miscommunication

Despite our wonderful relationships with *Corazón* co-researchers, we discuss some dilemmas to show divergent emic (insider) and etic (outsider) perspectives and goals, misunderstandings' influence on data gathering, and our growth.

Corazón leaders considered the children always. Thus, sometimes a leader told Kathy's research assistants to assist drop-in children (not part of the May project); teacher candidates (TCs) already had tutees. Yet research assistants' jobs involved gathering consent/assent forms and data and they scurried to complete work in the intensive three-week program. To address this challenge, Kathy would explain the time crunch to the leader and redirect Kathy's assistants. Because the leader did not want the children to miss tutoring or gardening, she would not allow Kathy's assistants to interview the children sometimes. These instances demonstrate the unpredictable nature of the research process. From these experiences, we learned to explain research assistants' roles in advance.

The next predicament related to Kathy's failure in seeking permission from all possible leaders. Kathy had had received one *Corazón* leader's permission to conduct research before seeking institutional review board (IRB) permission and had emailed this leader the university's IRB approval letter and IRB-stamped assent and consent forms, detailing all research procedures. However, Kathy did not inform the leader's supervisor, whom Kathy called a few days into data gathering about another matter. During the phone conversation, the supervisor asked, "You're not going to interview the children, are you?" Gathering her breath, Kathy explained to the supervisor that parents and children would sign consent/assent forms before data gathering, nothing would transpire without child and parent permission, and data would not reveal sensitive information. Immediately after the phone call, Kathy emailed interview questions to this supervisor, who then approved the research.

From this experience, it became clear one leader did not grant or restrict access to children and parents. Instead, data gathering presented complications because of various leaders, each of whom can steer researchers in different directions. Although Kathy did not need to seek permission from the leader's supervisor previously, we learned processes vary with people and time and we needed to involve all leaders from the onset.

The next interaction related to *confianza* [trust]. Kathy has interacted positively with *Corazón* leaders, e.g., presenting at conferences, eating at restaurants, and participating in *Afinidad's* fundraising luncheons and Tutorial Center's musicals and *tamaladas* [tamale Christmas celebrations]. María, second author, attended these *tamaladas*, also. One leader resided in *Corazón* and guarded families' privacy; she would not allow Kathy's students to call or talk to parents about the children's and families' strengths. Kathy reiterated the assignment was for TCs to prepare lessons focused on family and child assets, but perhaps the *Corazón* resident thought parents might reveal sensitive information, understandable because some researchers sensationalize marginalized communities (Agyeman, 2008). Because of professors' privilege, the academy does not deserve to read about the subaltern's pain (Tuck & Yang, 2014). Thus, we realized building trust takes time and that context influences perceptions. We learned to have contingency plans, also. For instance, Kathy asked TCs to write reflections on community strengths they witnessed as they drove to and from the Center instead of basing their funds of knowledge reflections on conversations with parents.

A little later in the conversation, the same leader asked Kathy what Krystal, third author, asked during child interviews. A few girls had remarked about their secret interview with Krystal; this concerned the leader, and rightly so. As a safeguard, children should disclose to leaders what outsiders ask them. Immediately, Kathy brought Krystal into the leader's office; Krystal said she did not tell the girls the interview was a secret. Krystal had interviewed two girls together, as the one fluent in English translated for the other. Grateful for their patience, Krystal offered both girls extra candy as a thank you and asked them not to tell the other children about the extra treat. The leader was fine with the interviews after Krystal's explanation. This instance taught us to expect (and embrace) leaders who question our procedures, as their goal is to protect children.

Another trust issue emerged when the same leader, Kathy, and TCs walked around *Corazón*. Meanwhile, Krystal was to conduct an English focus group with the children, and María a Spanish group. The discussions centered on youth drawings of *Corazón* because we wanted to learn the children's positive perceptions of their community to challenge outsiders' rumors. Unbeknownst to Kathy, María, and Krystal, the leader had asked two Tutorial Center assistants to supervise the focus groups. During the youth discussions, Krystal and María felt uncomfortable asking follow-up questions. The children, normally friendly and talkative with Krystal, clammed up. More than likely, the leader had placed monitors in the rooms to ensure children's safety, as per *Protecting God's Children*, standards for Catholic clergy and laity (National Catholic Risk Retention Group, n.d.); see Chapter 4. Additionally, we realized having the children discuss their colonia might be misconstrued because many outsiders pathologize it. Thus, the following year Kathy asked the children to discuss what Spanish meant to them.

While Krystal served as research assistant and had interacted with the leader and children often, María had little contact with *Corazón* since 2011, and the new children and staff did not know María well. Kathy introduced María to the leader just before the focus group, explaining María would conduct a Spanish youth focus group. The leader's face drew a blank when she took in María. María explained she conducted her dissertation fieldwork in *Corazón* and had volunteered and researched often in *Corazón*. Still blank. María mentioned attending the *tamalada* about five months earlier, and then the leader knew her; see Chapter 1 regarding María's field entry.

In retrospect, we learned to sit alongside leaders before data gathering to introduce all researchers involved and ask permission for every research aspect, as some leaders had changed over the years. We realized we needed to ensure leaders had read and understood all procedures, as they juggle multiple responsibilities. Last, we realized leaders' loyalty to *Corazón* children. Even Kathy's TCs acknowledged one leader's role when they explained their visual metaphors; "[She is] the tree. She is from the colonia. She is grounded … She is protecting the kids." We cared for the children, but we faced challenges and rhizomed around them to gather data.

Belief Challenges

While we expect dilemmas in processes wherein the researchers are outsiders, dilemmas over beliefs surprised us, as we (the authors) focused on community strengths, including culture and language. However, it became apparent our beliefs did not align always. Specifically, we discuss challenges related to one male co-researcher's language and cultural beliefs and some university administrators' pedagogical beliefs.

Krystal met the man in June 2015. As with previous interviewees, Krystal asked him how he believed *Corazón* residents maintain Spanish and their culture. He responded that residents should learn English and assimilate to American culture to prosper. His beliefs related his deep care for *Corazón* and he discussed how many outsiders stereotyped Mexicans and colonia residents. He said, "I'm not anti-Spanish. I know who I am. *Soy indio*" [I am indigenous Mexican]. "I do understand that I must assimilate." He continued:

> I don't know if you remember a while back we were out there demonstrating for amnesty. We had the Mexican flags. The people up there in Washington get scared of us. Then we took the national anthem and translated it to Spanish. It scares people and then we have 10 babies. [The Anglos think] we're taking it over; Mexico is coming back to reclaim Texas.

Actually, many Mexican-heritage people in the Southwest possess ambivalent beliefs about Mexican nationalism, as they straddle the Mexico-U.S. fissure (D. Gutiérrez, 1999). Nevertheless, Krystal could sense the older man appropriating the interview because of his assimilation and bilingual education passions. To him, discrimination related minimally to social injustice. While Krystal had aimed to focus on *Corazón* strengths, including Spanish, Krystal used her better judgement to evaluate the situation and to listen actively, without challenging him or losing sight of her own position as a researcher. This situation taught us to see things from participants' perspectives. For example, this man has labored to empower *Corazón* people. He encourages them to vote and to seize educational opportunities. His love for *Corazón* propelled his beliefs and words.

Kathy faced challenges, also. She experienced difficulty convincing some university administrators to value community service learning (CSL). Some preferred that she operate in a school, believing teacher candidates (TCs) learn more about teaching in school settings. These administrators said the National Council of Accreditation of Teacher Education (NCATE) wanted only school-based experiences for TCs. Kathy shared her published articles with some administrators, demonstrating TCs learned much from CSL. As one TC said, "Some teachers don't even allow you to work one-on-one with the students. You just sit there and watch. It doesn't help."

Yet, because Kathy's findings did not convince some superiors, Kathy contacted an NCATE-affiliated representative and forwarded his email to administrators; his email stated CSL complemented and augmented TCs' school-based experiences. Others worry what the Texas Education Agency, one of our many governing bodies, will say about CSL. Thus, the panopticon, an all-seeing control mechanism, churns in educational institutions (Foucault, 1991) and administrators have power over researchers. Unfortunately, some may abandon beneficial projects because of fear. However, we discovered risk-taking and perseverance can improve our field and we learned to challenge commonly-held pedagogical assumptions that privilege school-based knowledge over home and community knowledge.

Theorizing Dilemmas

We learned many things from these challenges. First, leaders may perceive us as outsiders, despite the time we spend in a neighborhood. Second, although professors may uphold a community's best interests, we must balance data gathering with community privacy and perceptions. Third, we should not assume participants share our beliefs and we should respect their views. Last, we must be prepared to defend a community-based pedagogy and encourage other educators to take risks with us to advance the education field for diverse communities. In Third Space theory, disagreements provide intersubjective researchers with lessons. Bhabha (2004) referred to "... those moments or processes ... produced in the articulation of cultural differences" as "in-between spaces" (p. 2). These Third Space cultural conflicts can help us to outgrow ourselves.

Emic and Etic Perspectives

Emic (insider) and etic (outsider) dichotomies affected our research process, as some colonia leaders' perceptions of these binaries can present barriers and opportunities and can shape our research (McAreavey & Das, 2013). Claudia, book contributor and long-time *Corazón* resident, influenced our research findings. Although we live outside of *Corazón*, we do not consider ourselves as complete outsiders. Instead, we have straddled a liminal space as community-involved university researchers. Additionally, the complex fusion of *Corazón* people and our backgrounds and beliefs determine our positionality. At any given moment, we (the authors) might exist as insiders and outsiders simultaneously or we may straddle the two positions. These dual emic/etic roles may have confused leaders.

Power

Although Kathy, María, and Krystal connected to *Corazón* residents throughout the research, we realized our personal and social power, some participants' views, and the impact of both real and perceived power on interactions. Despite growing up working class and starting in *Corazón* as an untenured assistant professor, Kathy is white and now is a middle-class full professor. She has garnered privilege from these contexts. *Corazón* residents may have seen Kathy as powerful and may have withheld information. Next, María hails from Uruguay, one of Latin America's most European countries (Eakin, 2007). Since María speaks Uruguayan Spanish, border-Spanish speakers may believe María's dialect as more prestigious because of colonialism (Anzaldúa, 2007). Krystal comes from the mid-Rio Grande Valley (RGV) and does not speak much Spanish, so *Corazón* residents may have believed she held more status, as English serves as the language of power.

Kathy, María, and Krystal are light-skinned. Skin color, even between Latinos/as, relates to power (Ortiz & Telles, 2012). Last, we possessed more formal education than most *Corazón* residents, which can also cause power imbalances.

Undoubtedly, power pervades life. Power flip-flops between researchers and participants. Krystal could not ask many questions when an older male appropriated the interview; thus, he held power over a 30-year-old female researcher. Certainly, respondents can bite back. They can refuse to participate and answer questions, and may withdraw completely. Some teacher candidates (TCs) and *Corazón* residents refused to sign consent forms. "Refusal in research makes way for other r-words—for resistance, reclaiming, recovery, reciprocity, repatriation, regeneration" (Tuck & Yang, 2014, p. 244).

Moje (2000a) engaged in a tenuous research project with a middle school language arts teacher; Moje asked us to consider how we negotiate and contest positions and power in research. Critical pedagogue Shor (1997) experienced curricular conflicts with his students, also. Moje and Shor grew from these disagreements and interrogated their practices. Undoubtedly, fieldwork should change us. Our research challenges humbled us and helped us to consider how insiders might perceive us. We attempted reflexivity by making adjustments and we endeavored an ethic of care to adjust for imbalances.

Kathy appeared dirty and she smelled stinky from gardening with TCs, children, and parent volunteers, which may have decreased her lofty professorial status. Yet the ultimate power imbalance transpires when we write about a community and re-present their images and words (Neilsen, 2014). Thus, we invited Claudia as co-author. Due to her teaching job, rigorous master's program, and family commitments, Claudia could contribute only. However, she and two participants read a manuscript draft and we made substantial changes from their suggestions.

Rhizome

Moreover, these rhizomic principles presented themselves through our dilemmas: assigning rupture (working around and through challenges), heterogeneity (each leader followed different practices), multiplicity (valuing divergent perspectives), and not a tracing, but a map; for the latter we realized practices change with people and contexts. Next, the rhizomic principle of connection proved vital. Connection involved seeing more similarities than differences and realizing we needed to explain all procedures and researchers explicitly to all leaders. We valued these challenges because they caused us to grow new branches with the community (Deleuze & Guattari, 1987).

Major Implications

Welcome to (Third) Space

Imagine your bewilderment in a distant land. You stop to ask for directions. Are you close to your destination? Suddenly you see a billboard advertising, in your mother tongue, "Lost? Come here. We do not care from whence you came or the jingle in your pocket. We will get you where you want to go." A beaming building beckons around the corner, with a Martian green sign, "Welcome to Third Space." Are you in *Oz*? Once inside, you gain power. The experience transforms you and you transform others. Everyone inside aims to empower the community as a whole and to transform individual lives through the acknowledgement and appreciation of the cultures that bind them.

These types of spaces abounded in *Corazón*. If we were creating a list of Third Spaces, the Tutorial Center would be number one. Kathy's May Session program offered many opportunities for children to create resistant academic identities, but the Center did not limit its function as an in-between space for children. Adults used the Center for meetings and classes. Although the Center is Catholic-affiliated, staff welcome non-Christians. A Jewish Holocaust survivor related his harrowing tale to the Catholic youth group, priest, and volunteers; see Chapter 4. Father John told Kathy he chose the tutorial building as a neutral, respectful space for the Jewish man.

Yet Third Space exists as an uneasy place because boundaries meander and evolve. Incongruent phenomena, ideas, and people may occupy Third Space. Third Space can be virtual and imagined (Soja, 1996), not just something physical. Anzaldúa (2002) called Third Space *nepantla* to signify the borderlands. This is because Third Space comprises tension and growth, hope and loss in the diaspora (Clifford, 1994).

Joy and Claudia, teachers in the local school district, created a Third Space in their public school classrooms. Joy and Claudia chose to work through the social inequalities, including test-prep curricula, typically seen in classrooms serving low-income Latino/a children (Gándara, 2010). In contrast to a decontextualized curriculum, Joy provided her students with an education that was both culturally relevant and multimodal. Claudia taught

English-dominant students Spanish and involved them in many collaborative, authentic activities.

Giving Back

In Chapter 8, we discussed how the community service learning (CSL) benefitted teacher candidates (TCs) and children. For liberatory CSL and research, all parties must benefit, including the researchers and community (Maynes et al., 2013). Thus, we took reciprocal, equal partnership stances). Because we believe in social justice and Third Space in education, we reject a banking notion and realize co-researchers have many gifts and are experts (Freire, 2000).

The CSL project Kathy has implemented since 2006 has been helpful to *Corazón's* Tutorial Center regarding beautification of the grounds, increased children attendance during the May program, books for the Center library, and increased funding from agencies and foundations. News reports have featured the project and Kathy and Alma (inaugural tutorial coordinator), with others, organized a national funders' visit to the Center. The walking path we designed and created in 2007 has provided a central, safe place for outdoor exercise, helping female walkers emotionally, physically, and socially (Bussert-Webb, 2012). Community organizer Janie said she and other walkers (mostly women) use the mile/kilometer signs (which a colonia business installed) to set distance and time goals for exercise.

Furthermore, an instructor's presence during the CSL demonstrates an instructor's passion and commitment, which can motivate co-researchers. Our personas were different in the CSL project as well; we knew each other more deeply than in classroom settings. As TC Lorena explained, "Not only was it fun, it also helped to bond us, not only with my colleagues but with the students as well." Lorena's quote relates to the social aspects of learning and building community. Indeed, class discussions have consisted mostly of dialogue and group work. TCs, trusting each other and Kathy, took risks. Shared practices and visions become inseparable in collective Third Space, which transforms relationships (K. Gutiérrez, 2008).

Next, as teacher-researchers of communities and in community, we must continue the CSL at the same site for trust and long-term neighborhood benefits. Kathy stays in contact with residents and staff, has students enrolled in her courses do activities with Tutorial Center children throughout the year, assists the Center with projects, and acts as a liaison between the Center and

Kathy's university. We participated in a National Endowment for the Arts grant and Kathy and Alma co-organized a colonia visit of over 15 nationwide foundation representatives.

Kathy's former students maintain long-term relationships with *Corazón's* Tutorial Center; staff members have mentioned Kathy's students continue to volunteer. A few weeks after our 2015 course ended, Kathy saw Rachel, who had continued tutoring Sonrisa. "See," Rita, current tutorial coordinator, said pointing to the pair, "they come back." Kathy visited with Rachel, who said, "This [May 2015 course] is the best class I've had. I came back because I love this place." Sonrisa had drawn an interpretation of a story and a representation of herself; Rachel had learned this reader response strategy in our course. Rachel had continued to embrace multimodal literacy instruction. Earlier, Kathy doubted Rachel would return. Rachel wrote this reflection two days into the CSL program: "I know that the neighborhood doesn't have a good reputation, so I went into the class, thinking a bit negatively." Seeing Sonrisa, who was finished with summer coursework, return to work with Rachel, confirmed this CSL program made a difference in Sonrisa, also. Perhaps the abounding strengths emanating from children, staff, and parents in a marginalized community caused TCs to make a commitment to social justice.

We return to our Third Space and Social Justice visual model, Figure I.1 from our Book Introduction. To make education stronger, we need three legs—universities, schools, and homes. While *Corazón* possesses a powerful voice, praxis or reflection and action (Freire, 2000) require universities, schools, and neighborhoods collaborating. Kania and Kramer (2011) described collective impact versus individual intervention. Collective impact involves much more than universities and schools, however. Businesses, governments, organizations, and individuals can collaborate to combat social issues, such as poverty. Five collective impact conditions involve constant communication, a backbone support organization, reinforcing activities, and common agendas and measurements. Thus, to meet *Corazón's* and other communities' needs, we may co-create an organized, continuing process, instead of single solutions with less impact.

Closing the Margins

Corazón five-year-olds' stellar performance on an early-childhood test demonstrated school-readiness skills. However, a system they depend on desperately—formal education—has shunned them. Many global issues widened colonia residents' achievement gaps, which demonstrates that the global influences the local. Out-of-school factors, such as poverty, immigration, and neighborhood status, influenced *Corazón* residents' educational achievement. School-related injustices left them behind, also. Inadequate, inauthentic digital school experiences and a test-prep milieu starved many colonia youth and increased their academic disconnections. Although most residents in the surrounding city and *Corazón* are Latinos/as, *Corazón* residents experienced much lower high school and college graduation rates than the surrounding city. Thus, the educational disparity between the colonia and city does not appear to relate to race.

Most local public school teachers are Latinos/as, also. Yet perhaps some of these educators lack training and knowledge to recognize and address *Corazón* youth's gifts. Although nondominant educators usually possess more activist and diversity outlooks than white educators (Boyle-Baise & Langford, 2004), not all nondominant educators affirm diversity. This void may relate to the coloniality of power, e.g., assimilation pressures that nondominant educators experience (Quijano, 2000). However, pathway projects can prepare equity-oriented Latinos/as for the teaching profession.

We can reflect on our own perceptions and practices, also. We realize universities and teacher-education programs must take action to redress inequalities. As educators and community members, we may create a Third Space for students and families by building on diversity and strengths. Families must feel comfortable connecting to schools and communities, the antithesis of marginalizing diverse families (Rubin, Abrego, & Sutterby, 2012). One way to affirm and cultivate diversity involves recursive, dynamic polylingual education, which builds on translanguaging (García, 2009). "The greater the power of self-expression, the fuller the being" (Holquist, 1996, p. 141).

Together we can close opportunity gaps. For example, educators, such as Joy and Claudia, focused on the whole child and empowered and challenged students intellectually, socially, and emotionally (Ladson-Billings, 2009). Both educators crafted a Third Space by tapping into students' prior knowledge and engaging them in authentic, transformative learning. Joy incorporated Mexican-heritage literature and engaged students in multimodal projects, such as video inquiries and painting. She taught students the pragmatic cueing system and how cell-phone texting and other ways to write and speak depend on audience and purpose. In this way, Joy built on children's out-of-school contexts, but she encouraged them to be bi-dialectical and savvy. Claudia challenged students through group work and taught her students to value their mother tongue. Joy and Claudia understood students' cultural and linguistic diversity influenced learning processes.

Like Joy and Claudia, we strive to mediate and extend nondominant youth practices (Gutiérrez, Morales, & Martínez, 2009). Whatever our role—administrator, advocate, instructor, student, or family member—we must repel banking education because it alienates youth from school and it alienates the youth—period (Freire, 2000).

Why is education so important for Latinos/as? By 2060 Latinos/as will constitute one-third of the USA (U.S. Census Bureau, 2012b). Thus, we must understand this group. New immigrants help countries where they live with innovation, courage, and diversity. Indigenous people and immigrants who arrived many years ago have much to contribute, also. This diversity is our past, present, and future, and it relates to the disciplines. Quigley (2011) caused us to ponder this: What would happen to subject areas over time if nondominant people no longer enriched them? Although most of our participating parents were Spanish dominant and could not help their children with English homework in the disciplines, tutorial staff enriched parents' academic understanding. Staff taught parents to ask for their children's homework sheets and to monitor completion. The staff instructed parents how to read report cards, as one parent believed a grade of an A (or 90–100%) signified something bad, such as *ausente* [absent]. Tutorial staff encouraged parents to be their children's advocates in schools. Communities can also form their own Parent Teacher Associations (PTAs) outside of schools, such as *Afinidad's* PTA, and can make nondominant parents aware of unjust laws, such as House Bill 5 (HB 5) (Texas Education Agency, n.d.). Latino families possess many strengths and Latino parents care about their children's education and college attainment (Nora & Crisp, 2009).

This bulleted list represents our vision for equitable schooling practices:

- We make schools and other places fit—and build upon—nondominant people's linguistic and cultural strengths and practices, not vice-versa.
- We engage in loving dialogue with the subaltern so they can realize and resist oppression.
- Students and we use authentic, challenging, collaborative, generative multimodalities and digital instruction and assessment.
- We ask learners (perhaps privately) if they have technology access or if they can find access. If they cannot find access, we find or make access available and we mentor youth to use technology for rigorous academic purposes. We hold high-expectations, but scaffold.

- We collaborate with businesses, educators, organizations, governments, and others for collective impact and kinship, versus isolated efforts.
- We know our students and we use their and their family and neighborhood strengths in our curricula. We visit their homes, when possible.
- We value and engage with learners in critical exploration of evolving, relational local and global issues, spaces, and places
- We realize learners and families value education.
- We take risks to help the subaltern and to push the education field in positive directions; we resist fear related to colonialism (e.g., questioning authority).
- We make multiple curricular and textual entry points through universal design, or accessibility, so diverse people can achieve success. Some websites offer materials at various reading levels, including words, images and videos.

Final Words

We posed these research questions at our book's outset: What are *Corazón* strengths? How do we work in relationship with a community, while coming clean with power and privilege imbalances? How do residents engage in hybrid practices to confront obstacles? We may have illuminated some answers as qualitative researchers sharing kinship with co-researchers (Moje, 2000b). Hopefully, we raised questions to ponder as well. We offer this book, this bridge, to engage you in the practice of freedom (Freire, 2000).

Corazón residents demonstrated power and resourcefulness. They bypassed barriers and connected with others—slantwising to achieve goals most outsiders would value, e.g., getting a formal education, insisting on their rights, and supporting families. From our data, we realized bridging, rhizoming, and slantwising are literacies or situated practices. Campbell and Heyman (2007) referred to slantwise as a noun, but we made slantwise an action, a verb, to increase its purposefulness. After all, why cannot slantwising be an intentional disruption of norms, a deliberate challenge to authority? As mentioned in Chapter 8, teacher candidate Ella transformed rhizome into a verb as she created theory.

In a Freirean sense, many *Corazón* residents, especially adults, acted critically and creatively to transform their world. In a rhizomic sense co-researchers branched, connected, and refused containment. "The rhizome ...

acts on desire by external, productive outgrowths" (Deleuze & Guattari, 1987, p. 14). However, much work remains regarding youth conscientization, as many stopped short of analyzing systemic inequalities related to their schooling experiences and neighborhood's marginalization. The children, families, staff, parents, and others created an activist path for teacher candidates (TCs), also. We hope *Corazón* children and families have nestled into TCs' hearts, so these new educators can resist pathologizing portrayals and low expectations of nondominant children wherever they teach.

Coloniality and the emergence and continuation of colonias are not incidental (Anzaldúa, 2007). We offer this book as a theoretical Third Space betwixt structuralism, poststructuralism, postmodernism, and postcolonialism because we forced theories—kicking and hollering—into the same room. And now as we bid adieu, we hope our book functions in between the binaries that may exist where you live—so you may dialogue about beliefs and ideals—so you may take action. In this transformative space, the most powerful weapon is not anger. It is love. *Desde el corazón* [from the heart].

Questions to Ponder

1. What theoretical assumptions would cause us to discuss dilemmas? What are benefits to the reader when authors mention research challenges?
2. Describe a nondominant youth you know in the social injustice cycle, and the youth's academic identities and affiliations.
3. From a decolonizing research perspective, why is it important to discuss the specific, direct benefits of research on a community?
4. What research would you like to conduct about a marginalized community? What would your theoretical framework(s) be, and your ontological (relational) and epistemic (knowledge) assumptions? How would these frameworks and assumptions influence your research processes, from the onset?

REFERENCES

Acosta, T. P. (2011, August 17). Crystal City revolts. *Handbook of Texas Online*. Austin, TX: Texas State Historical Association.

Agyeman, G. S. (2008). White researcher-Black subjects: Exploring the challenges of researching the marginalised and "invisible." *The Electronic Journal of Business Research Methods*, 6(1), 77–84.

Ahlstrom, S. E., & Hall, D. D. (2004). *A religious history of the American people*. New Haven, CT: Yale University Press.

Allensworth, E., & Easton, J. Q. (2005). *The on-track indicator as a predictor of high school graduation*. Chicago, IL: University of Chicago. Retrieved from https://consortium.uchicago.edu/publications/track-indicator-predictor-high-school-graduation

Allington, R., & McGill-Franzen, A. (2008). Got books? *Educational Leadership*, 65(7), 20–23.

Anzaldúa, G. (1990). En rapport, in opposition: Cobrando cuentas a las nuestras. In G. Anzaldúa (Ed.), *Making face, making soul/Haciendo caras: Creative and critical perspectives by feminists of colors* (pp. 142–148). San Francisco, CA: Aunt Lute Books.

Anzaldúa, G. (2002). Preface: (Un) natural bridges, (Un) safe spaces. In G. Anzaldúa & A. L. Keating (Eds.), *This bridge we call home: Radical visions for transformations* (pp. 1–5). New York, NY: Routledge.

Anzaldúa, G. (2007). *Borderlands/La frontera: The new mestiza* (3rd ed.). San Francisco, CA: Aunt Lute Books.

Aquino-Sterling, C. R., Garrity, S., & Day, A. (2015). "We are heritage speakers and we are all diverse": Language mediating teachers' identities in a multilingual infant classroom *International Journal of Language and Linguistics*, 2(1), 1–14.

Arizmendi, L., Arizmendi, D., & Donelson, A. J. (2010). Colonia housing and community development. In A. J. Donelson & A. X. Esparza (Eds.), *The colonias reader: Economy, housing, and public health in U.S.-Mexico border colonias* (pp. 87–100). Tucson, AZ: The University of Arizona Press.

Ayón, C., & Villa, A. Q. (2013). Promoting Mexican immigrant families' well-being: Learning from parents what is needed to have a strong family. *Families in Society: The Journal of Contemporary Social Services, 94*(3), 194–202.

Bakhtin, M. M. (1986). The problem of speech genres (V. W. McGee, Trans.). In C. Emerson & M. Holquist (Eds.), *Speech genres & other late essays* (pp. 60–102). Austin, TX: University of Texas Press.

Baquedano-López, P., & Ochs, E. (2002). The politics of language and parish storytelling: Nuestra Señora de Guadalupe takes on "English Only." In P. Linell & K. Aronsson (Eds.), *Selves and voices: Goffman, viveka, and dialogue* (pp. 173–191). Linkoping, Sweden: Linkoping University.

Bartolomé, L. (2011). Literacy as *comida*: Learning to read with Mexican novelas. In M. L. Reyes (Ed.), *Words were all we had: Becoming biliterate against the odds* (pp. 49–59). New York, NY: Teachers College Press.

Barton, D., & Hamilton, M. (2012). *Local literacies: Reading and writing in one community* (2nd ed.). London, UK: Routledge.

Batibo, H. M. (2009). Poverty as a crucial factor in language maintenance and language death: Case studies from Africa. In W. Harbert (Ed.), *Language and poverty* (pp. 23–49). Bristol, UK: Multilingual Matters.

Berliner, D. C. (2009). Poverty and potential: Out-of-school factors and school success. *Education Policy Research Unit*. Retrieved from http://nepc.colorado.edu/files/PB-Berliner-NON-SCHOOL.pdf

Bhabha, H. (2004). *The location of culture* (2nd ed.). New York, NY: Routledge.

Bomer, R., & Maloch, B. (2013). Research and policy: Lunch, teeth, body, and mind: Children's learning and well-being. *Language Arts, 90*(4), 273–280.

Boyle-Baise, M. (2002). *Multicultural service learning: Educating teachers in diverse communities.* New York, NY: Teachers College Press.

Boyle-Baise, M., & Langford, J. (2004). There are children here: Service learning for social justice. *Equity & Excellence in Education, 37,* 55–66.

Brandes, S. (2000). El día de los muertos, el Halloween y la búsqueda de una identidad nacional mexicana. *Red de Revistas Científicas de América Latina y el Caribe, 10*(20), 7–20.

Brezosky, L. (2012, July 28). Texas still looking for a solution for colonias. *Houston Chronicle.* Retrieved from http://www.chron.com/news/houston-texas/article/State-still-seeks-solution-for-colonia-communities-3743612.php

Burke, D. (2015, June 18). Pope Francis: 'Revolution' needed to combat climate change. *CNN.* Retrieved from http://www.cnn.com/2015/06/18/world/pope-francis-climate-technology-encyclical/

Burrows-Goodwill, S. L. (2009). *Making the margin visible: Out-of-school literacy practices among Mexican heritage English learners in an English-only district* (Doctoral dissertation). Retrieved from ProQuest Dissertations and Theses Global. (UMI No. 3387391)

Bussert-Webb, K. (1999). To teach or to test? Reflections from a holistic teacher-researcher in south Texas. *Journal of Adolescent and Adult Literacy, 42*, 582–585.

Bussert-Webb, K. (2008). Gardening hope: How a tutoring and native garden project impacted preservice teachers. *The Journal for Civic Commitment, 11*, 1–15.

Bussert-Webb, K. (2009). ¿Qué hago? Latino/a children describe their activities in an "exemplary" school. *Journal of Latinos & Education, 8*(1), 38–54.

Bussert-Webb, K. (2011). Becoming socially just disciplinary teachers through a community service learning project. *Journal of Language and Literacy Education, 7*(2), 44–66.

Bussert-Webb, K. (2012). "So they can feel sure of themselves": Community service learning impact on female walkers. *Journal for Civic Commitment, 18*, 1–25.

Bussert-Webb, K. (2014). Problems and possibilities: Emergent bilinguals and multimodalities. *The Tapestry Journal: An International Multidisciplinary Journal on English Language Learner Education, 6*(1), 35–44.

Bussert-Webb, K. (2015). Parrying the pathologization of a strong, unified Mexican-American community. *Creative Approaches to Research, 8*(2), 46–69.

Bussert-Webb, K., & Díaz, M. E. (2012). New literacy opportunities and practices of Latino/a children of poverty in and out of school. *Language and Literacy, 14*(1), 1–25.

Bussert-Webb, K., & Díaz, M. E. (2013). Digital literacy, language, and Latinos: L1.4Word. *The Journal of Literacy and Technology, 14*(1), 2–50.

Caelli, K., Ray, L., & Mill, J. (2003). "Clear as mud": Toward greater clarity in generic qualitative research. *International Journal of Qualitative Method, 2*(2), 1–24.

Camarota, S. A. (2012). Immigrants in the United States, 2010: A profile of America's foreign-born population. *Center for Immigration Studies*. Retrieved from http://cis.org/2012-profile-of-americas-foreign-born-population

Campano, G., Ghiso, M. P., & Welch, B. J. (2016). *Partnering with immigrant communities: Action through literacy*. New York, NY: Teachers College Press.

Campbell, H., & Heyman, J. (2007). Slantwise: Beyond domination and resistance on the border. *Journal of Contemporary Ethnography, 36*(1), 3–30.

Cherland, M. R., & Harper, H. (2007). *Advocacy research in literacy education: Seeking higher ground*. Mahwah, NJ: Lawrence Erlbaum.

Cho, G. (2000). The role of heritage language in social interactions and relationships: Reflections from a language minority group. *Bilingual Research Journal, 24*(4), 369–84.

Chuang, H. K., Joshi, R. M., & Dixon, L. Q. (2012). Cross-language transfer of reading ability. *Journal of Literacy Research, 44*(1), 97–119.

Clifford, J. (1994). Diasporas. *Cultural Anthropology, 9*(3), 302–338.

Cline, Z., & Necochea, J. (2003). My mother never read to me. *Journal of Adolescent & Adult Literacy, 47*(2), 122–126.

Cohen, D. A., McKenzie, T. L., Sehgal, A., Williamson, S., Solinelli, D., & Lurie, N. (2007). Contribution of public parks to physical activity. *The American Journal of Public Health, 97*(3), 509–514.

Comber, B. (2016). *Literacy, place, and pedagogies of possibility*. New York, NY: Routledge.

Continuum. (n.d.). *Pedagogy of the oppressed: About Paulo Freire*. New York, NY: Author.

Conway, W. (1990). La quinceañera: Segundo artículo en una serie [The fifteenth birthday: Second article in a series]. *New Catholic Explorer, 5*.

Coronado, I. (2003). La vida en las colonias de la frontera/Life in the colonias on the border. *Latino Studies, 1*, 193–197.

Danet, B., & Herring, S. C. (2007). *The multilingual Internet: Language, culture, and communication online*. New York, NY: Oxford University Press.

Darvin, R., & Norton, B. (2012). Transnational identity and migrant language learners: The promise of digital storytelling. *Education Matters, 2*(1), 55–66.

Dávalos, K. M. (1996). "La quinceañera": Making gender and ethnic identities. *Frontiers: A Journal of Women Studies, 16*(2/3), 101–127.

Day, M. (1971). *Forty acres: César Chávez and the farm workers*. New York, NY: Praeger Publishers.

Day, S. A. (2004). Staging politics in Mexico: The road to neoliberalism. Cranbury, NJ: Rosemont Publishing and Printing Corp.

de la Piedra, M. T. (2013). "Consejo" as a literacy event: A case study of a border Mexican woman. *Language Arts, 90*(5), 339–350.

Deleuze, G., & Guattari, F. (1987). *A thousand plateaus: Capitalism and schizophrenia*. Minneapolis, MN: University of Minnesota Press.

Dennis, A. R., Bhagwatwar, A., & Minas, R. K. (2013). Play for performance: Using computer games to improve motivation and test-taking performance. *Journal of Information Systems Education, 24*(3), 223–231.

Diamond, P. (2012, January 24). *The amazing and miraculous image of Our Lady of Guadalupe*. Fillmore, NY: Most Holy Family Monastery. Retrieved from https://www.youtube.com/watch?v=xTgSSuuR1Jw

Díaz, M. E. (2011). *A case study of Spanish language use in a Texas border colonia* (Unpublished doctoral dissertation). The University of Texas at Brownsville, Brownsville, Texas.

Díaz, M. E., & Bussert-Webb, K. (2013). Reading and language beliefs and practices of Latino/a children in a border community. *Journal of Latinos and Education, 12*(1), 59–73.

Dolhinow, R. (2010). *Jumble of needs: Women's activism and neoliberalism in the colonias of the southwest*. Minneapolis, MN: University of Minnesota Press.

Duffy, J. N. (2014). *Who's your paddy? Racial expectations and the struggle for Irish American identity*. New York, NY: New York University Press.

Duménil, G., & Lévy, D. (2013). *The crisis of neoliberalism*. Cambridge, MA: Harvard University Press.

Durand, T. M. (2010). Latina mothers' school preparation activities and their relation to children's literacy skills. *Journal of Latinos and Education, 9*(3), 207–222.

Eakin, M. C. (2007). *The history of Latin America: Collision of cultures*. New York, NY: Palgrave Macmillan.

Eaton, D. K., et al. (2008). Youth risk behavior surveillance: United States, 2007. *Morbidity and Mortality Weekly Report, 57*(SS-4). Retrieved from http://www.cdc.gov/mmwr/preview/mmwrhtml/ss5704a1.htm

Ek, L. (2009). "Allá en Guatemala": Transnationalism, language, and identity of a Pentecostal Guatemalan-American young woman. *The High School Journal, 92*(4), 67–81.

Farr, M., & Guerra, J. C. (1995). Literacy in the community: A study of Mexicano families in Chicago. *Discourse Processes, 19,* 7–19.

Federal Reserve Bank of Dallas. (2015, April). *La colonias in the 21st century: Progress along the Texas-Mexico border.* Dallas, TX: Author. Retrieved from http://www.dallasfed.org/assets/documents/cd/pubs/lascolonias.pdf

Fernández, R. (2001). *Imagining literacy.* Austin, TX: University of Texas Press.

Fishman, J. A. (2001). *Can threatened languages be saved? Reversing language shift, revisited: A 21st century perspective.* Clevedon, UK: Multilingual Matters.

Fleischman, H. L., Hopstock, P. J., Pelczar, M. P., & Shelley, B. E. (2010). *Highlights from PISA 2009: Performance of U.S. 15-year-old students in reading, mathematics, and science literacy in an international context (NCES 2011-004).* Washington, DC: U.S. Department of Education, National Center for Education Statistics.

Flyvbjerg, B. (2006). Five misunderstandings about case-study research. *Qualitative Inquiry, 12*(2), 219–245.

Foucault, M. (1972). *The archeology of knowledge.* (A. M. Sheridan Smith, Trans.). New York, NY: Pantheon Books/Random House. (Original work published 1969).

Foucault, M. (1980). Lecture two: 14 January 1976. In C. Gordan (Ed.), *Power/knowledge: Selected interviews and other writings, 1972–1977* (pp. 92–108). (C. Gordon, L. Marshall, J. Mepham, & K. Soper, Trans.). New York, NY: Pantheon Books.

Foucault, M. (1991). *Discipline and punish: The birth of a prison.* London, UK: Penguin.

Fraser, N. (1997). *Justice interruptus: Critical reflections on the "postsocialist" condition.* New York, NY: Routledge.

Freire, P. (1994). *Pedagogy of hope: Reliving pedagogy of the oppressed* (R. R. Barr, Trans.). New York, NY: Continuum.

Freire, P. (1997). *Pedagogy of the heart* (D. Macedo & A. Oliveira, Trans.). New York, NY: Continuum.

Freire, P. (2000). *Pedagogy of the oppressed: 30th anniversary edition* (M. B. Ramos, Trans.). New York, NY: Continuum.

Freire, P., & Macedo, D. (2000). *Ideology matters.* (M. B. Ramos, Trans.). Boulder, CO: Rowman & Littlefield.

Gadotti, M. (1994). *Reading Paulo Freire.* (J. Milton, Trans.). Albany, NY: SUNY Press.

Gándara, P. (2010). Special topic: The Latino education crisis. *Educational Leadership, 67*(5), 24–30.

García, O. (2009). *Bilingual education in the 21st century: A global perspective.* Malden, MA: Wiley/Blackwell.

García, O., & Kleifgen, J. A. (2010). *Educating emergent bilinguals: Policies, programs, and practices for English Language Learners.* New York, NY: Teachers College Press.

Gee, J. P. (2007). *What video games have to teach us about learning and literacy* (2nd ed.). New York, NY: Palgrave.

Gee, J. P. (2012). *Social linguistics and literacy: Ideology in discourses.* (4th ed.). New York, NY: Routledge.

Giroux, H. (2016). *The Giroux reader.* (2nd ed.). New York, NY: Routledge.

Goldenberg, C., Reese, L., & Rezaei, A. (2011). Contexts for language and literacy development among dual-language learners. In A. Yücesan Durgunoglu & C. Goldenberg (Eds.), *Language and literacy development in bilingual settings* (pp. 3–25). New York, NY: Guilford Publications.

Goldhaber, D., Lavery, L., & Theobald, R. (2015). Uneven playing field? Assessing the teacher quality gap between advantaged and disadvantaged students. *Educational Researcher, 44*(5), 293–307.

González, J. M. (2011). Words were all we had: Reflections on becoming biliterate. In M. L. Reyes (Ed.), *Words were all we had: Becoming biliterate against the odds* (pp. 26–35). New York, NY: Teachers College Press.

Gorski, P. C. (2013). *Reaching and teaching students in poverty: Strategies for erasing the opportunity gap.* New York, NY: Teachers College Press.

Greenberg, J. B., Browning-Aiken, A., Alexander, W. L., & Weaver, T. (2012). Conclusion: Structural adjustment, structural violence. In T. Weaver, J. B. Greenberg, W. L. Alexander, & A. Browning-Aiken (Eds.), *Neoliberalism and commodity production in Mexico* (pp. 315–341). Boulder, CO: University Press of Colorado.

Gutiérrez, D. (1999). Migration, emergent ethnicity, and the "third space": The shifting politics of nationalism in greater Mexico. *Journal of American History, 86*(2), 481–517.

Gutiérrez, G. (1973). *A theology of liberation.* Maryknoll, NY: Orbis.

Gutiérrez, G., & Müller, G. L. (2015). *On the side of the poor: The theology of liberation* (2nd ed.). (R. A. Krieg & J. B. Nickoloff, Trans.). Maryknoll, NY: Orbis.

Gutiérrez, K. (2008). Developing a sociocritical literacy in the third space. *Reading Research Quarterly, 43*(2), 148–164.

Gutiérrez, K., Baquedano-López, P., & Tejada, C. (1999). Rethinking diversity: Hybridity and hybrid language practices in the third space. *Mind, Culture, and Activity, 6*(4), 286–303.

Gutiérrez, K., Baquedano-López, P., & Turner, M. G. (1997). Putting language back into language arts: When the radical middle meets the third space. *Language Arts, 74*(5), 368–378.

Gutiérrez, K., Morales, P., & Martínez, D. (2009). Re-mediating literacy: Culture, difference, and learning for students from nondominant communities. *Review of Research in Education, 33*, 212–245.

Hadaway, N. L., Vardell, S. M., & Young, T. A. (2009). *What every teacher should know about English language learners.* Boston, MA: Pearson.

Hall, E. T. (1976). *Beyond culture.* Garden City, NY: Anchor Books.

Hames-García, M. (2011). *Identity complex: Making the case for multiplicity.* Minneapolis, MN: University of Minnesota Press.

Hardon, S. J. (2003). *The Blessed Virgin Mary and the Catholic discovery of America.* Lombard, IL: The Real Presence Association. Retrieved from http://www.therealpresence.org/archives/Christopher_Columbus/Christopher_Columbus_004.htm

Harrington, D. W., & Elliot, S. J. (2009). Weighing the importance of neighborhood: A multi-level exploration of the determinants of overweight and obesity. *Social Science & Medicine, 68*(4), 593–600.

Hassan, I. H. (1987). *The postmodern turn: Essays in postmodern theory and culture*. Athens, OH: Ohio University Press.

Haycock, K. (2001). Closing the achievement gap. *Educational Leadership, 58*(6), 6–12.

Henry, L. A. (2007). *Exploring new literacies pedagogy and online reading comprehension among middle school students and teachers: Issues of social equity or social exclusion?* (Doctoral dissertation). Retrieved from http://digitalcommons.uconn.edu/dissertations/AAI3282520/

Hernández, R. B. (2003). *Culture clash in a south Texas colonia: Teachers' and parent's attitudes and practices regarding parental involvement* (Doctoral dissertation). Retrieved from ProQuest Dissertations and Theses Global (UMI No. 3107383)

Hinrichs, L. (2006). *Codeswitching on the web: English and Jamaican Creole in e-mail communication*. Amsterdam, NL: Benjamins.

Hispanically Speaking News. (2013). *Immigration rallies planned on Virgen de Guadalupe feast day*. Chicago, IL: Author. Retrieved from http://beforeitsnews.com/alternative/2013/12/immigration-rallies-plan-on-virgin-de-guadalupe-feast-day-2838020.html

Holquist, M. (Ed.) (1996). *The dialogic imagination: Four essays by M. M. Bakhtin* (10th ed.). (C. Emerson & M. Holquist, Trans.). Austin, TX: University of Texas Press.

Hornberger, N. H. (2006). Voice and biliteracy in indigenous language revitalization: Contentious educational practices in Quechua, Guarani, and Maori contexts. *Journal of Language, Identity, and Education, 5*(4), 277–292.

Hornberger, N. H. (2014). The continua of biliteracy and the bilingual educator: Educational linguistics in practice. *International Journal of Bilingual Education and Bilingualism, 7*(2 & 3), 155–171.

Hurtado, A., & Vega, L. A. (2004). Shift happens: Spanish and English transmission between parents and their children. *Journal of Social Issues, 60*(1), 137–155.

Hyde, J. S., & Else-Quest, N. M. (2013). *Half the human experience* (8th ed.). Belmont, CA: Wadsworth Cengage.

Internet Live Stats (2015). *Internet users*. Retrieved from http://www.internetlivestats.com/internet-users/

Janus, M., & Offord, D. R. (2007). Development and psychometric properties of the Early Development Instrument: A measure of children's school readiness. *Canadian Journal of Behavioral Science, 39*(1), 1–22.

Jiménez, F. (1997). *The circuit: Stories from the life of a migrant child*. Albuquerque, NM: University of New Mexico Press.

Jiménez, R. T. (2003). Literacy and Latino students in the United States: Some considerations, questions, and new directions. *Reading Research Quarterly, 38*(1), 122–128.

Jiménez, R. T., Smith, P. H., & Teague, B. L. (2009). Transnational and community literacies for teachers. *Journal of Adolescent & Adult Literacy, 53*(1), 16–26.

Johnson, J. R., & Ingram, J. E. (2013). Anatomy of a modern-day lynching: The relationship between hate crimes against Latina/os and the debate over immigration reform. *North Carolina Law Review, 91*, 1613–1656.

Joshi, P., Hardy, E., & Hawkins, S. (2009). *Role of religiosity in the lives of the low-income population: A comprehensive review of the evidence final report*. Washington, DC: U.S. Department of Health & Human Services. Retrieved from http://aspe.hhs.gov/sites/default/files/pdf/75821/report.pdf

Juarbe, T., Turok, X. P., & Pérez-Stable, E. J. (2002). Perceived benefits and barriers to physical activity among older Latina women. *Western Journal of Nursing Research, 24*(8), 868–886.

Kania, J., & Kramer, M. (2011). Collective impact. *Stanford Social Innovation Review, Winter.* Retrieved from http://ssir.org/images/articles/2011_WI_Feature_Kania.pdf

Kellinger, J. J. (2012). The flipside: Concerns about the "new literacies" paths educators might take. *The Educational Forum, 76*(4), 524–536.

Kelman, H. C. (1971). Language as an aid and barrier to involvement in the national system. In J. Rubin & B. H. Jernudd (Eds.), *Can language be planned? Sociological theory and practice for developing nations* (pp. 21–51). Honolulu, HI: University of Hawaii Press.

King, K. A., & Punti, G. (2012). On the margins: Undocumented students' narrated experiences of (il)legality. *Linguistics and Education, 23*(3), 235–259.

Kingston, M. (1976). *The woman warrior: Memoirs of a childhood among ghosts.* Vintage Books (2nd ed.). New York, NY: Vintage books.

Knoll, B. R. (2012). ¿Compañero o extranjero? Anti-immigrant nativism among Latino Americans. *Social Science Quarterly, 93*(4), 911–931.

Kress, R., & Lake, T. (2013). *Paulo Freire's intellectual roots: Toward historicity in praxis.* New York, NY: Bloomsbury Publishing.

Labor Archives Research Center. (2007). *Cultivating creativity: The arts and the farm workers' movement during the 1960s and '70s—The Virgin of Guadalupe.* San Francisco, CA: Labor Archives and Research Center. Retrieved from http://130.212.18.164/exhibits/cultivating/intropages/delanomarch.html

Ladson-Billings, G. (2009). *The dreamkeepers: Successful teachers of African American children* (2nd ed.). San Francisco, CA: Josssey-Bass Publishers.

Landry, R., & Bourhis, R. Y. (1997). Linguistic landscape and ethnolinguistic vitality: An empirical study. *Journal of Language and Social Psychology, 16*(1), 23–49.

Lange, E. (1998). Fragmented ethics of justice: Freire, liberation theology and pedagogies for the non-poor. *Convergence, 31,* 81–94.

Lankshear, C., & Knobel, M. (2006). *New literacies: Everyday practices and classroom learning* (2nd ed.). New York, NY: Open University Press.

Leu, D. J., O'Byrne, W. I., Zawilinski, L., McVerry, J. G., & Everett-Cacopardo, H. (2009). Comments on Greenhow, Robelia, and Hughes: Expanding the new literacies conversation. *Educational Researcher, 38*(4), 264–269.

Lilley, S. (2012, September 12). Poll: 1 out of 3 Americans inaccurately think most Hispanics are undocumented. *NBC Latino.* Retrieved from http://nbclatino.com/2012/09/12/poll-1-out-of-3-americans-think-most-hispanics-are-undocumented/

Lilley, S. (2014, April 14). Latino college completion rates low despite enrollment. *NBC News.* Retrieved from http://www.nbcnews.com/news/latino/latino-college-completion-rates-low-despite-enrollment-n80326

Lockeman, K. S., & Pelco, L. E. (2013). The relationship between service-learning and degree completion. *Michigan Journal of Community Service Learning, 20*(1), 18–30.

Luke, A. (2005). Foreword. In K. Pahl & J. Rowsell (Eds.), *Literacy and education: Understanding the new literacy studies in the classroom* (pp. x–xiii). London, UK: Paul Chapman.

Macedo, D. (2000). Introduction to the anniversary edition. In P. Freire (Ed.). *Pedagogy of the oppressed: 30th anniversary edition* (3rd ed., pp. 11–27). New York, NY: Continuum.

Madden, M., Lenhart, A., Duggan, M., Cortesi, S., & Gasser, U. (2013, March 13). *Teens and technology: Main findings.* Pew Research Center. Retrieved from http://www.pewinternet. org/2013/03/13/main-findings-5/

Martínez, M. (2013, July 24). Valley woman fought discrimination as a child and won. *Valley Central.* Retrieved from http://www.valleycentral.com/news/story.aspx?id=925663#. VdQYyV9RGM8

Martini, N. F. (2012). "La iglesia" in politics? Religion and Latino public opinion. *Social Science Quarterly, 93*(4), 988–1006.

Matthiesen, H. (1997). What now for the Texas colonias? *New Mexico Law Review, 27,* 1–31.

Maynes, N., Hatt, B., & Wideman, R. (2013). Service learning as a practicum experience in a pre-service education program. *Canadian Journal of Higher Education, 43*(1), 80–99.

Mays, V. M., & Comas-Díaz, L. (1988). Feminist therapy with ethnic minority populations: A closer look at blacks and Hispanics. In M. A. Dutton-Douglas & L. E. Walker (Eds.), *Feminist psychotherapies: Integration of therapeutic and feminist systems* (pp. 228–251) Norwood, NJ: Ablex Publishing Corp.

McAreavey, R., & Das, C. (2013). A delicate balancing act: Negotiating with gatekeepers for ethical research when researching minority communities. *International Journal of Qualitative Methods, 12*(1), 113–131.

McElwee, J. J. (2013, September 25). Pope meets with liberation theology pioneer. *National Catholic Reporter.* Retrieved from http://ncronline.org/news/theology/pope-meets-liberation-theology-pioneer

Mignolo, W. D. (2006). Citizenship, knowledge, and the limits of humanity. *American Literary History, 18*(2), 312–331.

Mignolo, W. D. (2011). *Local histories/global designs: Coloniality, subaltern knowledges, and border thinking.* Princeton, NJ: Princeton University Press.

Mitchell, K. (2005). Hybridity. In D. Atkinson, P. Jackson, D. Sibley, & N. Washbourne (Eds.), *Cultural geography: A critical dictionary of key concepts* (pp. 188–193). New York, NY: Palgrave Macmillan.

Mitchell, W. (1995). Translator translated: Interview with cultural theorist Homi Bhabha. *Artforum, 33*(7), 80–84.

Moje, E. B. (2000a). Changing our minds, changing our bodies: Power as embodied in research relations. *Qualitative Studies in Education, 13*(1), 25–42.

Moje, E. B. (2000b). Critical issues: Circles of kinship, friendship, position, and power. Examining the community in community-based literacy research. *Journal of Literacy Research, 32*(1), 77–112.

Moje, E. B. (2007). Developing socially just subject-matter instruction: A review of the literature on disciplinary literacy teaching. *Review of Research in Education, 31*(1), 1–44.

Moje, E. B., Young, J. P., Readence, J. E., & Moore, D. W. (2000). Reinventing adolescent literacy for new times: Perennial and millennial issues. *Journal of Adolescent & Adult Literacy, 43*(5), 400–410.

Moraga, C., & Anzaldúa, G. (1983). *This bridge called my back: Writings by radical women of color* (2nd ed.). New York, NY: Kitchen Table: Women of Color Press.

Morrow, R. (2013). Rethinking Freire's "oppressed": A "southern" route to Habermas's communicative turn and theory of deliberative democracy. In R. Kress & T. Lake (Eds.), *Paulo Freire's intellectual roots: Toward historicity in praxis* (pp. 65–88). New York, NY: Bloomsbury Publishing.

National Catholic Risk Retention Group. (n.d.). *Protecting God's children*. Tulsa, OK: Author. Retrieved from https://www.virtus.org/virtus/protecting_children.cfm

National Center for Education Statistics. (2013). *Table 306.10. Total fall enrollment in degree-granting postsecondary institutions, by level of enrollment, sex, attendance status, and race/ethnicity of student*. Washington, DC: Author. Retrieved from https://nces.ed.gov/programs/digest/d13/tables/dt13_306.10.asp

Neilsen G. L. (2014). Poetic inquiry. In P. Albers, T. Holbrook, & A. S. Flint (Eds.), *New methods of literacy research* (pp. 133–149). New York, NY: Routledge.

Nichols, S. L., Glass, G. V., & Berliner, D. C. (2012). High-stakes testing and student achievement: Updated analyses with NAEP data. *Education Policy Analysis Archives, 20*(20), 1–30.

Nieto, S., & Bode, P. (2008). *Affirming diversity: The sociopolitical context of multicultural education* (5th ed.). New York, NY: Longman.

Nora, A., & Crisp, G. (2009). Hispanics and higher education: An overview of research, theory, and practice. In J. C. Smart (Ed.), *Higher education: Handbook of theory of research* (Vol. 24, pp. 317–353). New York, NY: Springer.

Norton, B. (2013). *Identity and language learning: Extending the conversation* (2nd ed.). Bristol, UK: Multilingual Matters.

Novak, K. (2013). Preventative patrol and beyond. In G. Bruinsma & D. Weisburd (Eds.), *Encyclopedia of criminology and criminal justice* (pp. 3921–3931). New York, NY: Springer.

O'Brien, D., & Scharber, C. (2008). Digital literacies. *Journal of Adolescent and Adult Literacy, 52*(1), 66–68.

O'Connor, N. (2009). Hispanic origin, socio-economic status, and community college enrollment. *The Journal of Higher Education, 80*(2), 121–145.

Oakes, J. (2005). *Keeping track: How schools structure inequality* (2nd ed.). New Haven, CT: Yale University Press.

Ogbu, J. U. (1992). Understanding cultural diversity and learning. *Educational Researcher, 21*(8), 5–14.

Orellana, M. F. (2009). *Translating childhoods: Immigrant youth, language, and culture*. New Brunswick, NJ: Rutgers University Press.

Orfield, G. (2014). Tenth annual Brown lecture in education research: A new civil rights agenda for American education. *Educational Researcher, 43*(6), 273–292.

Ortiz, M. T. (2014, October 17). New border voices reflects life in a third space. *The Texas Observer*. Retrieved from http://www.texasobserver.org/author/mnica-teresa-ortiz/

Ortiz, V., & Telles, E. (2012). Racial identity and racial treatment of Mexican Americans. *Race and Social Problems, 4*(1), 41–56.

Ovando, C. (1994). Insights on diversity: Reflections of an involuntary voluntary immigrant. *Bilingual Research Journal, 18*(3–4), 115–117.

Palmer, D., & Lynch, A. W. (2008). A bilingual education for a monolingual test? The pressure to prepare for TAKS and its influence on choices for language of instruction in Texas elementary bilingual classrooms. *Language Policy, 7,* 217–235.

Palmer, D., & Rangel, V. S. (2011). High stakes accountability and policy implementation: Teacher decision making in bilingual classrooms in Texas. *Educational Policy, 25*(4), 614–647.

Paolillo, J. C. (1996). Language choice on soc.culture.punjab. *Electronic Journal of Communication/La Revue Electronic de Communication, 6*(3). Retrieved from http://www.cios.org/EJCPUBLIC/006/3/006312.HTML

Paris, D., & Winn, M. T. (2014). Preface: To humanize research. In D. Paris & M. Winn (Eds.), *Humanizing research: Decolonizing qualitative inquiry with youth and communities* (pp. xiii–xx). Thousand Oaks, CA: Sage.

Passel, J. S., & Cohn, D. (2009). *A portrait of unauthorized immigrants in the United States.* Washington, DC: Pew Research Center. Retrieved from http://www.pewhispanic.org/2009/04/14/a-portrait-of-unauthorized-immigrants-in-the-united-states/

Paugh, P., & Moran, M. (2013). Growing language awareness in the classroom garden. *Language Arts, 90*(4), 253–267.

Payne, R. (2005). *A framework for understanding poverty* (4th ed). Highlands, TX: Aha! Process.

Peña, D. G. (1999). *Chicano culture, ecology, politics: Subversive kin.* Tucson, AZ: University of Arizona Press.

Perry, K. H., & Homan, A. (2014). "What I feel in my heart": Literacy practices of and for the self among adults with limited or no schooling. *Journal of Literacy Research, 46*(4), 422–454.

Pew Research Center. (2014, May 7). *The shifting religious identity of Latinos in the United States.* Washington, DC: Author. Retrieved from http://www.pewforum.org/2014/05/07/the-shifting-religious-identity-of-latinos-in-the-united-states/

Poetry Foundation. (2010). *Naomi Shihab Nye.* Chicago, IL: Author. Retrieved from http://www.poetryfoundation.org/bio/naomi-shihab-nye

Putnam, R. D. (1995). Bowling alone: America's declining social capital. *Journal of Democracy, 6*(1), 65–78.

Quigley, C. (2011). Pushing the boundaries of cultural congruence pedagogy in science education towards a third space. *Cultural Studies of Science Education, 6*(3), 549–557.

Quijano, A. (2000). Coloniality of power, Eurocentrism, and Latin America. *Nepantla: Views from South, 1*(3), 533–580.

Ramshaw, E. (2011, July 7). Improvement comes up short in south Texas colonias. *The Texas Tribune.* Retrieved from http://www.nytimes.com/2011/07/08/us/08ttconditions.html

Rangel, E. (2015, May 26). Controversial immigration bills die in Texas Senate. *Amarillo Globe News.* Retrieved from http://amarillo.com/news/latest-news/2015-05-26/controversial-immigration-bills-die-texas-senate

Rappaport, J. (2000). Community narratives: Tales of terror and joy. *American Journal of Community Psychology, 28*(1), 1–24.

Reese, L., & Goldenberg, C. (2006). Community contexts for literacy development of Latina/o children: Contrasting case studies. *Anthropology and Education Quarterly, 37*(1), 42–61.

Richardson, C., & Pisani, M. J. (2012). *The informal and underground economy of the south Texas border.* Austin, TX: University of Texas Press.

Rideout, V. J., Foehr, U. G., & Roberts, D. F. (2010). *Generation M²: Media in the lives of 8- to 18-year olds.* Menlo Park, CA: Henry J. Kaiser Family Foundation. Retrieved from http://www.kff.org/entmedia/upload/8010.pdf

Rosenblatt, L. M. (1978). *The Reader, the text, the poem: The transactional theory of the literacy work.* Carbondale, IL: Southern Illinois University Press.

Rothstein, R. (2014). The racial achievement gap, segregated schools, and segregated neighborhoods—a constitutional insult. *Race and Social Problems, 6*(4), 21–30.

Rubenstein-Ávila, E. (2003–2004). Conversing with Miguel: An adolescent English language learner struggling with later literacy development. *Journal of Adolescent & Adult Literacy, 47*(4), 290–301.

Rubin, R., Abrego, M. H., & Sutterby, J. A. (2012). *Engaging the families of ELLs: Ideas, resources, and activities.* New York, NY: Routledge.

Santos, M. (2004). The motivations of first-semester Hispanic two-year college students. *Community College Review, 32*(3), 18–34.

Satija, N., & Ura, A. (2015, March 8). Undrinkable. *The Texas Tribune.* Retrieved from http://apps.texastribune.org/undrinkable

Scholastic & Bill and Melinda Gates Foundation (2014). *Primary sources: America's teachers on teaching in an era of change* (3rd ed.). Seattle, WA: Author. Retrieved from http://www.scholastic.com/primarysources/PrimarySources3rdEdition.pdf

Sharkey, P. (2013). *Stuck in place: Urban neighborhoods and the end of progress toward racial equality.* Chicago, IL: University of Chicago Press.

Shirley, D. (2002). *Valley Interfaith and school reform: Organizing for power in south Texas.* Austin, TX: University of Texas Press.

Shor, I. (1997). *When students have power: Negotiating authority in a critical pedagogy.* Chicago, IL: The University of Chicago Press.

Shor, I., & Freire, P. (1987). *A pedagogy for liberation.* Westport, CT: Bergin & Garvey.

Showstack, R. E. (2012). Symbolic power in the heritage language classroom: How Spanish heritage speakers sustain and resist hegemonic discourses on language and cultural diversity. *Spanish in Context, 9*(1), 1–26.

Skogan, W. G. (2006). Community policing and the new immigrants. In M. King (Ed.), *Justice and safety in America's immigrant communities* (pp. 43–64). Princeton, NJ: Princeton University.

Smith, P. H., & Murillo, L. A. (2012). Researching transfronterizo literacies in Texas border colonias. *International Journal of Bilingual Education and Bilingualism, 15*(6), 635–651.

Smith, P. H., & Valenzuela, A. V. (2012). Literacies on the margins: Border colonias as sites for the study of language and literacy. In P. J. Dunston, S. K. Fullerton, C. C. Bates, K.

Headley, & P. M. Stecker (Eds.), *61st yearbook of the Literacy Research Association* (pp. 335–346). Oak Creek, WI: Literacy Research Association.

Soja, E. W. (1996). The trialectics of spatiality. In E. W. Soja (Ed.), *Thirdspace: Journeys to Los Angeles and other real-and-imagined places* (pp. 54–82). Cambridge, MA: Blackwell.

Soja, E. W. (2009, March 12–14). *The city and spatial justice* [La ville et la justice spatiale]. (S. Didier, & F. Dufaux, Trans.) (pp. 1–5). Presented at the conference Spatial Justice, Paris, France. Retrieved from http://www.jssj.org/wp-content/uploads/2012/12/JSSJ1-1en4.pdf

Solomon, D. (2015, January 22). The FBI's list of the most dangerous cities in Texas. *Texas Monthly*. Retrieved from http://www.texasmonthly.com/daily-post/fbis-list-most-dangerous-cities-texas

Sparapani, E. F., Perez, D. C., Gould, J., Hillman, S., & Clark, L. (2014). A global curriculum? Understanding teaching and learning in the United States, Taiwan, India, and Mexico. *SAGE Open, 4*(2), 1–15.

Sparks, A., & Reese, E. (2013). From reminiscing to reading: Home contributions to children's developing language and literacy in low-income families. *First Language, 33*, 89–110.

Street, B. (2003). The limits of the local—"Autonomous" or "disembedding"? *International Journal of Learning, 10*, 2825–2830.

Strick, B. R. (2012). Equitable access to college: evidence for the influence of school context. *Education Policy Analysis Archives, 20*(35), 1–20.

Strife, S., & Downey, L. 2009. Childhood development and access to nature: A new direction for environmental inequality research. *Organization Environment, 22*(1), 99–122.

Suárez, D. (2007). Second and third generation heritage language speakers: HL scholarship's relevance to the research needs and future directions of TESOL. *Heritage Language Journal, 5*(1), 27–49.

Texas Department of Transportation. (2004). *2004 Border Colonias Access Program (BCAP) population*. Retrieved from http://ftp.dot.state.tx.us/pub/txdot-info/tpp/bcap/bcap2004.pdf

Texas Education Agency. (n.d.). *House Bill 5: Foundation high school program*. Retrieved from http://tea.texas.gov/Curriculum_and_Instructional_Programs/Graduation_Information/House_Bill_5__Foundation_High_School_Program

Texas Secretary of State. (n.d.). *What is a colonia?* Austin, TX: Author. http://www.sos.state.tx.us/border/colonias/what_colonia.shtml

The Economist. (2011, January 27). *The colonias of the Mexican border: Paving the way*. Retrieved from http://www.economist.com/node/18013822

Thelwall, M. (2008). Fk yea I swear: Cursing and gender in MySpace. *Corpora, 3*(1), 83–107.

Thomas, W. P., & Collier, V. P. (2003). *A national study of school effectiveness for language minority students' long-term academic achievement*. Final Report. Santa Cruz, CA: Center for Research on Education, Diversity & Excellence.

Tuck, E., & Yang, K. W. (2014). R-words: Refusing research. In D. Paris & M. T. Winn (Eds.), *Humanizing research: Decolonizing qualitative inquiry with youth and communities* (pp. 223–247). Thousand Oaks, CA: Sage.

Turner, C., & Kamenetz, A. (2015, January 9). A "sizable decrease" in those passing the GED. *National Public Radio*. Retrieved from http://www.npr.org/sections/ed/2015/01/09/375440666/a-sizable-decrease-in-those-passing-the-ged

U.S. Census Bureau. (2000). *American FactFinder: Profile of selected social characteristics. Census 2000, summary file*. Washington, DC: Author. Retrieved from http://factfinder2.census.gov

U.S. Census Bureau. (2010). *American FactFinder*. Washington, DC: Author. Retrieved from http://factfinder.census.gov

U.S. Census Bureau. (2012a). *The foreign-born population in the United States: 2010 American community survey reports*. Washington, DC: Author. Retrieved from https://www.census.gov/prod/2012pubs/acs-19.pdf'

U.S. Census Bureau. (2012b). *U.S. Census Bureau projections show a slower growing, older, more diverse nation a half century from now*. Washington, DC: Author. Retrieved from https://www.census.gov/newsroom/releases/archives/population/cb12-243.html

U.S. Customs and Border Protection. (n.d.). *Visa Waiver Program (VWP) countries*. Washington, DC: Author. Retrieved from https://www.cbp.gov/travel/international-visitors/visa-waiver-program

U.S. Department of Housing and Urban Development. (2014). *State community development block grant colonias set-aside. HUD Exchange*. Washington, D. C.: Author. Retrieved from https://www.hudexchange.info/programs/cdbg-colonias/

U.S. Department of Labor. (2015a). *Employment projections: Earnings and unemployment rates by educational attainment*. Washington, DC: Author. Retrieved from http://www.bls.gov/emp/ep_chart_001.htm

U.S. Department of Labor. (2015b). *Local area unemployment statistics: Unemployment rates for metropolitan areas*. Washington, DC: Author. Retrieved from http://www.bls.gov/web/metro/laummtrk.htm

U.S. Department of Labor. (2015c). *Occupational employment and wages, May 2014: 27–3091 interpreters and translators*. Washington, DC: Author. Retrieved from http://www.bls.gov/oes/current/oes273091.htm

Valenzuela, A. (2008). Uncovering internalized oppression. In M. Pollock (Ed.). *Everyday antiracism: Concrete strategies for successfully navigating the relevance of race in school* (pp. 50–55). New York, NY: The New Press.

Vasilachis de Gialdino, I. (2009). Ontological and epistemological foundations of qualitative research. *Forum Qualitative Sozialforschung/Forum: Qualitative Social Research, 10*(2). Retrieved from http://www.qualitative-research.net/index.php/fqs/article/view/1299/3164

Vega, S. (2015). *Latino heartland: Of borders and belonging in the Midwest*. New York, NY: New York University Press.

Ward, P. M. (1999). *Colonias and public policy in Texas and Mexico: Urbanization by stealth*. Austin, TX: University of Texas Press.

Warschauer, M. (2011). *Learning in the cloud: How (and why) to transform schools with digital media*. New York, NY: Teachers College Press.

Warschauer, M., & Matuchniak, T. (2010). New technology and digital worlds: Analyzing evidence of equity in access, use, and outcomes. *Review of Research in Education, 34*(1), 179–225.

White-Kaulaity, M. (2007). Reflections on Native American reading: A seed, a tool, and a weapon. *Journal of Adolescent & Adult Literacy, 50*(7), 560–569.

Williams, E. E. (2000). Liberation theology and its role in Latin America. *The Monitor: Journal of International Studies, 7*(1). Retrieved from http://web.wm.edu/so/monitor/issues/07-1/6-williams.htm

Wyner, J. S., Bridgeland, J. M., & DiIulio, J. J. (2007). *The achievement trap: How America is failing millions of high-achieving students from lower-income families*. A report by the Jack Kent Cooke Foundation. Retrieved from http://www.usc.edu/dept/chepa/IDApays/publications/Achievement_Trap.pdf

Yore, L. D., Pimm, D., & Tuan, H. L. (2007). The literacy component of mathematical and scientific literacy. *International Journal of Science and Mathematics Education, 5*, 559–589.

Zatz, M. S., & Smith, H. (2012). Immigration, crime, and victimization: Rhetoric and reality. *Annual Review of Law and Social Science, 8*, 141–159.

Zinn, M. B. (1982). Familism among Chicanos: A theoretical review. *Humboldt Journal of Social Relations, 10*(1), 224–238.

INDEX

W

X

Y

Z

Yolanda Medina and Margarita Machado-Casas
GENERAL EDITORS

Critical Studies of Latinos/as in the Americas is a provocative interdisciplinary series that offers a critical space for reflection and questioning what it means to be Latino/a living in the Americas in twenty-first century social, cultural, economic, and political arenas. The series looks forward to extending the dialogue to include the North and South Western hemispheric relations that are prevalent in the field of global studies.

Topics that explore and advance research and scholarship on contemporary topics and issues related with processes of racialization, economic exploitation, health, education, transnationalism, immigration, gendered and sexual identities, and disabilities that are not commonly highlighted in the current Latino/a Studies literature as well as the multitude of socio, cultural, economic, and political progress among the Latinos/as in the Americas are welcome.

To receive more information about CSLA, please contact:

Yolanda Medina (ymedina@bmcc.cuny.edu) &
Margarita Machado-Casas (Margarita.MachadoCasas@utsa.edu)

To order other books in this series, please contact our Customer Service Department at:

(800) 770-LANG (within the U.S.)
(212) 647-7706 (outside the U.S.)
(212) 647-7707 FAX

Or browse online by series at:

WWW.PETERLANG.COM